FACT
& FICTION

FACT & FICTION

THE NEW JOURNALISM AND THE NONFICTION NOVEL

by John Hollowell

THE UNIVERSITY OF NORTH CAROLINA PRESS
Chapel Hill

The author is grateful for permission to reprint passages from the following: From the book
Fictions and Events: Essays in Criticism and Literary History by Warner Berthoff. Copyright ©
1971 by Warner Berthoff. Reprinted by permission of the publishers, E. P. Dutton & Co., Inc.,
and *New Literary History*, in which the essay "Witness and Testament: Two Contemporary
Classics" originally appeared, by permission of the editor, Ralph Cohen.

In Cold Blood by Truman Capote, copyright © 1965 by Truman Capote and "The Duke in His
Domain" and "The Muses Are Heard" from *Selected Writings of Truman Capote*, copyright ©
1963 by Random House, Inc., reprinted by permission of Random House, Inc.

From *Armies of the Night* by Norman Mailer. Copyright © 1968 by Norman Mailer. By
arrangement with The New American Library, Inc., New York, N.Y. Reprinted by permission of
the author and the author's agents, Scott Meredith Literary Agency, Inc., 845 Third Avenue,
New York, N.Y. 10022. From *Miami and the Siege of Chicago* by Norman Mailer. Copyright ©
1968 by Norman Mailer. By arrangement with The New American Library, Inc., New York,
N.Y. Reprinted by permission of the author and the author's agents, Scott Meredith Literary
Agency, Inc., 845 Third Avenue, New York, N.Y. 10022. From *Of a Fire on the Moon* by
Norman Mailer, copyright © 1969, 1970 by Norman Mailer, by permission of Little, Brown and
Co. Reprinted by permission of the author and the author's agents, Scott Meredith Literary
Agency, Inc., 845 Third Avenue, New York, N.Y. 10022.

From "Double Perspective on Hysteria" by Robert Scholes, copyright © 1968 by Saturday
Review, Inc., reprinted by permission of Saturday Review, Inc.

From *The Elements of Fiction* by Robert Scholes, copyright © 1968 by Oxford University Press,
Inc., reprinted by permission of Oxford University Press, Inc.

Reprinted with the permission of Farrar, Straus & Giroux, Inc., from *The Electric Kool-Aid
Acid Test* by Tom Wolfe, copyright © 1968 by Tom Wolfe, copyright © 1967 by the World
Journal Tribune Corporation. From *Radical Chic & Mau-Mauing the Flak Catchers* by Tom
Wolfe, copyright © 1970 by Tom Wolfe. *The New Journalism, with an Anthology Edited by Tom
Wolfe and E. W. Johnson*, copyright © 1973 by Tom Wolfe and E. W. Johnson, reprinted by
permission of Harper & Row, Publishers, Inc.

© 1966/1969 by The New York Times Company. Reprinted by permission: "The Story behind a
Nonfiction Novel" by George Plimpton, January 16, 1966; and "The Literary Sixties: When the
World Was Too Much with Us" by Alfred Kazin, December 21, 1969.

Manufactured in the United States of America
Library of Congress Catalog Card Number 76-20826
ISBN 0-8078-1281-1

Library of Congress Cataloging in Publication Data

Hollowell, John, 1945–
  Fact and fiction.

  Bibliography: p.
  Includes index.
  1. American fiction–20th century–History and
criticism. 2. Journalism–United States. I. Title. II. New
journalism and the nonfiction novel.
PS379.H63   813'.5'409   76-20826
ISBN 0-8078-1281-1

For TOM
who lived most of his life
during the perilous nineteen-sixties

Contents

PREFACE

THIS STUDY PROPERLY BEGINS with the pervasive social changes in America during the 1960s and the responses of novelists and journalists to those dislocations. A most interesting response has been a form of nonfiction that relies upon the narrative techniques and intuitive insights of the novelist to chronicle contemporary events. Critics who have praised such works as Truman Capote's *In Cold Blood*, Norman Mailer's *The Armies of the Night*, and Tom Wolfe's *The Electric Kool-Aid Acid Test* have seen in them a new fusion of reporting and fiction and have called them "nonfiction novels" and "new journalism." Some detractors have labeled them "pop sociology" and "parajournalism."

Although books and articles that blend the empirical sense of the journalist and the fictional technique of the novelist continue to appear in the 1970s, I begin my discussion with the promise of new hope ushered in by John Kennedy's election in 1960 and conclude with the period marked by the American landing on the moon in the summer of 1969. It was during this decade that major changes in journalistic conventions and a new involvement of novelists in current history coalesced in a unique way.

To discuss such a contemporary literary development has inherent risks. The critic, without the clarity of perspective provided by intervening years, may fall prey to the distorting proximity of a decade just past. Yet our present literary climate is a precarious one for writers and critics alike. And the forms and styles of all art are shifting rapidly, perhaps more rapidly than ever before. Such hybrid forms as the nonfiction novel demand examination not only for the vivid portrait of contemporary life they provide, but also for what they may tell us about the direction of American writing. Raymond M. Olderman contends in his study of the novel of the 1960s that

it is no longer cutting it too fine to talk about the vision of a single decade. Writers more than ever have become conscious of history and the symbolic value of turning points. Decades are treated with the same sense of symbolic new directions as centuries have been treated in the past. . . . The novel of the 1960s decidedly turns away from the many sacred values of the novel written in the 1950s; and nothing seems more certain than that the novel of the 1970s will similarly turn from its predecessor.*

Olderman's point can be made equally of the nonfiction of the past decade.

The nonfiction novel and the new journalism are significant for three main reasons: (1) they reflect changes in the style and form of traditional journalism; (2) nonfiction novels demonstrate a changing relationship between the writer's conception of his role and the production of art in a mass society; and (3) the writer's choice of documentary forms rather than imaginative fiction raises important questions about the direction of writing in America.

From all the excellent nonfiction of the 1960s, I have selected works by Truman Capote, Norman Mailer, and Tom Wolfe for close analysis. Such books as *In Cold Blood*, *The Armies of the Night*, and *The Electric Kool-Aid Acid Test* are among the best written of the nonfiction novels and they are fairly representative of the themes that such books present. Also, each writer figures significantly in the general trend since each has formulated a tactical definition of the genre. Capote coined the phrase "nonfiction novel," and, in a series of interviews, defined his work as a fusion of journalistic and fictional narrative forms. Norman Mailer wrote three nonfiction novels during the 1960s, each a curious blend of essay, memoir, reportage, and autobiography. Like Capote, Mailer contributed to the aesthetic definition of the form, calling his work a history "in the form of a novel." Tom Wolfe, while not a novelist, has become almost synonymous with the term *new journalism*.

*Raymond M. Olderman, *Beyond the Waste Land: The American Novel in the 1960s* (New Haven: Yale University Press, 1972), p. x.

Wolfe's ambitious thesis is that varieties of journalism have replaced the realistic novel as the dominant form of writing in America.

The dilemmas of our present situation, which seems so much to be one of transition in literature, demand a multifaceted critical perspective. In *The Novelist at the Crossroads*, David Lodge makes an analogy to painting that I would like to adopt here. "One may stand with his nose to a painting to admire its detailed brushwork," writes Lodge, "or at the other side of the gallery to appreciate its arrangement of shapes and color. Both are legitimate ways of looking at the painting, whether one stands close up or far away (or somewhere in between) depends entirely on what one is interested in at the time."† My own interests lead me in both directions at once. I attempt to take a long view to determine the nonfiction novel's place in contemporary writing and the changes in the writer's relationship to history that it reflects. The short view permits the close reading of particular texts.

The new fusion of novelistic technique and factual reporting raises complex questions beyond the scope of a strictly literary study. The traditional distinctions between elite art forms and the popular arts, and between "art" and "non-art," seem continually to be evaporating. The writer's position in society as a public figure whose reputation may have nothing whatever to do with his artistic accomplishment is a significant feature of our literary scene. I rely upon insights drawn from social history and the history of American journalism wherever they appear relevant. The risks of adopting the speculations of social scientists, of historians, and of students of journalism for literary study is a necessary complexity, but a fruitful one, I hope, for the critic to employ.

†David Lodge, *The Novelist at the Crossroads, and Other Essays on Fiction and Criticism* (Ithaca: Cornell University Press, 1971), p. x.

Acknowledgments

IN THE COURSE of writing this study, I have incurred debts both large and small that cannot fully be repaid. Several colleagues at the University of Michigan read earlier versions of this manuscript with care and suggested useful directions for further study. Ira Konigsberg helped me particularly in the refinement of the critical problems and steered me from many unfruitful paths. Marvin Felheim proved himself a rich source of information about the popular culture and provided needed encouragement, especially in the early stages of my work. To Stephen Dunning, who guided my three years of doctoral study and who read an earlier version of the manuscript with utmost care, I owe a permanent debt. Joseph Blotner provided me always with sound critical advice. Without the benefits of his knowledge and scholarly judgment at every stage of the research and writing, this study would be much impoverished.

My colleague at the University of Arizona, Rex Pemberton, played a vital role during the final revision of this book. His extensive knowledge of Tom Wolfe's work and his interest in contemporary literature were sources of encouragement and often lively debate. Our talks over a wide range of critical issues allowed me to refine and clarify my ideas. My students in an English 4 course dedicated to the "new journalism" gave my notions about this genre of writing the special tests that only classroom discussion can provide. Their comments on the works analyzed here spurred their instructor to new insights and broader reading.

Others assisted me significantly at various stages of my work. I am grateful to the Dean of the College of Liberal Arts, the University of Arizona, for a grant that supported the final stages of my research. Linda Compton and Suzanne Taylor of the University of Michigan typed the preliminary versions of the manuscript expertly. Patricia White of the English Department of the University of Arizona prepared the final manuscript with patience and good humor. I am indebted to the staff of The University of North Carolina Press—and, in particular, to my editor Sandra Eisdorfer— for patient guidance and counsel in the preparation of this book. Finally, my wife, Eileen, read this study in each of its several transformations and always suggested changes worth making. More than that, she and my son, Daron, kept the demands of everyday existence within manageable bounds while I wrote. To all these, and to those not specifically mentioned here, I give my sincere thanks.

FACT
& FICTION

I

NOVELISTS AND THE NOVEL IN A TIME OF CRISIS

There is no more fiction or
nonfiction—only narrative.
—E. L. DOCTOROW, *in an*
acceptance speech for the best
novel of 1975, awarded by the
National Book Critics Circle

THE DOMINANT MOOD of America in the 1960s was apocalyptic. Perpetual crisis seemed in many ways the rule. Throughout the decade the events reported daily by newspapers and magazines documented the sweeping changes in every sector of our national life and often strained our imaginations to the point of disbelief. Increasingly, everyday "reality" became more fantastic than the fictional visions of even our best novelists. When a twisted assassin fired upon the presidential motorcade in Dallas in November of 1963, events that seemed before beyond our wildest fantasies became a part of everyday reality.

A killer in a tower shot randomly into a crowd and slaughtered a dozen people. In New York a young woman was stabbed to death in full view of thirty-eight witnesses who did nothing. As American involvement in Vietnam heightened, young people on college campuses banded together in radical and often violent demonstrations

bystander effect (also this story is exaggerated see K. Genovese)

against the government. When the gains of the nonviolent Civil Rights movement did not end poverty and racial discrimination, angry black people burned and looted the urban ghettos that confined them. Perhaps more than at other times in American history, public events were bewildering, chaotic, almost random, and without meaning.

Even more important were changes in life-style and in the values and attitudes of Americans that appeared fundamental and comprehensive. The drug culture. The sexual revolution. The age of Aquarius. Such phrases became the watchwords to describe basic changes affecting every area of our national life. Young people and minority groups sought radical solutions to their problems and rejected, at least in part, the American dream of material success. Turning their backs on wealth and work they found meaningless, college students were attracted to communal living, Eastern religions, and consciousness-altering drugs. By the mid-sixties, political groups of every stripe had developed as individuals sought alternative solutions to the problems that beset society. Brightly colored clothing and long hair reflected a new freedom in personal style from the conservatism of the past. Whatever these pervasive changes in the social fabric of America might augur for the future, it was apparent that comprehensive changes in our consciousness and in the patterns of our national life were occurring. And like many of the rest of us, American novelists were confused.

I

Although the social ferment of the sixties revived old dilemmas and imposed special demands on writers of fiction, it also generated new possibilities. Many of the popular books of the last decade reflect an increased concern for social issues and an awareness of the individual's relationship to an explosive social history. Brooding about the sweeping changes in social values, mores, and life-styles, some of our best novelists complained about the difficulty of writing fiction at all in a period in which daily events seemed to preempt the possibilities of the novelist's imagination. Many novelists, in fact, temporarily turned away from the creation of fiction toward forms of social commentary, documentary, and a vigorous kind of reportage. The American novelist's preoccupation with the rush and frenzy of events in the sixties diverted the impulse for fiction into the special kind of journalism that is the subject of this book.

One significant direction the new writing took was toward documentary forms, eyewitness reports, and personal and confessional narratives. The work of certain novelists, as well as that of certain journalists, reflects an unusual degree of self-consciousness about the writer's role in society and the unique character of American life. Many novelists confronted directly in their works the problem of writing fiction in such an era, since literature, like the American experiment of democracy itself, seemed to rest on such a precarious foundation. If anarchy reigned, the argument might have gone, then written literature itself was threatened with disruption or extinction.

This doesn't seem like an immediate effect of anarchy

While such fears now seem highly exaggerated, the social pressures on novelists and the novel form were to many observers unprecedented. Perhaps it is a common tendency of a nation to find its historical situation unique and unparalleled, and during the sixties this apocalyptic fervor pervades much of our best writing. The familiar arguments about "the death of the novel" were revived with a new kind of validity. The most frequently cited difficulty for writers of fiction was that of defining just what "social reality" was. Everyday events continually blurred the comfortable distinctions between reality and unreality, between fantasy and fact. In a society so fluid and so elusive, the creation of social realism seemed continually to be upstaged by current events. Philip Roth expressed the frustration of many novelists of his generation in a 1961 article:

The American writer in the middle of the 20th century has his hands full in trying to understand, then describe, and then make *credible* much of the American reality. It stupefies, it sickens, it infuriates, and finally it is even a kind of embarrassment to one's own meager imagination. The actuality is continually outdoing our talents, and the culture tosses up figures almost daily that are the envy of any novelist.[1]

Roth's complaint about the competition of fiction with the events broadcast daily by the news media reverberated in public statements by other novelists, and was often reflected in fiction itself. In "The Man Who Studied Yoga," an ambitious prologue to a projected eight-part novel, Norman Mailer's protagonist Sam Slovoda is himself a frustrated writer. In an early sequence of the story, the narrator reports Sam's difficulty in writing realistically: "Marvin asks Sam if he has given up on his novel, and Sam says, 'Temporarily.' He cannot find a form, he explains. He does not want to write a realistic novel, because reality is no longer realistic."[2] This perceived unreality of contemporary life and the problems it poses for the novelist is, of course, nothing new in American literature. Even our earliest novelists—Cooper, Hawthorne, and to an extent, Melville—complained that American society did not offer the depth and stability of cultural materials to sustain a national literature. In a 1966 paper Norman Mailer succinctly summarized this viewpoint:

[American social realism] was a literature which grappled with a peculiarly American phenomenon—a tendency of American society to alter more rapidly than the ability of its artists to record that change. . . . The American phenomenon had to do with the very rate of acceleration. It was as if everything changed ten times as fast in America, and this made for extraordinary difficulty in creating a literature.[3]

Since the beginnings of the novel in the eighteenth century, of course, it has periodically become fashionable for critics to speak of the form's imminent death. In a 1923 essay T. S. Eliot declared that the novel had ended with Flaubert and with James. At about the same time, Spanish critic Ortega y Gasset formulated a particularly influential argument in "Notes on the Novel."[4] Ortega pointed to what he called the increasing dehumanization of art in industrialized society, and went on to proclaim that the novel was dying since it had been cut off from the middle-class roots that had originally fostered its development. In metaphors comparing the source of fiction to a mine of ore, Ortega suggested that the plots and techniques available to novelists would soon become exhausted. Although contemporary critic Louis Rubin, Jr., vehemently disagrees with the conclusion that the novel is dying, he has nonetheless ironically summarized the argument: "The novel was a nineteenth-century phenomenon which depended for its life on the breakdown of the traditional class structure, and now that the class structure is permanently fluid, . . . there is no place for the novel."[5]

Since about the mid-fifties, the arguments of Eliot and Ortega have been endorsed in varying degrees by influential modern critics. Some have found the suggestion of the novel's death to be exaggerated, but have nonetheless agreed that certain possibilities for fictional realism and certain possibilities of language are reaching exhaustion. In a provocative collection of essays entitled *Waiting for the End* (1964), Leslie Fiedler declares that if the novel dies two root causes will be paramount: "First because the artistic faith that sustained its writers is dead, and second because the audience-need it was invented to satisfy is being better satisfied otherwise."[6]

A 1967 article by John Barth called "The Literature of Exhaustion" is indicative of what Fiedler terms the writer's lack of faith. Barth argues persuasively that what is significant is not whether the novel is dead, but *why* so many writers *feel* as if it were:

Literary forms certainly have histories and historical contingencies, and it may well be that the novel's time as an art form is up, as the "times" of classical tragedy, grand opera, or the sonnet sequence came to be. No necessary cause for alarm in this at all, except perhaps to certain novelists, and one way to handle such a feeling might be to write a novel about it. Whether historically the novel expires or persists seems immaterial to me: if enough writers and critics *feel* apocalyptic about it, their feeling becomes a considerable cultural fact, like the *feeling* that Western civilization, or the world, is going to end rather soon.[7]

In terms of the audience need traditionally fulfilled by the novel, Fiedler means that movies and television have supplanted the novel's cognitive function as "news" or "the portrait of provincial life." Marshall McLuhan's series of prophetic books have reinforced this viewpoint in even more emphatic terms. In *The Gutenberg Galaxy* (1962) and *Understanding Media* (1964), McLuhan speculates that Western man, who was traditionally visually oriented and bound to print media, has switched his "sensory balance" from the eye to the ear. Now Western man, according to McLuhan, is attuned to the drumbeat of television and film and is unconsciously bound to a new worldwide unity—"the global village." Despite the fact that McLuhan's speculations are not founded upon empirical research, his conclusions provided new ammunition to those who argued that the traditional audience for fiction was turning elsewhere. More than that, McLuhan's theories undermined further the novelist's artistic faith in himself and his medium.

What began as the American novelist's plaintive cry about the pressures on the writing of fiction has, in recent years, been increasingly endorsed by literary critics and social historians. One unmistakable trend to emerge from the writing of the fifties and sixties has been the growing popularity and significance of nonfiction. This, too, has diverted the writer's impulse away from fiction. In an influential review of sociologist David Riesman's *The Lonely Crowd*, Lionel Trilling praised the book's literary quality and suggested that the novel's traditional function of examining morals and manners was being better served by the social sciences. Similarly, *Commentary* editor Norman Podhoretz argued in 1958 that the most interesting writing done in the fifties was not fiction, but the frequently confessional and autobiographical essays to be found between magazine covers.[8] Podhoretz singled out for praise the "discursive prose" of such writers as Isaac Rosenfeld and James Baldwin. The magazine article, Podhoretz predicted, would become the prevailing art form in America. Novelists who must compete with the electronic media for fame and dollars, would become too impatient to suffer the long incubation periods required by fiction. They would opt instead, said Podhoretz, for the success and immediate fame afforded them by magazine journalism.

The celebration of the rise of nonfiction in recent years led quite naturally to a fierce critical backlash. In a 1965 article entitled "Who's Killing the Novel?," Robert Brustein charged that critics like Podhoretz were actually hastening the decline of the novel by making it increasingly difficult for the young writers who might revitalize fiction to publish their work. Even worse, the preference for nonfiction over fiction constituted the subversion of the public taste. Yahoos like Podhoretz who consciously promoted "the article as art," Brustein concluded, would usher in an era of philistinism.[9]

Somewhere between such celebration and such contempt for the increasing popularity of nonfiction lies a less hysterical middle ground. Clearly, the novel did not die in the mid-sixties; too many well-written novels dispute this claim. Yet the demands placed upon novelists, both in terms of audience need and the importance of alternative media, were real and felt pressures. And it was clear that at least certain conventions of social realism, as well as certain possibilities of language and technique, were less well suited to the radically different character of the American reality.⌋

The growing popularity of nonfiction in recent decades is apparent from even the most cursory review of magazine trends. Until about the forties, in fact, magazines printed about one-third nonfiction and two-thirds fiction. By the mid-sixties, however, this proportion had nearly reversed itself.[10] Similarly, a perusal of best-seller lists for the last decade reveals a concomitant rise in memoirs, confessions, autobiographies, and a host of "how-to" books by psychologists, doctors, and others. Even contemporary poetry shows a similar tendency toward autobiographical and confessional themes. Although these trends do not foreshadow the death of fiction, the increasing proportion of nonfiction reflects a new confrontation with public statements and social issues.

Certain shared assumptions that have previously bound novelists together *do* appear to be on the decline. Novelists writing today, for example, seem less willing to make assumptions about what "reality" is. The familiar technique of authorial omniscience has declined in recent novels, perhaps implying a reluctance to affirm the God-like knowledge that the technique implies. The contradictory impulses to be found in recent fiction make critical affirmations about the values and techniques it embodies practically impossible. Yet Marcus Klein's introductory statement in *The American Novel since World War II* is illustrative of the antithetical directions in recent fiction:

In the years since the end of World War II the novel in America has been: nihilistic, existential, apocalyptic, psychological; it has withdrawn from social considerations; it has been radical and conservative. In form it has been loosely picaresque, it has returned to its beginnings in myth, it has been contrived with a cunningness of technique virtually decadent, it has been purely self-reflexive and respondent to its own development. And the novel has died.[11]

In an important way, the lack of a clear direction in postwar fiction reflects a period of transition and experimentation in a variety of narrative forms. Certain conventions and techniques of traditional realism have declined, but this does not imply the imminent demise of fiction. Rather we have entered a period of widespread literary experimentation in which a variety of forms coexist side by side.

2

The ferment of social change of the last decades, and the exhaustion of certain forms of fiction that have dominated the novel since World War II, have created new opportunities for writers. One of the most interesting responses has been the creation of hybrid forms that combine fictional techniques with the detailed observation of journalism. Perhaps more than the novels of the last two decades, these nonfiction works have successfully conveyed the national confusion and the cataclysmic tenor of American life. Significantly, novelists have turned away from the necessity of inventing plots and characters to direct confrontations with social reality. The varieties of these works of fictionalized social history have been called by a number of terms—"higher journalism," "new journalism," "the literature of fact." By whatever name we call them, however, these forms of narrative reportage have capitalized upon the growing popularity of nonfiction. They reflect an increasing tendency toward documentary forms, toward personal confession, toward the exploration of public issues. Perhaps most important, the best of such works have been written not only by journalists but by novelists who have temporarily abandoned fiction to explore the social issues and moral dilemmas that confront us.

This still-evolving form of nonfiction has not, as its advocates would claim, replaced the function of fiction, but it has already become an important feature of recent literary history. Truman Capote called *In Cold Blood*, his account of the multiple murder of a Kansas farm family, a "nonfiction novel." Norman Mailer wrote a series of books during the sixties that similarly blend the empirical eye of the reporter with the moral vision of the novelist. Perhaps in response to Capote's tremendous success, Mailer subtitled his *The Armies of the Night* "history as a novel, the novel as history." Both writers undoubtedly wanted to attach the prestige of the novel to works of nonfiction, but more important, they wanted to underscore the claim that nonfiction is capable of the moral seriousness of the novel.

In addition to the novelists Capote and Mailer, reporters Tom Wolfe, Jimmy Breslin, Joan Didion, Gay Talese, and Hunter Thompson have experimented with fictional techniques by rebelling against the conventional standards of "objective reporting." Works by these writers have collectively been labeled "new journalism," since they have brought to reporting the personal commitment and moral vision frequently found only in fiction. Together these writers have generated a new kind of nonfiction that defies our usual classifications of "fiction" and "nonfiction," since they combine elements of both genres in a variety of ways.

Throughout the sixties, in fact, a number of writers who have traditionally thought of themselves as novelists have been turning to documentary forms as an alternative to fiction. Although the works I shall examine in detail in subsequent chapters are not, strictly speaking, novels, they confound the critical distinctions commonly drawn between "fiction" and "nonfiction." *In Cold Blood* and *The Armies of the Night* are perhaps only the best examples of a whole series of recent books that have captured our attention in a special way. More than the novels of the sixties, the new journalism and the "nonfiction novels" have served the function of fiction; they have illuminated the ethical dilemmas of our time and conveyed the major concerns of these years.

Besides *In Cold Blood* and *The Armies of the Night*, a number of recent books have blurred the distinctions between fact and fiction. Anthropologist Oscar Lewis portrayed vividly the lives of the poor of Mexico and Puerto Rico in *The Children of Sánchez* (1961) and *La Vida* (1966), respectively. Lewis's documentaries *read* more like novels than like works of social science. He translated and transcribed tape-recorded monologues of his subjects telling their own poignant stories, then "fictionalized" them, and inevitably heightened their dramatic impact. Perceiving himself in conscious competition with literature, Lewis has insisted that "*his* material was not to be duplicated elsewhere, that he was working out of a whole new literary domain."[12] Such highly revealing social documents amply demonstrate Trilling's assertion that fiction must now compete with sensitively written social science.

While the white intellectual presented "the culture of poverty" to a largely uninitiated middle class, the extreme experiences of blacks and other minorities have appeared directly in confessions, personal essays, and thinly veiled autobiographical novels. In *Notes of a Native Son* (1957) and *The Fire Next Time* (1963), James Baldwin fiercely documented the harsh realities of the black man in America. Malcolm X's powerful *Autobiography* (1965) proved a candid testament of his climb from squalor and street crime to political and religious leadership. Claude Brown's *Manchild in the Promised Land* (1965) and Piri Thomas's *Down These Mean Streets* (1967) depicted street life in Harlem from the viewpoints of blacks and Puerto Ricans, respectively. From behind the walls of a California prison came the anguished cry of "I am" from Black Panther Eldridge Cleaver in *Soul on Ice* (1968). These confessional and autobiographical books brought to the attention of white audiences the neglected plight of American minorities. Without the intervention of the fictional imagination, these accounts explored subjects and attitudes neglected for the most part in the novels of the period.

The themes of racial fear and violence that have lain dormant in our literature for a century were imprinted in our consciousness in important books of the sixties. Like Capote and Mailer, novelist John Hersey temporarily abandoned fiction to write a documentary account of the Detroit riots in *The Algiers Motel Incident* (1968). Hersey's interpretation of the mutual suspicions of blacks and whites and police brutality employed brilliantly many of the techniques pioneered by John Dos Passos in his *U.S.A.* trilogy. Reflecting the growing trend toward the treatment of minority experiences, William Styron's *The Confessions of Nat Turner* (1967) proved a powerful and provocative historical novel about the suppressed powers and dreams of a black man.

Literary critics, too, wrote personal accounts about the social issues and the current events of the late sixties. Leslie Fiedler chronicled the imbroglio surrounding his drug arrest in *On Being Busted* (1969), and John Aldridge assessed the changes brought about in society by radical youth in the controversial *In the Country of the Young* (1970). Susan Sontag's *A Trip to Hanoi* (1968) and parts of her *Styles of Radical Will* (1970) provide us with an insider's look at Vietnam and an analysis of the increasing radicalism of youth. Like novelists and journalists, these critics spoke out in essays that reflect a personal commitment and involvement in the crucial moral issues of the decade.

In a 1970 article comparing *The Armies of the Night* and *The Autobiography of Malcolm X*, Warner Berthoff contends that they are merely the most conspicuous examples of a series of recent books that cast the writer in the role of moral witness to our times. Their importance is not that such books represent a retreat from fiction, Berthoff argues, but that they demonstrate a new trend toward the affirmation of a moral position:

A great many books have recently been claiming our attention in this way; and it is of special interest that literary men and women, as distinct from plain journalists, have been drawn into writing them, as if to satisfy some new, or revived, test of occupational seriousness. So we find an old-school man of letters like Robert Penn Warren turning out a collection of interviews on segregation and race consciousness; a book it is possible to think as nicely fitted to Warren's raconteur's talent as any he has ever given us. . . . Those novels and poems, too, that show some special boldness of ambition are likely to have, or move toward, the form of public statement.[13]

Writing in a similar vein, Alfred Kazin concludes in a summary article on the writing of the sixties in the *New York Times Book Review* that "the world was too much with us" for the necessary detachment and the usual osmotic process of art to take place. Despite the many fine novels published during the decade, Kazin observes that the dominant trend is the increasing power and significance of nonfiction writing in a form that he calls "the imagination of fact." The important dimension of this change in direction from fiction to nonfiction, Kazin notes, has to do with the writer's lack of confidence in his ability to produce the "great novel" of his predecessors:

If anything is clear about American writing and literary culture at this moment, it is that with the possible exception of Vladimir Nabokov, a special case in every way, ... none of the many gifted American novelists today gives even the impression of believing that he will create a masterpiece. Perhaps you don't have to believe in masterpieces in order to create one. ... In any event to talk about masterpieces now is to think of oneself as possessing not merely wholly original powers but a kind of inviolability from the age. ... I can't connect the many strong works of fiction in the 1960's with the old-fashioned belief in oneself as a genius.[14]

[handwritten marginalia: a fundamental disconnect w/ the purpose of the writer, their work and art in general]

Significantly, then, the nonfiction novel has provided novelists with "a disguise and retreat from fiction while permitting them to maintain their interest in fiction."[15] Norman Mailer's attraction to such books as *The Armies of the Night* is that they permit the writer "to have one's immediate say on contemporary matters"[16] and to retain at the same time a loyal readership.

The passion for documentary forms, for eyewitness accounts, and for the affirmation of values provides at least tentative solutions to two dilemmas faced by novelists: (1) how to find a form more closely attuned to the altered nature of reality in America than the conventional realistic novel; and (2) how to secure and maintain an audience. The novelist or critic who can write of his own commitments and actions in the social sphere makes of himself, in effect, his own protagonist. More important, narratives that dramatize social forces and public events can portray actions too broad to be represented by the actions of a single hero. The traditional novel has been concerned with the individual's fate, but many of the important events of the sixties were *collective* experiences—mass political protests, urban riots, the war in Vietnam. Kazin speculates in *Bright Book of Life* that for this reason the nonfiction novel has flourished in the last decade:

The reason for the "non-fiction novel" (and documentary plays, movies, art works) is that it reproduces events that cannot be discharged through one artist's imagination. Tragedy exists in order to be assimilated by us as individual fate, for we can identify with another's death. Death in round numbers is by definition the death of strangers, and that is one of the outrages to the human imagination in the killing after killing which we "know all about," and to which we cannot respond.[17]

Generally for a novel to succeed, the writer must first comprehend a social "reality" and then create a plausible fictional world that bears some resemblance to that world. During the sixties, however, when the differences between "reality" and "fantasy" had blurred, novelists were often unable or unwilling to claim such knowledge.] Even the adoption of the technique of omniscient narration commonly found in realistic novels implies a comprehensiveness of knowledge that many writers refused to accept. In contrast, the writer of the nonfiction novel says, in effect: *"This I saw* and *this I did and felt.* My book implies only whatever impressions and observations I can make about my own experience." If reality and even the "facts" become suspect, then the writer of the nonfiction novel chooses a confessional tone. In Sartre's terms, his stance becomes *engagé* in the world of events.

The writers of works that have been classified as the "literature of fact," the "nonfiction novel," or the "new journalism" do not in any real sense constitute a school or movement. And yet, despite the stylistic and thematic differences of the writers I have mentioned, their works do reflect shared assumptions and techniques that are the direct products of the turbulence of recent life in America. Five main elements characterize the nonfiction novel and its writers:

1. Novelists who have temporarily turned away from fiction have created documentary forms and varieties of public testimony in which the writer is placed in the role of witness to the moral dilemmas of our times.

2. The writer of the nonfiction novel declines to invent fictional characters and plots in order to become instead his own protagonist, frequently as a guide through a region of a contemporary hell.

3. As a narrative form, the nonfiction novel combines aspects of the novel, the confession, the autobiography, and the journalistic report. This deliberate blending of narrative form prompts such critical questions as: What is a novel? What are the differences between fiction and nonfiction? When is something *literature* and when is it *mere* journalism?

4. A sense of ultimacy or a concern with "last things"—a mood of impending apocalypse—pervades such works. The increasing depersonalization of man in mass society, the threat of cultural

anarchy, the fear of the obsolescence of literature, often with the writer as "last man," are among these ultimate concerns.

5. The nonfiction novel is at least a tentative solution to the problems that confront writers of realistic fiction. It has proved to be an appropriate narrative form for the radically altered reality of America in an era of intense social change.

These characteristics, of course, do not apply in the same way to each of the writers I shall be discussing in detail in subsequent chapters. Yet, in general, these common elements do reflect one dominant pattern of recent American writing.

The best nonfiction novels reveal a moral vision that may serve as a guide to the persistent human dilemmas common to men in all eras. And like the best literature of any period, these works are preoccupied ultimately with the nature of man and his power to shape solutions, however tentative, to the difficulties that confront him. Warner Berthoff believes that such books as *The Armies of the Night* and *The Autobiography of Malcolm X* belong to the central tradition of American literature:

Calling them "classics" is not merely pitchman's slang. I am simply persuaded that these two books do in fact have a central place in the continuing major history of American writing; that they are works of formed imaginative argument as powerfully developed and sustained as any we have had during the past quarter century; works organized and deepened by imaginative conceptions of the story to be told which have in the end not only a tough interior truthfulness but also, emerging as determining themes, a visionary force, a transforming authority. And what precisely do we mean by high literature if not work of this character?[18]

3

If I have spoken until now of the growing popularity and importance of socially committed nonfiction to the exclusion of fiction, I have done so chiefly for emphasis. There were of course important and well-crafted novels written during the sixties, many of which reflect themes similar to those treated in the nonfiction novels. Saul Bellow, Bernard Malamud, Philip Roth, William Styron, and John

Updike—to name only a few of the best novelists of the postwar period—wrote new novels that reflect a broadened vision of existence. Then, too, a new group of writers came into prominence in the sixties. Joyce Carol Oates's *Garden of Earthly Delights* (1967), *Expensive People* (1968), and *Them* (1969) expressed many of the concerns that dominate the nonfiction novels and received impressive critical receptions. Joan Didion, whose reputation as a new journalist was established with *Slouching towards Bethlehem* (1967), wrote a beautifully spare portrait of the desperation of a Hollywood woman in *Play It As It Lays* (1970). Yet some of the most popular writers of the fifties were casualties of the altered nature of contemporary life. J. D. Salinger, for example, ceased to write fiction after 1963 and retreated to the woods of New England. And Ralph Ellison and Joseph Heller failed to produce subsequent novels that lived up to the promise of *Invisible Man* or *Catch-22*.

Perhaps a more significant trend in the fiction of the last decade has been experimentation in a variety of fictional forms that demonstrates a dissatisfaction with the assumptions of the realistic novel. A new group of writers, responding in a different way to the social pressures of the decade, created darkly surrealistic works dominated by a sense of black humor and the art of the absurd. Many of these works are revivals of the earliest narrative forms of fantasy, fable, romance, allegory, and myth. William Burroughs created strange fantasies of contemporary experience in *Naked Lunch* (1959) and *Nova Express* (1964). Thomas Pynchon's *V* (1963) and *The Crying of Lot 49* (1966) demonstrate, too, an inversion of time and space and the disruption of cause and effect in order to mirror the unreal quality of our experience. Such satirists and writers of black humor as Donald Barthelme and Kurt Vonnegut, Jr., generated much interest as well, particularly among younger readers. John Hawkes's *The Lime Twig* (1961) and *Second Skin* (1964), and John Barth's *The Sot-Weed Factor* (1960) and *Giles Goat-Boy* (1966), reveal a similar movement away from realism toward myth and fantasy.

Critic of contemporary literature Ihab Hassan contends that what connects these writers is that their works show a desire to reconceive fiction during a period of transition: "These novelists do not make a school. Nor are they committed to some abstract hypothesis concerning 'the death of the novel.' They are, however, all determined to reconceive fiction—the very nature of language and narrative—in terms more adequate to crucial changes in American culture and consciousness."[19] In *Beyond the Waste Land*, Raymond Olderman contends that the fictional vision and techniques of these new writers constitute a reaction against the outmoded or exhausted possibilities of social realism. In contrast, the novels of Bellow, Malamud, Roth, and Styron remain committed by and large to depicting the struggle of an essentially middle-class protagonist trapped or enervated by a confining environment. In *Radical Innocence* Hassan explains that this typical protagonist of postwar fiction recoils within himself, and in confrontation with experience, becomes either a rebel or a victim of society's destructive elements.[20] Although these viewpoints greatly reduce the complexity and variety of recent fiction, Olderman is correct to conclude that the new writers who have come to prominence in the sixties appear to be doing things differently from their predecessors. For although no clear pattern for the new kind of novel has emerged, the works of Hawkes, Barth, and Pynchon reflect the revival of older narrative forms in new combinations in preference to the conventions of realism.

On one level, these novels of the black humorists and satirists constitute a directly opposite approach to social "reality" from that reflected by the nonfiction novel. This is true, Olderman suggests, because "the criteria of what is realistic in a novel must necessarily become shaky when we lose our confidence in recognizable fact. If reality has become surrealistic, what must fiction do to be realistic?"[21] Such works as *The Lime Twig* or Pynchon's *V* do bear a relationship to the bizarre nature of contemporary life, but it is not a directly representational or mimetic one. In *The Nature of Narrative*, Scholes and Kellogg define two antithetical modes of narrative from which the novel has developed historically, the *empirical* mode and the *fictional* mode. This two-part scheme will allow us to see the relationship of nonfiction novels to the new direction in fiction. As Scholes and Kellogg define it, empirical narrative includes history and biography, documentary and journalism. Its commitment is to mimesis, or the realistic representation of experience. The fictional mode, in contrast, includes such forms as romance, fable, allegory, and myth. Its allegiance is to an imagined world distanced from the world of experience and less bound to the contingencies of everyday life.[22]

In his subsequent book *The Fabulators*, Scholes views such works as Barth's *Giles Goat-Boy* and Hawkes's *The Lime Twig* as modern transformations of the very old fictional mode that harkens back to the beginnings of all narrative art.[23] Scholes calls these forms that create imagined verbal worlds "fabulations." Fabulations are characterized by inversions of time and space, by the reversal of causality, and by the frustration of the reader's realistic expectations. Because the realistic novel is breaking up, according to Scholes, fabulistic fiction in the form of fantasy, myth, and fable is the likely direction for the future of American writing.

On the two-part scheme that Kellogg and Scholes propose in *The Nature of Narrative*, nonfiction novels are examples of the empirical mode. In "The Novelist at the Crossroads," however, British critic David Lodge observes that Scholes's prediction that fabulation will dominate the future of fiction tells only one side of the story. Citing *In Cold Blood* and *The Armies of the Night* as examples, Lodge contends that contemporary works tend toward *either* the fictional or the empirical mode, but that the movement is in *both* directions simultaneously:

Mr. Scholes may be right to see the novel as closer to disintegration today than it has ever been in its always hectic and unstable history, but his diagnosis of its direction in *The Fabulators* is one-sided. Since, in his view, the synthesis of empirical and fictional modes is no longer worth the trouble of maintaining, he recommends that narrative should exploit the fictional modes, for which he has a personal predilection, more or less exclusively. Logic suggests, however, that it would be equally possible to move in the opposite direction—towards the empirical narrative, and away from fiction. This is in fact what we find happening.[24]

If Lodge is correct, then the disintegration of the novel into empirical and fictional modes is a reversal of the historical synthesis of history, biography, and chronicle, on the one hand, and allegory, fable, and myth on the other, from which the novel originally grew.

If we wanted to represent the modes of narrative in a very rough way as points along a continuum, it might be diagrammed as follows:[25]

EMPIRICAL   FICTIONAL

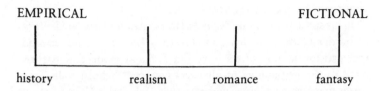

history   realism   romance   fantasy

Moving from left to right along the continuum, the direct representation of experience would be history or a purely empirical narrative. The opposite extreme at the right would be fantasy or a purely imaginary world. Between the extremes lie realism and romance. Realism strives to present the world "as it is" and is closely allied to history; romance presents the world "as it might be" or "as it should be." No actual narrative ever approaches the pure types suggested by the chart, however, since most narratives are combinations of the various elements. Yet it is possible to say that the central tradition of the novel is somewhere in the center, in the area encompassing realism and romance. Lodge's theory would suggest that fewer contemporary works are to be found at the center, and that the direction of change is toward the extremes. Such works as *The Lime Twig* or *V* tend toward fantasy, while *In Cold Blood* and *The Armies of the Night* tend toward history.

This splintering of the novel into the fictional and empirical modes does not necessarily foreshadow the death of the form, but it does represent an important shift in the relationship of literary art to experience. In the present period of literary transition, it seems clear that the realistic novel has declined because it has failed to give expression to the greatly altered consciousness of our experience. And the novelist's dissatisfaction with realism has led to experiments with language and with narrative form. While fabulism might be one solution to the novelist's present dilemma, by the end of the sixties such documentary forms as the nonfiction novel emerged as important alternatives.

THE DEVELOPMENT OF A "NEW" JOURNALISM

> *The status of the New Journalism*
> *is not secured by any means. In*
> *some quarters the contempt for it*
> *is boundless...even breathtaking....*
> *With any luck at all the new genre*
> *will never be sanctified, never be*
> *exalted, never given a theology.*
> –TOM WOLFE, The New
> Journalism

WHILE THE NOVELISTS OF THE SIXTIES were struggling to create narrative forms more closely fitted to the bizarre social reality of American life, a group of reporters began experimenting with fictional techniques in an effort to reconceive American journalism. Even Tom Wolfe, whose name has become almost synonymous with the term *new journalism*, readily acknowledges the inadequacy of the name. Like "the New Humanism, the New Criticism, and the New Frontier," Wolfe explains, "a movement, group, party, . . . philosophy, or theory with 'New' in it, is just begging for trouble."[1] Nonetheless, the variety of changes in reporting techniques and in the form and style of the journalistic article arising in the sixties have collectively been identified with that name. The new journalism differs from the conventional reporting practiced in most newspapers and magazines in two main ways: (1) the reporter's relationship to the people and events he describes reflects new attitudes and values; and (2) the form and style of the news story is radically transformed through the use of fictional devices borrowed from short stories and novels.

I

The most important difference between the new journalism and traditional reporting is the writer's changed relationship to the people and events he depicts. Traditionally, the straight news article is based upon an "objectivity" that requires a commitment to telling both sides of the story, and an impersonality on the part of the journalist characterized by the lack of value judgments and emotionally colored adjectives. Michael J. Arlen describes the standard journalistic practice in America until the changes of the last decade as the functional use of language: "The American press rested its weight on the simple declarative sentence. The no-nonsense approach. Who-what-where-when. Clean English, it was later called when people started teaching it at college. Lean prose."[2]

In sharp contrast to the "objectivity" that the reporter strives for in the standard news article, the voice of the new journalist is frankly subjective; it bears the stamp of his personality. Such colorful writers as Tom Wolfe and Norman Mailer openly flaunt their subjectivity. Less interested in official statements to the press corps by powerful spokesmen and the need for balance, the new journalist records his personal reactions to the people and events that make news.

The new journalist's stance is often openly critical of the powerful interests that control the dissemination of the news. By revealing his personal biases, the new journalist strives for a higher kind of "objectivity." He attempts to explode the myth that any report can be objective by freely admitting his own prejudices. The tradition of objectivity became a fact of life in American journalism about the turn of the century with the development of the major wire services.

Until the changes introduced in the last decade, it has dominated most of American journalism. With the ever-widening gap between the statements of official spokesmen and the events beneath the surface in the sixties, however, a new approach has emerged.[3]

Literary critic Robert Scholes has praised Wolfe and Mailer, calling them "hystorians," since they record the *hysteria* of contemporary life:

> The hystorian operates differently from the orthodox journalist. Perhaps the credulous believe that a reporter reports facts and that newspapers print all of them that are fit to print. But actually newspapers print all of the "facts" that fit, period—that fit the journalistic conventions of what "a story" is (those tired formulas) and that fit the editorial policy of the paper. The hystorian fights this tendency toward formula with his own personality. He asserts the importance of *his* impressions and *his* vision of the world. He embraces the fictional element inevitable in any reporting and tries to imagine his way toward the truth.[4]

In terms of the reporter's attitudes and values, the new journalism reflects a decreased deference toward public officials indicative of the decline in authority throughout society. The conventional reporter typically holds a deferential attitude toward public officials and must dutifully report their statements. The usual news article often reflects, unwittingly, the official attitudes of those with vested interests in how the news gets reported. The new journalist, in contrast, strives to reveal the story hidden beneath the surface facts. Michael J. Arlen describes a hypothetical city fire to illustrate the difference in approach. In the past, Arlen notes, a reporter's facts were based on the official statements made "on the record" by the fire commissioner. "At the Fire Commissioner's briefing, for the most part no one started his camera, or pencil, until the Fire Commissioner came into the room, and walked to the lectern, had opened his Bible, and began to speak."[5] In the new journalist's report, however, people "have a journalistic existence on either side of the event." The new kind of reporter is interested in "what went on before (and after) the Fire Commissioner came into the room. What did he do when he got on the elevator downstairs? Did he drop a quarter on the floor?"[6] This sensitivity to actions and statements that by tradition have been "off the record" makes for colorful reporting, but it also undercuts the authority of public officials.

The new journalism also represents a change in journalistic values on a broader scale. Tom Wolfe charges that the conventional journalistic practices reflected in who-what-where-when reporting usually serve to reinforce the middle-class reader's values. Most news articles, and many feature stories, are representative of what Wolfe calls "totem newspapers." They appear on coffee tables or are simply carried around, but seldom do they jar the reader's value assumptions about the figures and events in the news. By "totem stories," Wolfe means "all those nice stories on the first page of the second section about eighty-seven-year-old ladies on Gramercy Park who have one-hundred-and-two-year old turtles or about the colorful street vendors of Havana."[7] For Wolfe the typical newspaper until the early sixties was "the symbol of the frightened chair-arm-doilie Vicks Vapo-Rub *Weltanschauung* that lies in the solar plexus of all good gray burghers."[8] In contrast to this bland quality of conventional reporting, the best new journalists use a variety of writing techniques to place the reader "inside" a world he may find quite different from his own.

2

The second major area of change reflected in the new journalism lies in the style, language, and form of the journalistic article. Since about the forties, newspaper and magazine reporters have sporadically experimented with the storytelling techniques of fiction applied to the news feature stories. With the ever-increasing "knowledge explosion" in our society, readers have desired news coverage with greater depth and background, with psychological insights into the major figures behind the news, and with interpretation and analysis that place today's news in a broader context. The growing trend toward reporting in depth in newspaper and magazine journalism generally has led to greater freedom for writers in terms of style and form.

Such freedom has not always been the case, however. Despite

individual writers of talent, most newspaper and magazine reporting until the sixties had relied upon certain formulas and conventions fitted to the editorial policy of the publication and the readership. *Esquire* editor Harold Hayes explains that until the rise of the new journalism,

the magazine article was a convention of writing, and those who were successful at it were those who understood the convention. . . . There was an anecdotal lead opening into the general theme of the piece; then some explanation followed by anecdotes or examples. If a single individual was important to the story, some biographical material was included. Then there would be a further rendering of the subject, and the article would close with an anecdote.[9]

Although outstanding writers have often departed from the formula Hayes describes, not until the sixties have so many journalists used fictional techniques in such thorough and sophisticated ways. The new journalist's motive is to achieve a literary style comparable to fiction and to portray characters with psychological depth. The new journalism of Wolfe, Jimmy Breslin, Joan Didion, Gay Talese, and others seeks to elevate reportage to an art form by freeing it from the formulas of typical news writing. In the usual news story, the basic units are facts and quotations. In the new journalism, however, the writer attempts to *reconstruct* the experience as it might have unfolded. The new journalist uses literary techniques to convey information and to provide background not usually possible in most newspaper and magazine reporting.

Although he has a vested interest in the promotion of the new form, Wolfe usefully identifies four principal narrative devices common to realistic fiction as central to the new journalism: (1) portraying events in dramatic scenes rather than in the usual historical summary of most articles; (2) recording dialogue fully rather than with the occasional quotations or anecdotes of conventional journalism; (3) recording "status details," or "the pattern of behavior and possessions through which people experience their position in the world"; and (4) using point of view in complex and inventive ways to depict events as they unfold.[10] Closely related to the techniques Wolfe lists are two additional fictional devices that have been frequently employed by the new journalists: (5) interior monologue, or the presentation of what a character thinks and feels without the use of direct quotations; and (6) composite characterization, or the telescoping of character traits and anecdotes drawn from a number of sources into a single representative sketch.

In addition to these six basic techniques, the new journalists have also used such literary techniques as flashbacks, foreshadowing, inverted chronology, and a variety of others to achieve the vivid and colorful writing usually found only in fiction. Although these techniques have been used sporadically in newspapers and magazines since the forties, not until the sixties have they come together in such systematic ways. Let us look at how each of these techniques has been employed by a major new journalist.

1. The Dramatic Scene. Probably the most important fictional technique employed by the new journalists is the reconstruction of the story as the action unfolds, in dramatic scenes, rather than through a summary of the events. In the collection of his critical prefaces, *The Art of the Novel*, Henry James explains that the development of *scenic* depiction rather than historical summary is the distinguishing characteristic of the novel. Tom Wolfe, for example, develops the action at a party for the Black Panther Defense Fund given by conductor Leonard Bernstein in 1969 almost entirely in this way. Rather than merely summarizing the action for the reader, Wolfe shows the action moving from scene to scene as it unfolds. If the name of his protagonist had been a less famous one, Wolfe's opening paragraph might be mistaken for that of a short story:

At 2 or 3 or 4 a.m., somewhere along in there, on August 25, 1966, his forty-eighth birthday, in fact, Leonard Bernstein woke up in the dark in a state of wild alarm. That had happened before. It was one of the forms his insomnia took. So he did the usual. He got up and walked around a bit. He felt groggy. Suddenly he had a vision, an inspiration. He could see himself, Leonard Bernstein, the *egregio maestro*, walking out on stage in white tie and tails in front of a full orchestra. On one side of the conductor's podium is a piano. On the other is a chair with a guitar leaning against it. . . . He has an anti-war message to deliver to this great starched white-throated audience in the symphony hall. He announces to them: "I love." Just that. The effect is mortifying.[11]

By beginning with this scene of Bernstein's insomniac vision, Wolfe attempts to place the reader inside the conductor's consciousness and to reveal insights about his personality to be fully developed as the story proceeds.

2. *Recording Dialogue in Full.* The "straight news" story is traditionally developed in the familiar "inverted pyramid" format, with the most significant facts and quotations first. Although this practice is changing in America's best newspapers, still the conventional journalist usually strives to tell who-what-where-when in the first paragraph. Although news stories frequently quote key persons, space requirements do not allow for the fully developed dialogue that has been used by the new journalists. When James Mills took to the streets of New York to trail police detective George Barrett for five months, he wrote a particularly revealing article for *Life* called "The Detective." Much of the power of Mills's account lies in his ability to capture Barrett's "tough cop" talk, as in this exchange after breaking up a fight between two homosexuals:

Barrett starts toward them, and a pressman says, "Look out, he has a knife." Barrett grabs the Negro by the shirt, yanks him off the victim and slams him up against the theater wall. . . .

"Quiet!" Barrett orders. "No one talks unless I ask something. Because I won this little show, right? So we play this ball game my way." He writes their names and addresses in a notebook and then asks the one who was beaten if he wants to prefer charges. He says, "No, I just want to leave it where it's at." Barrett then asks each the same questions and gets from each the same answers:

"Are you male?"
"Yes."
"Are you a homosexual?"
"Yes."
"Are you a female impersonator?"
"No."

They have said no to the last because impersonating a female is a crime, but so long as they do not actually wear female clothes they cannot be arrested. . . .

"Hey, germ!" Barrett yells at him. "Come here!" . . .

"Now." Barrett says, indicating everyone except the attacker, "all of you germs walk up this street to Broadway and get lost. Don't come back." They take off.[12]

3. *Status Details*. Although the depiction of what Wolfe calls "status details" is hardly a *new* technique, many of the new journalists have achieved psychological depth to an unusual degree by recording "the everyday gestures, habits, manners, customs, styles of furniture, clothing, decoration . . . by which [people] experience their position in the world."[13] Rex Reed is among those new journalists who have used these realistic details very effectively. His portrait of Ava Gardner as an aging star begins with the following description of her physical surroundings:

She stands there, without benefit of a filter lens against a room melting under the heat of lemony sofas and lavender walls and cream-and-peppermint-striped movie-star chairs, lost in the middle of that gilt-edge birthday-cake hotel of cupids and cupolas called the Regency. There is no script. No Minnelli to adjust the CinemaScope lens. Ice-blue rain beats against the windows and peppers Park Avenue below as Ava Gardner stalks her pink malted-milk cage like an elegant cheetah. She wears a baby-blue cashmere turtleneck sweater pushed up to her Ava elbows and a little plaid mini-skirt and enormous black horn-rimmed glasses and she is gloriously, divinely barefoot.[14]

Reed brilliantly describes the colors and shapes of Ava's surroundings to provide the reader with an important introduction to her world. The style of decoration at the Regency and the clothing she wears tell us a great deal about her personality. As Wolfe readily concedes, status details have long been used in fiction to achieve a precision of characterization. With the new freedom and extended length possible in the new journalism, however, reporters are using these atmospheric details to an unprecedented degree.

4. *Point of View*. A fourth fictional device often used in the new journalism is the portrayal of character as if the reader understood the person's mental processes, or alternatively, from the viewpoint of others significant in his life. Tom Wolfe explains that the new journalist uses point of view to "present every scene to the reader through the eyes of a particular character, giving the reader the feeling of being inside the character's mind." The best new journalists such as Wolfe, Gail Sheehy, Gay Talese, and Jimmy Breslin often reveal the interior thoughts and emotions of the main charac-

ters in their stories in addition to their direct speech. The normal journalistic practice is to quote the subject directly, being careful to attribute each quotation. Yet in *In Cold Blood*, for example, Truman Capote generates sympathy for the killers by narrating their stories from the viewpoints of comforting women close to them. In Wolfe's *Esquire* article about stock-car driver Junior Johnson, the narrator feigns the voice of a character from Johnson's native Ingle Hollow, North Carolina:

Working mash wouldn't wait for a man. It started coming to a head when it got ready to and a man had to be there to take it off, out there in the woods, in the brush, in the brambles, in the muck, in the snow. Wouldn't it have been something if you could have just set it all up inside a good old shed with a corrugated metal roof and order those parts like you want them and not have to smuggle all the copper and all that sugar and all that everything out here in the woods and be a coppersmith and a plumber and a cooper and a carpenter and a pack horse and every other goddamned thing God ever saw in the world, all at once.[15]

downstage voice

By imitating the speech patterns and run-on sentences of a moonshiner, Wolfe conveys a sense of Johnson's background and attitudes without explicitly commenting upon them. Such a passage dramatizes his rise from a whiskey runner to well-known stock-car racer more effectively than a simple biographical summary could.

5. *Interior Monologue.* A distinctive use of point of view that can be considered a separate technique is interior monologue. Events are reported *as if* a subject were thinking them rather than through the direct quotations of the speaker. In *Honor Thy Father*, his account of gangland leader Joseph Bonanno, and *The Kingdom and the Power*, a "human history" of the *New York Times*, Gay Talese employs this technique quite effectively. In a panel discussion about the new journalism, Talese explained that the purpose of interior monologue is to reveal a character's thoughts and attitudes more completely and without the interruptions necessary with direct quotations:

"I rarely if ever will use a direct quotation any more. I'll use dialogue, but I would never, if someone that I may be following around, should say something, I would never quote as an old *New Yorker* profile might quote some fisherman for 8,000 words in a row. . . . I always take it out of direct quotations and use it without quotations but always attribute. . . . [When I interview a subject], I would ask him what he *thought* in every situation where I might have asked him in the past what he did and said."[16]

In *The Kingdom and the Power*, Talese employs the interior monologue to reveal the thoughts and attitudes of A. M. Rosenthal, whose new policies as assistant managing editor of the *Times* angered and upset many veteran reporters:

Seated behind his big desk in the middle of the newsroom, Rosenthal momentarily looked up from the stories that he was reading and gazed around the room at the distant rows of desks, the reporters typing, talking among themselves, sometimes looking at him in a way he suspected was hostile—*they must despise me*, he thought, being both irritated and saddened by the possibility, *they must really hate my guts*.[17]

6. *Composite Characterization*. A sixth literary technique often employed in the new journalism is the creation of a *composite character*, a person who represents a whole class of subjects. In the best articles, these "composites" are always supported by careful interviewing and research. Gail Sheehy uses this technique effectively in a series of articles on prostitution that appeared in *New York* magazine. Her subsequent book *Hustling* (1970) begins with a sketch of "Redpants," a composite of several Times Square prostitutes Sheehy had interviewed and followed around in researching her story. The opening scene depicts "Redpants" eluding the police:

The girl in red pants walks into the Belmont Plaza allnight drugstore.
    "Got a hammer? My heel came off in a chase."
    She is thin as a needle, tracked in the arms and urgent around the eyes. The druggist produces a hammer. She lifts one long, exquisitely bolted leg in an arabesque—every eye in the store bleeds because her legs are still dazzling— and she says to the druggist, "Tap it on for me, will you, sugar?"
    She is wearing Gucci shoes. Remnants of a near past when the girl they called Redpants lit up this street like fireworks.[18]

Critics of the new journalism have objected to the use of composite characters, feeling that the technique is dishonest if the reader may be deluded into thinking he is reading about an actual person.[19] Sheehy has defended her practice in the preface where she explains: "The widow in 'The Ultimate Trick' [and 'Redpants'] [are] composite[s] of several women, and the quotes and anecdotes supporting them are assembled from several years of acquaintance with their lives. The form is literary. The function is to present the life while protecting the privacy of perfectly decent people."[20] At its best composite characterization allows the journalist to compress documented evidence from a variety of sources into a vivid and unified telling of the story.

Although these "fictive" techniques have been used occasionally by journalists for decades,[21] not until the sixties have they coalesced in the unique and sophisticated style of the new journalists. In the best new journalism, vivid and colorful writing complements careful research. In the hands of less scrupulous reporters, however, the urge to "fictionalize" has led to the abuse and fabrication of dialogue.[22] In general, however, the new journalism requires extensive research and even more careful reporting than does the typical news article. In his work on *In Cold Blood*, Capote interviewed hundreds of individuals close to the Clutter family and to the killers, accumulating documents sufficient "to fill a small room." Wolfe's critics have charged that he was "piping it," or making up dialogue, in his article on Leonard Bernstein's radical chic party. He has defended his accuracy as follows: "I was also accused of sneaking a tape recorder into Bernstein's home in order to get the dialogue. . . . I took this as a great left-handed compliment to my accuracy, which I achieved in the oldest and most orthodox manner possible: I came . . . for no other reason than to write about it, arrived with a notebook and ballpoint pen in plain view and took notes."[23] By the mid-sixties such critics as Dwight Macdonald in the *New York Review of Books* attacked the new journalism for turning reporting of the news into mere entertainment.[24] Several critics have also felt that the new journalism style inspires fictionalizing, even when the reporter has been careful to verify the facts and to perform the background research necessary for the storytelling techniques the form relies on. In *Fame and Obscurity*, however, Gay Talese defends the new journalism against such charges and contends that the new form requires even more rigorous research than does conventional reporting:

The best new journalism, though often reading like fiction, is not fiction. It is, or should be, as reliable as the most reliable reportage although it seeks a larger truth than is possible through mere compilation of verifiable facts, the use of direct quotations, and adherence to the rigid organizational style of the older form. The new journalism allows, demands in fact, a more imaginative approach to reporting.[25]

The new journalism demands a more intense and personal kind of interviewing and research than does traditional reporting. Tom Wolfe's term is "saturation reporting," since in order to record accurately the scenes and dialogue of events as they occur, the journalist must saturate himself in a particular environment. This method frequently requires the reporter to follow his subject around for days or even months and years with a sensitivity to certain people and events and often to a special atmosphere. Capote spent six years researching *In Cold Blood* and formed many close friendships with the people of Holcomb, Kansas, where the murders took place. Similarly, Tom Wolfe's *The Electric Kool-Aid Acid Test* involved him to an unusual degree in the drug scene of California.

This kind of dogged "close-to-the-skin" reporting is the key to the success of most of the new journalists. Some writers are reluctant to follow their subjects around for extended periods of time, but Wolfe claims some kind of rapport must be established before the psychological depth of the new journalism can be achieved. "If a reporter stays with a person or group long enough," Wolfe explains, "they—reporter and subject—will develop a personal relationship of some kind, even if it is one of hostility."[26]

Although the changes in narrative techniques and method inherent in the new journalism represent important differences from conventional journalism, promoters of the genre overemphasize their originality. Such outstanding reporters as Wolfe, Talese, Breslin, Didion, and others are only the most conspicuous examples of more general changes that have been occurring over the last two decades in American journalism. Former editor of the *New York Times Magazine* Lester Markel believes that most accounts of the rise of the new journalism give the individual reporter too much credit:

What they [the new journalists] overlook too is that what they call "old" journalism is in the process of important change. Increasing emphasis is being put on interpretation—the effort to make news clear and relevant for the reader and, whenever possible, to provide an approximation of the truth. Reporting in depth—profiles with insights, round-ups, trend stories.... Such pieces do not appear as often as they should, but a start has surely been made. Reporters and editors have definitely progressed.[27]

3

Critics of the new journalism have been quick to point out that the personal style and fictional techniques that characterize the form are hardly "new."[28] Indeed, the historical roots of the present reporting are probably centuries old. Tom Wolfe argues in *The New Journalism* that an aggressive and ambitious group of feature writers at the *New York Herald Tribune* in the early sixties began to experiment with fictional techniques to create a livelier reporting that might save a dying newspaper. Yet in the history of journalism a number of writers and reporters have, at various times, employed the "scenic" methods and the fictive techniques that Wolfe describes. *Village Voice* reporter Jack Newfield defines the new journalism so broadly that writers as diverse as Daniel Defoe and Stephen Crane might qualify as practitioners:

To begin with there is not much that is new about New Journalism. Personal advocacy preceded the who-what-where-when formula of the AP by a couple of centuries. Tom Paine and Voltaire were New Journalists. . . . Objective journalism developed with the teletype and radio news.

Daniel Defoe, Stephen Crane, and Mark Twain were all New Journalists according to most contemporary definitions.[29]

Newfield is right that the fictional techniques of the new journalism derived from the combination of periodical journalism and storytelling that gave rise to the novel in the eighteenth century. Defoe's *Journal of the Plague Year* heaps realistic detail on detail to create the illusion of an eyewitness report of the Great Plague of 1665. While it was fiction masquerading as fact, Defoe's account was long regarded as an accurate historical record. Addison and Steele's periodical journalism of the eighteenth century—particu-

[handwritten marginalia: bipolarity of literature — there is no gray area]

larly their *Sir Roger de Coverley Papers*—relies upon many of the techniques employed by today's new journalists. The nineteenth-century essays of Carlyle, De Quincey, Ruskin, and others show some affinity for today's form of reporting. The most frequently cited example of "old" new journalism is William Hazlitt's 1822 essay called "The Fight," which treats the classic battle of boxers Bill Neate and the Gas-man. Hazlitt provides the "subjective atmosphere" surrounding the event and the you-are-there immediacy that Wolfe and Mailer strive for.[30]

The long tradition of travel literature and local-color sketches also yields examples that prefigure the new journalist's concerns and methods. Dickens's *Pictures from Italy*, written in 1846, vividly depicts the hanging of a highwayman in Rome with the realistic detail and emotional impact one finds in his later novels. Nineteenth-century literature and periodical journalism, too, reveal examples of personal reporting and colorful sketches that rely on fictional techniques, but usually as warm-up exercises for short stories and novels.

In America a reciprocal relationship has always existed between our literary and journalistic traditions. The best American novelists and short story writers have used their narrative gifts to create "sketches" and local-color stories, often as preludes to fiction. In parts of Mark Twain's *Roughing It* and *Life on the Mississippi*, for example, one is hard pressed to distinguish factual reporting from what Twain called "stretchers." Stephen Crane's sketches and newspaper articles of the 1890s, especially, bear a strong resemblance to today's new journalism. Factual reporting and fictionalized storytelling blend thoroughly in many of his tales. Writing for American and British newspapers, Crane invented characters, used himself as a "stranger" in the background, and rendered impressionistic and dramatic dialogue. Such New York sketches as "In a Park Row Restaurant" or "Mr. Binks' Day Off" might easily pass for short stories.[31] In fact, it is difficult to think of very many American writers who have not, at one time or another, been journalists. In addition to Mark Twain and Stephen Crane, such novelists as Henry James, Dreiser, and, of course, Hemingway, have also written nonfiction that closely resembles the new journalism.

The muckraking journalism of the reform period from 1890 to 1912 reveals some works that are very similar to certain varieties of the new journalism. Vivid exposés of city life and the corruption of government and big business, such as Ida Tarbell's *The History of the Standard Oil Company*, Upton Sinclair's *The Jungle*, and Lincoln Steffens's *The Shame of the Cities* are forebears of the advocacy journalists of the sixties. The muckraking spirit is still very much alive today, especially in magazines like *Ramparts* and in the underground press. Although Tarbell and Steffens were more concerned with social reform than with literary style, their work involves the scene setting and narrative passages common to the articles of Wolfe, Talese, Sheehy, and others.

The American "reportage school" of the thirties and the Federal Writers' Project, which chronicled among other things the plight of America's poor during the Great Depression, bears a strong similarity to the new journalism. Walker Evans and James Agee's *Let Us Now Praise Famous Men* explores the lives of sharecroppers in Mississippi with stirring vividness and documentary detail.

see Zavarzadeh's discussion of this book

Several writers of fiction have previously created nonfiction works that closely resemble the nonfiction novels of Capote, Mailer, and Wolfe. Perhaps the most notable example is George Orwell, whose *Down and Out in London and Paris* and *Homage to Catalonia* rely heavily upon the "close-to-the-skin" reporting that characterizes the new journalism. A few of Hemingway's war reports, and especially such nonfiction as *Green Hills of Africa* and *Death in the Afternoon*, develop from intentions similar to those of Capote and Mailer. In the foreword to *Green Hills of Africa*, Hemingway compares his book explicitly to the novel: "The writer has attempted to write an absolutely true book to see whether the shape of a country and the pattern of a month's action can, if truly presented, compete with a work of the imagination." Meyer Levin's account of the sensational Leopold-Loeb murder case in Chicago in 1924 uses many of the fictional techniques found in *In Cold Blood*. Throughout much of American literature, isolated works by a variety of writers closely parallel the new nonfiction of the sixties.

Although the new journalism did not *flourish* in newspapers and magazines until the last decade, many talented free-lance writers successfully used fictional techniques thirty years earlier. For although objective reporting has been the dominant trend in American journalism, writers for the *New Yorker* as early as the thirties were intent on making reportage more literary. In the thirties and forties, St. Clair McKelway, Joseph Mitchell, Lillian Ross, and A. J. Liebling virtually pioneered a new form of magazine journalism in the *New Yorker* "Profiles." These writers combined careful research, fictionalized scenes, and extensive dialogue to bring a new level of sophistication to the personality piece. Liebling's series of articles on New York life, or his depiction of "Colonel Stingo," employ nearly all the techniques later used by Wolfe and Talese. Gay Talese admitted as much in a 1970 panel discussion on the new journalism:

"When he was writing shorter pieces for *The New Yorker*, you got the sense that Joe Liebling had established himself as sort of the fat man on the scene; it was, The Fat Man Goes to a Fight, The Fat Man is in Parie Restaurants, or The Fat Joe Liebling is down in New Orleans with Huey Long. Liebling had established himself to a lesser degree than Mailer to be sure, but he established himself as a character in the action."[32]

By the forties the American magazine began to change dramatically. Although Wolfe dates the beginnings of the new journalism in the sixties, fictional techniques are apparent in the magazine articles of the forties and fifties. The immediate predecessors of today's new journalism may date from the *New Yorker* articles, such as John Hersey's "Hiroshima" to which an entire edition of the magazine was devoted in 1946. Lillian Ross's narrative reporting in "Picture," her account of the filming of *The Red Badge of Courage*, is another early example.

4

Although the roots for a new journalism have long been present in American writing, the forces that coalesced in the sixties fostered a rebellion against conventions and formulas on a wide scale. Tom Wolfe thinks that the new style began early in the decade when his friends writing for the *New York Herald Tribune*'s Sunday supplement—Jimmy Breslin, Dick Schaap, Charles Portis—began experimenting with fictional techniques in news feature stories and columns. The new art journalism began, in Wolfe's view, as a competition among newspaper writers based primarily in New York. It was not based on the familiar "scoop competition"—getting the exclusive story first—that inspires most movie plots about reporters. Instead, it was, in Wolfe's view, a literary struggle among columnists and news feature reporters. Unlike the "straight news" story, Wolfe explains,

feature stories gave a man a certain amount of room in which to write. Unlike scoop reporters, the feature writers did not openly acknowledge the existence of their competition, not even to one another. Nor was there any sort of scorecard. And yet everyone in the game knew precisely what was going on and went through the most mortifying sieges of envy, even resentment, or else surges of euphoria, depending on how the game was going.[33]

The phenomenon of fictional techniques used in nonfiction was occurring in many parts of the country, however, not just in New York. Free-lance writer André Fontaine explains that Wolfe's chronology is distorted: "Most accounts of new journalism said that it all started in the early sixties and all agreed that it was being practiced by a small group of New Yorkers that included Wolfe himself, Jimmy Breslin, Gay Talese, and a few others. But while these men are unquestionably new journalists, the list leaves out more names than it includes—David Smith and Stuart Loory of the *Los Angeles Times*, Ben Bagdikian and Joan Didion."[34]

Yet while Wolfe may be right that the new journalism got its impetus from news features and columns of metropolitan newspapers, it soon spread to magazines when Wolfe and Talese among others began free-lancing for *Esquire*. Wolfe recalls that an early piece by Talese called "Joe Louis: The King as a Middle-Aged Man" startled him when he first read it in *Esquire*, since it begins with dialogue between the ex-champ and his wife that one might find in a short story:

"Hi, sweetheart!" Joe Louis called to his wife, spotting her waiting for him at the Los Angeles Airport.
She smiled, walked toward him, and was about to stretch up on her toes and kiss him—but suddenly stopped.

"Joe," she said, "where's your tie?"

"Aw, sweetie," he said, shrugging, "I stayed out all night in New York and didn't have time—"

"All *night*!" she cut in, "When you're out here all you do is sleep, sleep, sleep."

"Sweetie," Joe Louis said, with a tired grin, "I'm an ole man."[35]

Although Wolfe's history of the new journalism stresses the creativity of the innovative reporters, the economics of publishing life and the financial plight of struggling newspapers and magazines also gave new impetus to experimentation. In the late fifties, such household names of American reading as *Collier's* and *Woman's Home Companion* ceased publication. In the sixties and seventies, giants of publishing such as the *Saturday Evening Post* (1969), *Look* (1971), and *Life* (1972) gave way to financial pressures throughout the industry. Newspaper mergers, too, were common in recent years due to increased costs of production and loss of advertising revenue to electronic media.[36] Although television advertising is far more expensive, many advertisers prefer to focus their campaigns upon a potential viewing audience of forty million as compared with the fifteen- to twenty-million readers that the largest-circulating magazines can produce.

Although this economic pattern eventually led to the death of certain general magazines, specialized magazines that appeal to specific groups of consumers have remained alive. The magazine that can deliver a specific advertising market can receive an even larger share of the advertising dollar. Such magazines as *Playboy* and *Esquire*, directed toward a young, predominantly male audience under thirty-five continue to prosper even in years of high inflation. Sophisticated marketing research has persuaded advertisers to become more selective and to invest in magazines with distinct appeals to particularly affluent consumers.

One outcome of this struggle for financial survival has been the widespread experimentation in nonfiction. Younger editors at the *Atlantic*, *Harper's*, *Esquire*, and, later, *New York* magazine encouraged the greater freedom in the form and style than had previously been the case. Harold Hayes, the *Esquire* editor from 1956 to 1973, actively promoted experimentation with the form of the nonfiction article and nourished the development of superior writers like Wolfe and Talese. In a 1972 interview, Hayes emphasized the economic factors in the rise of the new journalism: "If there's been any great change to accelerate the possibility of writers dealing more flexibly with the language and with form, it's not because of the birth of a new journalism form, but because there is a commercial disposition among magazines to see that imaginative writing now is more appealing to their readers."[37] A southerner in his thirties at the time, Willie Morris served as editor of *Harper's* from 1967 to 1971 and revitalized that magazine's format by encouraging lengthy nonfiction. Morris encouraged such writers as Larry King and David Halberstam during his tenure. And it was he who suggested to Norman Mailer the possibility of a long article on his 1967 march on the Pentagon, which later became the Pulitzer Prize-winning *The Armies of the Night*.

Former *Esquire* editor Clay Felker helped to launch *New York* magazine in 1967, with a staff that included Wolfe, Gail Sheehy, Gloria Steinem, and refugees from the *Herald Tribune*'s Sunday supplement staff. Other editors who have played critical roles in the rise of the new journalism include William Shawn at the *New Yorker*, who strongly supported the writing of *In Cold Blood*, and Dan Wolf at the *Village Voice*.

Beyond the economic necessities and the enterprising editors of the sixties, the rapidly developing underground press contributed to the general atmosphere of freedom from which the new journalism grew. Increasingly, even the more established media are rescinding the restrictions on the use of language, although when the *Village Voice* began in 1955 it was one of the few American newspapers to have no restrictions of any kind. By the mid-sixties, however, underground papers such as the *Berkeley Barb*, the *Boston Avatar*, and the *Los Angeles Free Press* became popular with young readers who were distrustful of official versions of the news and who yearned for alternative life-styles. Although underground papers are often poorly written and edited, their opposition to the Vietnam War and their freedom from journalistic conventions helped to counteract the pervasive tradition of objective reporting. By the end of the decade, over five hundred affiliate underground papers were receiving copy from two full-time wire services founded by former college editors, the Liberation News Service and the Underground Press Syndicate.[38]

5

The variety of subjects treated by the writers makes generalization about the new journalism difficult. Yet in the three major anthologies that have appeared to date, certain dominant trends emerge.[39] The subject matter of articles and books in the new style is intimately bound to the extreme experiences of the social and political climate of the decade. The new journalists often treat subjects and personalities unfamiliar to middle-class readers. Tom Wolfe's subjects especially—stock-car racers, topless dancers with silicone-injected breasts, California surfers, the mafiosi, members of teen-aged subcultures—often relate to "new" and emerging patterns of social organization that deviate from the mainstream culture. In general, the subject matter of the new journalism can be classified into four main categories: (1) celebrities and personalities; (2) the youth subculture and the still-evolving "new" cultural patterns; (3) the "big" event, often violent ones such as criminal cases and antiwar protests; and (4) general social and political reporting.

First, the insatiable interest of Americans in celebrities and personalities in the news dominated our view of history to an unusual degree in the sixties. The best and the worst new journalism explores private lives hidden from the camera with an intensity barely short of libel. Talented interviewers such as Gay Talese and Rex Reed portrayed movie stars and culture heroes with a careful eye for nuances of language, clothing, and attitude. The star interview has a long history, of course, in such magazines as *Photoplay*, *Screen Romances*, and *Motion Picture*. Yet Reed's "Ava: Life in the Afternoon" and Talese's "Frank Sinatra Has a Cold," which both appeared in *Esquire*,[40] capture the personalities and habits of these stars in a more candid and less sentimental way than does the typical star interview.

The "genre" probably gained new sophistication in the *New*

Yorker "Profiles" since the forties. Lillian Ross's infamous sketch of Hemingway and Capote's treatment of Marlon Brando are well known. The reporter's method involves staying with the subject long enough for revealing scenes to take place before his eyes. As one critic puts it, "While the invisible and faceless reporter . . . allows his subject to manufacture the rope whereby he eventually hangs himself, said reporter . . . merely remain[s] an impartial witness to the suicide."[41]

John Gregory Dunne is another talented writer who creates vivid portraits of members of the Hollywood colony. His account of Twentieth Century Fox's eighteen-million-dollar children's movie, "Dr. Dolittle," is the classic centerpiece of his collection of sketches in *The Studio* (1969).[42] Many gifted writers produced sketches or "lives" of personalities for *Esquire* in the early sixties by acting on the theory that if a reporter followed a famous celebrity closely for twenty-four hours he could capture the significant details of his subject's "inner" life. By the end of the decade, the star interview had been transformed from low-level gossip and sentimentality to sensitively written assessments of character.

In the second major category of the new journalism attention is focused upon the "new"—patterns of social organization or trends that reflect important changes in our national manners and mores. Shifting patterns of life-style and leisure pursuits were among the most prominent. In his best-seller *Future Shock* Alvin Toffler contends that the variety of new subcultures that developed among teenagers and youth groups—often centered upon drugs, rock music, and new styles of dress—are among the most important changes for the sixties.[43] Tom Wolfe thinks that when major histories of this era are written, these changes and not the exploration of space or the war in Vietnam will be seen as major developments.

Wolfe's articles in *The Kandy-Kolored Tangerine-Flake Streamline Baby* treat these new life-style patterns with a special flair. Among the best is the lead article on custom-car designers whom Wolfe views as contemporary artists. His portraits of Las Vegas as the American Versailles, the teenage underground, topless dancers, and New York "etiquette" reflect an ironic attitude toward American culture almost like that of an anthropologist studying a rare tribe.

Another vivid depiction of the "youth culture" is Robert Christgau's haunting portrait of a young girl hooked on Eastern philosophy and a protein-less diet that leads to her death in "Beth Ann and Macrobioticism." Anthony J. Lukas's "The Life and Death of a Hippie" and Joan Didion's "Slouching towards Bethlehem" explore the drug culture as it developed in San Francisco's Haight-Ashbury district.[44]

Violent events both at home and in Southeast Asia provided a third arena for new journalistic explorations, many requiring considerable skill and courage by the participant-observer. Among the best reports from Vietnam was *M* (1967) by John Sack, who persuaded the U.S. Army to allow him to participate in basic training at Fort Dix, and then to follow a group of new recruits into the jungles of Vietnam. Sack's account conveys what it was like to be a line soldier, or "grunt," by recording events from the viewpoints of the men themselves. In California, a free-lance journalist named Hunter S. Thompson joined the violent motorcycle gang that had terrorized tourist resorts throughout the state. His first-person account in *Hell's Angels: A Strange and Terrible Saga* (1967) tells of his eighteen-month involvement with the group, which ended when he was "stomped" by gang members in a small town.[45] In a more playful but nonetheless violent way, dilettante George Plimpton persuaded the Detroit Lions to let him play professional football as a "rookie quarterback." In *Paper Lion* (1966), he gives us a vivid "insider's" view of the sport. Plimpton roomed with players, took part in practices, and played in one preseason game before being "retired."[46] These vivid accounts attest to the tenacity of reporters who participated in events in order to write about experiences often neglected or distorted by the traditional press.

John Hersey's *Algiers Motel Incident* (1968) explored the racial tensions between blacks and the police during the Detroit riots of 1967. The account of incidents shrouded in sexual fear and race prejudice, like *In Cold Blood*, was representative of the violent nature of life in the sixties. Hersey relied upon official records, court transcripts, and extensive interviews to provide a documentary history of the case. Although the book was carefully researched, Hersey presents the evidence and allows the reader to draw his own conclusions because he wanted to avoid the artifice of a "fictional-ized" reconstruction.[47]

A fourth category of the new journalism includes political and social reporting on subjects ranging from the Civil Rights movement to political conventions. Early in the decade, the movement for racial equality generated a series of reports from the voter registration efforts in the South, and later, reports on the Reverend Martin Luther King and other minority leaders. An interesting and well-written piece is Paul and Geoffrey Cowan's "Three Letters from the South," which describes the involvement of middle-class northerners in the "freedom rides" of the early sixties in the Deep South. Garry Wills wrote a series of excellent articles on the Southern Christian Leadership Council, culminating with "Martin Luther King Is Still on the Case."[48] Wills's moving account describes the Nashville garbage workers who traveled to the humble church where the slain leader's casket lay after his assassination. More than that, Wills reflects upon Dr. King's rhetorical power and the political strategies he employed in urging new rights for American minority groups.

The height of political reporting came in 1968, perhaps the focal point of the antiwar protest and the decade's most violent year. Consider the events that shook the nation in that year: April, the assassination of Dr. King; May, political disruption and a general strike at Columbia University; June, the assassination of Senator Robert Kennedy by Sirhan Sirhan in Los Angeles; August, the most violent presidential convention in recent memory, in Chicago.

Some of the best political reportage came at the Democratic convention in August. In addition to Mailer's book-length account in *Harper's* (which I shall discuss in detail in chapter 5), many novelists were dispatched by large-circulation magazines to cover the convention in anticipation of the violence that eventually erupted. *Esquire* alone enlisted the services of two novelists, a playwright, and well-known reporter for its November 1968 issue. Terry Southern depicted the general atmosphere of Chicago in "Grooving in Chi." William Burroughs's article, "The Coming of the Purple Better One," presents a surrealistic portrait of the candidates in the style of his *Naked Lunch*. Jean Genet sketched bizarre caricatures of the convention delegates in his "The Members of the Assembly," while John Sack's "In a Pig's Eye" focused upon the police brutality.[49]

Dan Wakefield's "Supernation at Peace and War," which first appeared in the *Atlantic*,[50] was an ambitious attempt to survey the general mood of the nation in 1968. Wakefield used the conventional reporter's technique of traveling around the country to interview Americans about their fears, concerns, hopes, and dreams. Frequently, he relied on the documentary techniques initiated by Dos Passos in *U.S.A.*, such as the juxtaposition of newspaper clippings, short biographical sketches, and panoramic sweeps of towns and cities. "Supernation" is a tremendous feat of reporting that gives an in-depth look at the nation in the most disruptive year of the decade. By 1968, most major magazines were hiring novelists, whenever possible, to write impressionistic versions of contemporary history.

6

The variety and vehemence of the criticism that the new journalism has provoked since the mid-sixties is an important indication of its impact. Dwight Macdonald, writing in the *New York Review of Books*, called Wolfe's first collection of articles "parajournalism," from the Greek, *para*, meaning "beside" or "against": something similar in form but different in function. "It's a bastard form," Macdonald concluded, "having it both ways, exploiting the factual authority of journalism and the atmospheric license of fiction."[51] Michael J. Arlen observed in the *Atlantic* that the new journalist is less of a reporter than an impresario:

Tom Wolfe presents . . . Phil Spector! Jack Newfield presents . . . Nelson Rockefeller! Norman Mailer presents . . . the Moon Shot! And the complaint is not that the New Journalist doesn't present the totality of someone's life, because nobody can do that—but that, with his ego, he rules such thick lines down the edges of his own column of print.[52]

By the end of the decade a variety of critics concluded that the new journalism was dangerous for a variety of reasons: it risked turning the reporting of news into mere entertainment; the new journalist's use of scenes and dialogue distorted the facts; the new reporting style would replace the hard-won tradition of objectivity with a cult of mere egotism.[53]

The new journalism also had its spirited advocates. Dan Wakefield argued in a 1966 article that Capote and Wolfe had created a new fusion of the journalist's eye for detail and the personal vision of the novelist:

Such reporting is "imaginative" not because the author has distorted the facts, but because he has presented them in a full instead of a naked manner, brought out the sights, sounds, and feel surrounding those facts, and connected them by comparison with other facts of history, society, and literature in an artistic manner that does not diminish but gives greater depth and dimension to the facts.[54]

While critics disagreed as to the merit and even a definition of the new journalism, by the end of the sixties there was little doubt that the varieties of reporting called "new journalism," "the nonfiction novel," and "the literature of fact" had stimulated a widespread reevaluation of traditional journalistic practice.

On balance, some of the critics are quite right to suggest that Wolfe's views, at least as they are presented in *The New Journalism*, are greatly exaggerated. Wolfe sometimes makes it appear that the new form has revolutionized journalistic practice to the extent that "straight news" is hopelessly old-fashioned. Nothing could be further from the truth, as Lester Markel, the former editor of the *New York Times Magazine*, makes clear:

How do the New Journalists propose to cover, for the same day or the next day's newspaper, stories such as the admission of China to the United Nations, or Phase III of the Big Freeze, or an Attica outbreak, or the shooting of a Kennedy?

Of the twelve to fourteen articles on the first page of the average newspaper, at least ten cannot be covered in the minute detail or with the dialogue and the colorful sidelights which the New Journalists prescribe. There is simply not the time to do this kind of job, desirable as it may be, unless the newspaper is willing to yield the news field entirely to television.[55]

Wolfe's exaggerated claims for the new form have been responsible for the virulence of the critical response. He writes, for example, that the new journalists "never guessed for a minute that the work they would do over the next ten years, as journalists, would wipe out the novel as literature's main event."[56] The new journalism has not replaced the novel, nor has it "wiped out" conventional journalism. The need for accurate and comprehensive news on page one is vital. To take a conspicuous example, the recent Watergate reports by Bob Woodward and Carl Bernstein in the *Washington Post* demanded rigorous investigative reporting without literary frills. The corruption of the Nixon administration was <u>simply too important</u> a story to allow the fictionalized approach of the new journalists.

Wolfe's inflated rhetoric has so angered some critics of the new journalism that they fail to grant its legitimate achievements. The most superficial charge critics frequently make is that the form is not new, and as we have seen, there are indeed many historical roots. But to dismiss the form merely because it is not new is too simple a rebuttal that misses the point, as Jay Jensen, professor of journalism at the University of Illinois, explains:

> One cannot dispose of the New Journalism in such a simple way, because old techniques are constantly being revived and used in new ways under new circumstances. That is what has actually happened in the case of the New Journalism, so it seems legitimate to call it "new" in that sense—new in the sense that it is something different from what we have been used to, and something that apparently has been accepted as journalism of a sort.[57]

The new journalism of the sixties is new in the limited sense that Jensen describes. Since it developed in the context of one of the most violent decades in American life, the rebellion from tradition it represents is a product of that social turbulence. First, the sheer number of new journalism articles and their impact on traditional practices is significant. Today it is hard to read a newspaper or magazine without finding in several articles the "art leads," the detailed characterization, and the scenic reconstruction that characterize the form. This was not the case two decades ago. The new journalism has also played a role in changing even the most conservative of newspapers. It is not uncommon to find in the *New York Times* or the *Wall Street Journal* stories on page one that reflect greater depth and interpretation than was previously true.

Second, Wolfe is right when he says that today's new journalism differs from the frequently cited examples of "old" new journalists. This is true for two reasons. Such writers as Wolfe, Breslin, Talese, Didion, and Sheehy are using fictional techniques in more complex and sophisticated ways than did their predecessors. The works of Stephen Crane and Mark Twain, for example, were often sketches written as preliminary exercises to fiction. In A. J. Liebling's or Joseph Mitchell's articles, for example, one finds long passages of straight historical narration, indicative of the older journalistic tradition. The techniques of interior monologue and stream of consciousness, as employed by Wolfe or Talese, have seldom been used in the sustained ways that these writers employ them. Most important, the best contemporary new journalists are primarily reporters who strive to convey information. They use novelistic techniques in order to provide greater psychological depth and to portray dramatically important social issues. Third, the new journalism is new in the sense that a variety of forces coalesced in the sixties to nourish the form. As the hostile criticism of Wolfe and others shows, seldom has there been so much interest in nonfiction and activity among writers of nonfiction as in the last decade.

Finally, the new journalism has evolved in a period of intense experimentation and critical confusion in fiction. Had there been a significant movement in literature, or a dominant direction of paramount importance, it is unlikely that the new reportage would have received all the attention it has. The rise of the new journalism, however, has closely paralleled explosive changes in society generally, and by the end of the sixties, some of the best writing of the decade was clearly nonfiction. The use of fictive techniques has occasionally led to abuses, and in the hands of careless reporters, the results have sometimes been disastrous. Yet the best writing in the new style has been well-researched and carefully documented. The new journalism has not replaced conventional objective reporting nor was that ever the intention of its writers. Yet in the relatively staid, formula-ridden world of traditional journalism a new voice is being heard. More important, established novelists turned temporarily from fiction to write about contemporary issues. Those critics who have praised the vitality of the new journalism have seen in it a fusion of the journalist's passion for detail and the novelist's personal vision. And more so than before, the once clearly demarcated differences between *mere* journalism and literature, between elite art and the popular arts, have become increasingly difficult to distinguish.

Is this really the case? In Cold Blood. Where is Capote?

3

PROMOTION AND PUBLICITY: THE REPORTER AS STAR

> *In our post-industrial society, then, we no longer need public figures to revere or to emulate. Instead, they are there as temporarily interesting equals, to entertain us.* —EDWIN DIAMOND, Columbia Journalism Review

UNTIL RECENTLY, the popular notion of the reporter in our culture might have conjured up the late-night movie image of a dashing young man with a "press" sticker in his hatband from the films of the thirties. In a movie like *The Front Page*, the reporter is portrayed as a workaday creature who chases firetrucks, interviews potential suicides on high ledges, and pounds a typewriter in a cramped city room. Less dramatically, the average American might think of the journalist as a hard-working professional who remains an anonymous part of a huge news-producing organization. For every reporter who makes a "name" for himself, thousands work quietly and efficiently far from public attention to bring us the day's news. In recent years, however, the image of the journalist seems to be changing so that the handsome television anchorman may be replacing the newspaperman. Yet seldom do we think of reporters as literary men, and only rarely have they become stars.

Since the sixties, however, the new journalists have been part of a vanguard that is changing the way in which we think of journalists. Tom Wolfe, Truman Capote, Norman Mailer, and a few others, have become part of the star world that is usually reserved for movie idols and politicians. In our era as in no other in history, we are bombarded daily with images of personalities and events. In *The Image*, American historian Daniel Boorstin calls these media images of personalities and events "pseudo-events," since they inevitably become distorted through their projection by the mass media. Because of our insatiable demand for news and gossip, Boorstin writes, we have moved from news gathering to literally "making news":

We expect the papers to be full of news. If there is no news visible to the naked eye, or to the average citizen, we still expect it to be there for the enterprising newsman. The successful reporter is one who can find a story, even if there is no earthquake or assassination or civil war. If he cannot find a story, then he must make one—by the questions he asks of public figures, by the surprising interest he unfolds from some commonplace event. . . . This change in our attitude toward "news" is not merely a basic fact about the history of American newspapers. It is a symptom of a revolutionary change in our attitude toward what happens in the world, how much of it is new, and surprising, and important. . . . Demanding more than the world can give us, we require that something be fabricated to make up for the world's deficiency.[1]

By turning attention upon himself and how he "got the story," the new journalist has himself become a product in this image-making world Boorstin describes. The attention the new journalism has received in magazine interviews and picture spreads, on television talk shows, and in literary gossip columns has transformed some journalists into celebrities. I am not arguing here that this is good or bad, nor do I wish to detract from the real accomplishments of the best new journalists. It is simply a fact of our present experience, as critic John Aldridge observed in 1964,[2] that literary production in our society can no longer be separated from its promotion. Three factors concerning the publicity about the new journalism and its major practitioners deserve special attention: (1) the new journalist's own aspirations for stardom; (2) the perpetual demand for novelty in the arts as in other aspects of our national life; and (3) Capote's, Mailer's, and Wolfe's attempts to define the new journalism as a *new* literary genre.

Tom Wolfe's flamboyant style, in particular, has done much to change the public's perception of the reporter. In his account of the rise of the new nonfiction in the early sixties, Wolfe confesses that reporters have long yearned for the kind of fame usually available only to novelists. Wolfe tells us that his dream, one shared by many of his contemporaries, was to write the magic book that would free him from newspaper work and confer fame and fortune upon him: "On newspapers very few editorial employees at the bottom—namely, the reporters—had any ambition to move up, to become city editors, managing editors, editors-in-chief, or any of the rest of it. Editors felt no threat from below. . . . Reporters didn't want much . . . merely to be stars!"[3]

Like many of the new journalists, Wolfe nourishes the romantic myth of the writer. When he describes the beginnings of the competition among New York journalists in the early sixties, for example, he portrays colleague Jimmy Breslin at the *Herald Tribune* as a kind of hero:

Breslin worked like a Turk. He would be out all day covering a story, come back in at 4 p.m. or so and sit down at a desk in the middle of the city room. It was quite a show. He was a good-looking Irishman with a lot of black hair and a great wrestler's gut. When he sat down at his typewriter he hunched himself over into a shape like a bowling ball. He would start drinking coffee and smoking cigarettes until vapor started drifting off his body. He looked like a bowling ball fueled with liquid oxygen![4]

The one-sidedness of Wolfe's celebration of the rise of the new journalism reads, in the words of one reviewer, as "how my friends and I made literary history."[5]

Although in a less emphatic way than contemporary novelists, perhaps, Wolfe has become part of the celebrity myth that permeates every sector of society. His flamboyant public persona has helped to introduce the *auteur* principle now common to filmmaking into newspaper and magazine journalism. Nicolaus Mills notes that with regard to traditional journalism, "We generally think of newspapers, e.g., the *New York Times*, the *St. Louis Post-Dispatch*, the *Christian Science Monitor*; but when we think of the new journalism, it is generally the writer who comes to mind first."[6]

Like the novelist, the reporter has created a public reputation for himself in the same way that movie stars and politicians have for some time. Like Capote's image as friend to the "beautiful people," or Mailer's "tough-guy intellectualism,"[7] Wolfe's role as the modern dandy helps to promote interest in his work and to publicize his personality. Decked out in imported Italian shoes and English hand-tailored suits with *real buttonholes*, Wolfe cuts a stylish, aloof figure that sharply contrasts with our usual expectations of the hard-working reporter. He has appeared frequently in panel discussions at major universities and journalism schools, fascinating students on the campus lecture circuit. His knowledge of the popular culture and the suave demeanor he projects in his vanilla ice-cream suits have generated much of the interest in the new journalism. Like so many other aspects of our culture, the reporter is now on public display. Michael J. Arlen writes of this change in the reporter's role: "Writers. Writer-journalists. It is clearly a splendid thing, a sexy thing, to be a writer-journalist these days. Admirals, aviators, bishops—everyone has his day. Today it is the journalist (and a few others)."[8]

Even more than Wolfe and Breslin, some journalists from the underground press have achieved folk-hero status in recent years. Perhaps the most infamous example is Hunter S. Thompson, "national affairs" reporter for the rock-music newspaper *Rolling Stone*. The image Thompson has created for himself as a drug-crazed, demented genius in his rambling, impressionistic articles on current affairs has made him a legend with his young following and a much sought-after speaker on the college lecture circuit. His first success as a new journalist came in 1967 with *Hell's Angels: A Strange and Terrible Saga*, which he wrote as a participant-observer in the notorious activities of motorcycle gangs in California. Since then, he has written about Las Vegas, and most recently, an inside account of the 1972 presidential campaign, *Fear and Loathing on the Campaign Trail*. Thompson's variety of the new journalism—which he calls "gonzo journalism"[9]—is probably the most extreme form since it calls for the writer to provoke many of the incidents that he describes.

When the "gonzo journalist" visited the University of Michigan in 1974, the campus newspaper described the mayhem that ensued as follows:

The frantic scene before 1,500 people at Hill Auditorium was one of delight for the author of "Fear and Loathing on the Campaign Trail." Playing the media hero to the hilt, Thompson entered, stretched his arms in a "V" sign, and anticipated the adulation the audience readily accorded him. . . . The crowd, in an atmosphere of idolitry [*sic*] cheered whenever Thompson spoke in the style he writes, . . . ready to lap up everything he said.[10]

The star status of the new journalist meshes perfectly with the personal style of his reporting. Since the writer is often a participant in the events he depicts, his tendency for self-display and exhibitionism becomes "part of the action." At the 1968 Democratic convention, for example, Mailer could hop up to the speaker's stand to harangue against the atrocities of the war in Vietnam and, at the same time, provide himself with "material" to write about. Even less well-known journalists have become participant-observers; some have even staged events in order to write about them. Tom Wolfe tells an anecdote about Michael Mok of the *New York Daily News*, for example, who dived into the icy water of Long Island Sound to get the story of a diet fanatic who had marooned himself on a sailboat:

The motorboat they hired conks out about a mile from the fat man's sloop, with only four or five minutes to go before the deadline. This is March, but Mok dives in and starts swimming. The water is about 42 degrees. He swims until he's half dead . . . [but] . . . Mok gets the story. He makes the deadline. There are pictures in the *News* of Mok swimmming furiously through Long Island Sound in order to retrieve this great blob's diet saga for two million readers.[11]

Our usual vision of the journalist as a dispassionate observer who gathers the facts but stays out of the action himself has yielded to that of the participant-observer. The best reporters of the sixties actively sought out "the story" and often made news themselves in the process. In the Columbia University disruptions in May 1968, for example, some of the best reporting came from the staff members of the underground Liberation News Service and from reporters of the *Columbia Daily Spectator* who were inside the commandeered buildings along with the protestors. The established press, represented most visibly by the *New York Times*, reported on the number of arrests and the damage to university buildings. These reports reflected the administration's viewpoint and, generally, told only of events that occurred outside the occupied buildings. According to Robert Glessing's history of the underground press, reporters within the "liberated" university buildings "sent reams of copy across the country, recounting poetry readings, dancing, and political developments inside Columbia. . . . *Life* magazine bid large sums for the 200-odd pictures taken by the underground photographers."[12]

[handwritten margin note: This isn't surprising. You have to be there to report well on action.]

2

Although the reporter's involvement in the story is often legitimate, the new journalism also reflects the growing tendency toward exhibitionism in all aspects of culture. Avant-garde filmmaker and pop artist Andy Warhol once remarked that in the future "everyone will be famous for fifteen minutes." Indeed, given the present tenor of American life, his prediction might well come true. In 1969, for example, a couple fornicated on the off-Broadway stage, and nudity became more and more fashionable in film and in the theater. Morris Dickstein comments in a review of Philip Roth's *My Life as a Man* that there is a growing tendency toward self-display throughout our culture:

Never in our history have Americans been so driven to expose themselves; in our recent revaluation of all values, privacy has been one of the big losers. Everywhere we turn in society and the arts people are baring their privates or spilling their guts, from the vogue of confessional poetry to the pervasiveness of pornography, *from the New Journalism with its lens turned inward on the reporter himself* to the new assertiveness of homosexuals and other increasingly proud minorities. (italics mine)[13]

As part of the pervasive changes of the sixties, once-private acts have been pushed fully into the public domain. Perhaps because we sense that our era is unique, our society has developed a passion for recording practically everything. A documentary television program a few years ago recounted the day-by-day activities of the Loud family of Santa Barbara, California. Things began happening right before the camera eye; a son revealed himself to be a homosexual, and before the end of the series, Mrs. Loud had requested a divorce from her husband in full view of forty million television watchers. Extraordinary as the history of Watergate has been, even Richard Nixon's ill-fated tape recording of White House conversations reflects the growing tendency for self-exposure throughout society.

The new journalists have entered a publicity world that has long been a part of our literary tradition. Certain novelists and journalists have projected, consciously or unconsciously, public images that were quite distinct from their literary reputations. In the nineteenth century, Emerson and Thoreau were public lecturers. Such journalists as Stephen Crane and Richard Harding Davis achieved a kind of notoriety that went far beyond their writings. Rumors that Crane was an adulterer or a drug addict followed him until his death in 1900. Then, too, such novelists as Hemingway and Fitzgerald cultivated images that were projected to the public via the mass media. According to John Raeburn in an article on Hemingway's public reputation, the difference in the meaning of "celebrity" from the nineteenth to the twentieth century is one not only of degree but of kind. Since the development of radio and television, Raeburn contends, the writer has become a commodity to be *consumed* by the public:

It is only with the rise of mass media [in the twentieth century] and all their powers of publicity that the famous person becomes a celebrity. The mass media creates the celebrity not so much by extolling his accomplishments, but rather by advertising his personality, for it is his personality above all else which distinguishes him in the eye of the public. The mass media and the celebrity have a symbiotic relationship: in return for the fame they bestow upon him, the celebrity allows his private life—his character, his tastes, and his attitudes—to become a commodity to be consumed by the mass audience.[14]

Although many writers and critics have deplored the commercialism of the literary marketplace, some have openly embraced its alluring force. And in the sixties, the new journalists and writers of nonfiction novels became public writers who thrived on publicity and the financial success they received. For the successful writer today, there are television talk shows, panel discussions, writer's workshops, and perhaps even a well-paid semester on a college campus. Moreover, the writer's private life becomes exposed in "in-depth" interviews. John Aldridge describes the contemporary writer of a successful first novel as follows:

A veneer of notoriety and celebrity is upon him. Now his name is mentioned whenever the current state of the novel is discussed. He is interviewed about his work habits, his sex life, what he thinks of his contemporaries. He engages in debates with other writers. . . . Perhaps he takes part in one of those big, nationally publicized panel discussions on large fateful topics like "Fiction in an Age of Acute Anxiety." . . . There may [develop] some real doubt in the young writer's mind about the necessity, or even the advisability, of settling down and doing that next book.[15]

Truman Capote's literary career, for example, closely adheres to the pattern Aldridge describes. In 1948, he appeared on the back cover of *Other Voices, Other Rooms* in a candidly seductive pose, stretched out on a couch, looking out at the reader with a boyish face that suggested a new genius had just arrived in the literary world. For more than twenty years Capote has artfully cultivated his public image while nurturing his literary talent. He has appeared on television talk shows, has debated with such contemporaries as Mailer and Gore Vidal, and has granted interviews about his jet-setter's life-style. Even before the publication of *In Cold Blood*, he had attained a reputation as an effete connoisseur of fine wines and "beautiful people."

The publication of *In Cold Blood* conferred full celebrity status upon Capote. Readers at all levels hungered for the gossipy details that lay "behind the nonfiction novel." How did he get to know the killers? How did such ruthless criminals react to his fastidious manner and small stature? How did he get the people of Holcomb, Kansas, to reveal so much about the Clutter case? As the title of a picture spread in *Life* magazine hinted, readers wanted to know "How the 'Smart Rascal' Brought It Off."[16] In literary columns and at cocktail parties, 1966 became the year of Truman Capote, not only for the literary accomplishment of *In Cold Blood* but also for the fame and fortune the book bestowed on its author. F. W. Dupee toyed ironically with the book's central theme when he titled his review "Truman Capote's Score." Although novelists had long enjoyed star status, seldom before had a book of nonfiction conferred such instantaneous celebrity on a writer.[17]

Capote's skill at self-promotion parlayed the interviews and photo-essays that surrounded the publication of *In Cold Blood* into dollars. When a *Newsweek* reporter asked about all of his public statements concerning *In Cold Blood*, Capote quipped: "A boy has to hustle his book."[18] Capote's hustler's instinct and promotional skill were, of course, nothing new. Steadily throughout his career, his literary accomplishment has been paralleled by his ability to convert novels, sketches, and stories into plays and movies. Robert K. Morris explains:

He has seen the airy *Grass Harp* and *House of Flowers* blown into spectaculars for the theatre, seen the shapely Holly Golightly emerge from a shapeless chrysalid novella and turn into the splendid butterfly Audrey Hepburn, Hollywood box-office and almost White Goddess on the Great White Way. Without a jot of envy, but clearly with some dismay, we saw it too; saw his success grow wider and his reputation boom disproportionately, saw what began as a trek become a lark, and the gold come down not as dust, but as nuggets.[19]

Since his best-selling war novel *The Naked and the Dead* (1948), Norman Mailer has thrived to an even greater extent on public exposure. In his autobiographical prefaces to *The Presidential Papers* (1963) and *Cannibals and Christians* (1966), Mailer retaliated vehemently against those critics who "misunderstood" his novels, and expounded at length upon such preoccupations as modern architecture, orgasm, Reichian psychology, marijuana, and leftist politics. In *Advertisements for Myself* (1959), he announced his ambition to create no less than "a revolution in the consciousness of our time." From *The Naked and the Dead* onward, Mailer has been our most exuberant and vocal, if not our best, novelist. In *The*

Presidential Papers he frankly admitted that he "had been running for President these years in the privacy of [my] own mind."

Throughout his commercially successful literary career, Mailer has kept dramatically in the public eye. In 1961, he was hospitalized for psychiatric observation after he stabbed his wife in public. He has twice won *Esquire* "Dubious Achievement Awards," and his reputation as a foul-mouthed barroom brawler is notorious. The heir apparent of the Hemingway myth of physical courage, Mailer likes to test his manhood dramatically in confrontations with experience that he calls "existential." Like the protagonists of his novels, Mailer relishes life at the edge, confirming his physical and psychic courage against hostile critics and the world at large. Mailer's appeal as a novelist and as a journalist is an outgrowth of his embrace of a strange amalgamation of existential philosophy, his idealization of the "hipster," and his mystical belief in personal heroism.

In 1969, after the critical success of *The Armies of the Night*, Mailer put his fantasies of political grandeur to the test by campaigning with Jimmy Breslin for mayor and city council president, respectively, of New York City. The Mailer-Breslin platform was based on the unorthodox idea that the city should secede from the rest of New York State and establish itself as the fifty-first state. Mailer's chief inspiration was a plan for decentralizing political power and developing local autonomy, under the banner of "power to the neighborhoods." Although New York's voters were not ready for Mailer's radical solutions to their problems (he finished fourth in a field of five), his attempt to convert literary celebrity to political power indicates a more general trend. Movie stars run for congress, baseball stars become broadcasters, and politicians become movie stars.[20] When the celebrity status itself seems the only common denominator, the original field in which stardom is achieved is almost beside the point.

Mailer's political campaign also underscores John Aldridge's observations about the celebrity status of writers. Mailer's career continually erases the barriers separating art and life, life-style and literary production. Not content to remain one of Shelley's "unacknowledged legislators," Mailer thrives on his role both as an important novelist and as a culture hero. Aldridge explained in 1964 that

one persistently must remember—that what we are dealing with here is actually not a literary world at all, but a publicity and celebrity world, in which the writer simply as personality or public phenomenon can achieve, if he is lucky, a status comparable in kind, if not in scope, to that of movie stars and political figures, but in which his status may have little or nothing to do with his contribution to literature.[21]

As I noted in chapter 2, the new journalism and the nonfiction novel are founded upon an engaged, socially committed stance of the writer-in-society. Richard Gilman contends that certain modern novelists like Mailer suffer from what he calls a "a confusion of realms," a decreasing distance between the artist's life and his art. In contrast to Mailer's attitudes, Gilman cites Flannery O'Connor's bitter distaste for Mailer's elaborate exhibitionism: "Why does he have to push himself forward all the time and make such a spectacle of himself. . . . Why can't he let his work speak for itself?" Miss O'Connor's antithetical attitude about the proper role of the writer, Gilman observes,

represents the "classic" attitude of distance, abnegation, impersonality and submission to the sovereignty of the imagination as reinventor of men's lives and not as meddler in the world's business. It is an attitude toward the relationship between art and life that has dominated most non-bohemian aesthetic enterprises; it is the characteristic stance of the great novelists of the modern era—James, Proust, Joyce, Mann and Kafka.[22]

By the mid-sixties, writers of fictionalized nonfiction and the new journalism had attained a distinctly *literary* acclaim. Favorable reviewers of Wolfe's two collections and *The Electric Kool-Aid Acid Test* no longer considered his work *mere* journalism. In cocktail parties and in publishing offices, editors and writers began to discuss the new journalism as part of the literary world.[23] Capote, Mailer, and Wolfe each formulated a tactical definition of the *new genre* that helped to spur the talk of a "higher journalism," a variety of nonfiction as stylistically fresh and as insightful as literature.

Although biography, autobiography, memoir, and confession have long been considered literary forms, the very word "nonfiction" implies that fiction—the novel—is the standard. In a 1966 article,

Dan Wakefield celebrated Capote's and Wolfe's journalism and observed that such works as *In Cold Blood* and *The Kandy-Kolored Tangerine-Flake Streamline Baby* were changing the status of nonfiction:

The negative sound of the term "nonfiction" always seemed to me a reflection of the common attitude toward that vast and various field of writing. The term itself indicates that "fiction" is the standard, central sort of serious writing, and that anything else is basically defined by being "not" of that genre. . . . Such fields as biography and history stand up as respectable, if somewhat plodding, cousins to the major literary practice of fiction. There is also an important and large but even less culturally stylish vein of the nonfiction field that, whether it is referred to as journalism, reporting, or, the fancier term, reportage, is usually preceded by the adjective "mere" in discussions of serious literature.[24]

Wakefield went on to say that works by Capote, Wolfe, and others were removing the long-standing stigma from nonfiction. The interest of novelists in reportage was making it a more legitimate literary activity.

Tactical definitions of the "genre" of the new journalism formulated by Capote, Mailer, and Wolfe also played an important role in its promotion. For the novelists who turned to "the imagination of fact," these definitions represent an attempt to appropriate the prestige of the novel to reporting. Although, as we saw in chapter 2, there have been many historical precedents for the new form, each major figure has claimed to invent "a new form." Promotional statements, interviews, and exposure on television contributed to the excitement that the new journalism generated both in the literary and in the journalistic worlds.

Capote insisted that *In Cold Blood* was not "mere journalism" but "a serious new art form." Although many critics dismissed the remark at first as "the alibi of a novelist . . . who was evidently between novels,"[25] Capote insisted upon recognition for novelty. His definition of the nonfiction novel was clever on two grounds. First, he wanted to suggest that *In Cold Blood* was an integral part of his lifetime work, not a mere diversion into journalism. Second, his assertion that he had "made it new"—a new art form—satisfied the pervasive demand for novelty in all the arts. It was calculated to bring his book special attention. While several talented journalists had pointed the way, Capote contended in an interview, no writer before him had so thoroughly blended journalistic techniques with the sophisticated narrative skills of the novelist.[26]

Moreover, he did not give the impression that he was part of any movement or school of reportage; his claims went much further. He said, in effect: "I have single-handedly created a new literary genre that is the envy both of novelists and reporters. They can equal neither my impeccable factuality nor the narrative skill with which I tell my story." He seemed to be saying that only Truman Capote could have written such a book.

The literary tradition of such tactical definitions is, of course, a very old one. Capote's assertion in 1966 echoes Fielding's claim in 1742 that *Joseph Andrews* was "a comic epic poem in prose," a hitherto unprecedented literary genre.[27] By positing his own definition, the writer anticipates the reader and critic and attempts to establish in advance the standards by which his work should be judged.

[margin annotation: Hyperbolic self-praise as promotion]

Mailer followed Capote's lead by concocting his own "aesthetic" for *The Armies of the Night*. His subtitle, "History as a Novel, the Novel as History," reflects his desire to promote the validity of his impressionistic journalism. Like Capote, Mailer did not want his nonfiction novel to be viewed by critics as merely a topical book by a well-known writer, but rather as the latest installment in what Mailer has called his "continuing vision of existence." Although *The Armies of the Night* was not the runaway best-seller that *In Cold Blood* was, it reaffirmed Mailer's power after the doubts that had been raised by two poorly conceived novels, *An American Dream* and *Why Are We in Vietnam?*.

Of course, *The Armies of the Night* was not Mailer's first foray into journalism. His previous political articles—notably "Superman Comes to the Supermarket," an account of John Kennedy's appeal as a presidential candidate, and "In the Red Light," an informal history of the 1964 Republican convention—were important precursors to his book-length excursions in journalism. In a 1964 interview Mailer had viewed journalism somewhat with disdain, as a brief respite from fiction, a way of "keeping in shape":

If what you write is a reflection of your own consciousness, then even journalism can become interesting. One wouldn't want to be caught justifying journalism as a major activity; it's obviously less interesting than to write a novel. But it's better to see journalism as a venture of one's ability to keep in shape than to see it as an essential betrayal of the chalice of your literary art.[28]

By the end of the decade, however, with three major nonfiction works to his credit, Mailer had begun to see his journalism as an integral part of his "vision." He writes in the preface to a recent collection of nonfiction articles: ["The moot desire to have one's immediate say on contemporary matters kept diverting the novelistic impulse into journalism. Such passing books began to include many of the themes of [a projected] big novel."[29]

Tom Wolfe's claims for the new journalism, while similar to those of the two novelists, are even more complex and extravagant. Wolfe launches a twin-edged attack on both the "pale beige tone" of the "old journalism" and upon the trend toward myth, fable, and romance in the contemporary novel. Wolfe views the new journalists as *lumpenproles*—lower-class writers making an assault on the literary temple—who have learned by experimentation all of the narrative devices of fictional realism. With the decline of the realistic novel and the anemia of the "old journalism," Wolfe argued in 1972, the new journalism became the dominant form of writing in America:

A new journalism was in the works in the 1950's, . . . except for one thing: during the 1950's the novel was burning its last bright flame as the holy of holies. The worship of the novel as a sacred form reaches a peak in that decade, then suddenly begins to tail off as it becomes apparent that there is to be no golden "Postwar Period" in the novel. By the early 1960's a more spectacular form of new journalism—more spectacular in terms of style—has begun.[30]

It is clear that Wolfe's polemical position arrogantly seeks to "win it all." He views writing in America as a great race for status and financial success and sees the new journalism as victorious on both counts. He has constructed a myth about the new journalism. The old journalism, he argues, is too feeble to explore the vibrant sixties. Realistic fiction has given way to nonhuman subjects and fantastic environments by relying on such uninteresting forms as myth and fable. Both of these kinds of writing, Wolfe asserts, bore readers. *Belles lettres* writers, old and doddering, are out of touch with current realities. With the possible exception of film, therefore, the new journalism wins the narrative "race" in a walk.[31]

Curiously, the insistence on uniqueness and novelty has led each of the three major writers of narrative journalism to ignore one another. For Wolfe, Mailer has some good insights, but he remains "a literary gentleman in the grandstand." His reporting ignores "the digging, the legwork" required for the new journalism at its best. Capote, on the other hand, dismisses Wolfe and Breslin since they are not novelists: "That crowd, they have nothing to do with creative journalism—in the sense I use the term—because neither of them [Breslin nor Wolfe], nor any of that school of reporting, has the proper fictional equipment."[32] Taken cumulatively, each of these tactical definitions of the genre reflects the writer's desire to be regarded as a literary pioneer, who charts alone the uninhabited regions of narrative art.

Despite the actual literary accomplishments of the best new journalism, then, the rhetoric of its promoters has greatly amplified its impact. It became a dominant form of writing in the sixties, not only because it describes the important changes that took place in that decade, but also because it was itself the object of such scrutiny. The new journalism as a cultural phenomenon, then, must be seen both as an agent and as an object in a society dedicated to making experience continually more surprising and exciting. As former *Esquire* editor Harold Hayes noted skeptically in a 1969 preface to a collection of the new journalism, "Separating the spurious from the authentic in most activities through this decade is a task continuing over into the future."[33] And it is with that task in mind that we turn to explorations of the nonfiction works of Capote, Mailer, and Wolfe.

4

TRUMAN CAPOTE'S "NONFICTION NOVEL"

*"It wasn't because of anything the
Clutters did. They never hurt me. . . .
Like other people have all my life.
Maybe it's just that the Clutters were
the ones who had to pay for it."*
—PERRY SMITH, *in his confession to
police,* In Cold Blood

ALTHOUGH IN THE FIFTIES there were promises of a new journalism
and early in the sixties newspapermen experimented with fictional
techniques, Truman Capote's *In Cold Blood* (1965) lent a new
seriousness to the talk about a "higher journalism." When its initial
printing of 100,000 copies sold out immediately, it became a literary
phenomenon almost overnight. The chilling account of two killers
and a slain Kansas family, which developed from an assignment for
the *New Yorker*,[1] attracted readers from all levels of taste. Although
Capote insisted upon the factual accuracy of all the situations and
dialogue that he depicted, his narrative *read* more like a novel than
like a historical account. Perhaps more than the political reportage
of Norman Mailer, or more than Tom Wolfe's new journalism, *In
Cold Blood* stimulated a critical debate about a new *form* of
literature that continued throughout the decade. The critics won-

dered: Is a book that relies upon documents and official records in any sense a novel? What are the boundaries between fiction and nonfiction? Is *In Cold Blood* the harbinger of an evolving new art form?[2]

Capote called his book a "nonfiction novel" and his literary ambitions went far beyond "mere" journalism. His pursuit of the Clutter case, which led him to Holcomb, Kansas, and eventually to an intimate relationship with the killers, began with the aesthetic premise that journalism could be raised to the level of art. He could accomplish this goal, he believed, by blending carefully recorded dialogue, psychological depth, and novelistic form with what he called "the realities of journalism." In an interview in the *New York Times Book Review* shortly after the book's appearance, he explained:

The decision [to write *In Cold Blood*] was based on a theory I've harbored since I first began writing professionally, which is well over twenty years ago. It seeeemed to me that journalism, reportage, could be forced to yield a serious new art form: the "nonfiction novel," as I thought of it. Several admirable reporters—Rebecca West for one, and Joseph Mitchell and Lillian Ross—have shown the possibilities of narrative reportage; and Miss Ross, in her brilliant "Picture," achieved at least a nonfiction novella. Still, on the whole, journalism is the most underestimated, the least explored of literary mediums.[3]

Capote's choice of the brutal murder of a family of four, which took place on 15 November 1959, mattered less to him than the artistic method by which the project was to be carried out. "The motivating factor in my choice of material—that is, choosing to write a true account of an actual murder case—was altogether literary."[4] Presumably, according to Capote's theory, the techniques of the nonfiction novel could be applied to any contemporary event.

Capote based his argument for a "new art form" on three crucial ingredients: (1) the timelessness of the theme; (2) the unfamiliarity of the setting; and (3) the large cast of characters that would allow him to tell the story from a variety of points of view.[5] Most reviewers praised *In Cold Blood*, but few were prepared to accept Capote's claims for a new literary form. "He calls it a 'new literary form'—'a nonfiction novel,' " wrote a *Time* magazine reviewer. "It is an unfortunate term, as contradictory as it is pretentious." Alfred Kazin expressed the skepticism of many when he called Capote's assertions "the alibi of a novelist whose last novel . . . had been slight and who was evidently between novels." Some commentators, however, saw a measure of validity in Capote's assertion. "He speaks of the book as a 'nonfiction novel'; if he means simply that there are few novels that have been more carefully structured," Granville Hicks wrote in *Saturday Review*, "I have no quarrel with the term." Hamilton Hamish in the *Times Literary Supplement* saw nothing new about the genre, but praised *In Cold Blood* as a work of art: "He has written about real life to make it seem like a novel: is that what the grandiloquent claims amount to? . . . The form is not new or remarkable, but it is handled here with the narrative skill of delicate sensibility that make this re-telling of a gruesome murder into a work of art." Perhaps Rebecca West's praise in *Harper's* was the most extravagant: "There are occasions when it is comprehensible why Plato felt fear lest the poets corrupt the minds of the people. But at any rate nothing but blessing can flow from Mr. Capote's grave and reverend book."[6]

Whether or not *In Cold Blood* is a new literary form, an important question to which I shall return, his achievement rests upon his gifts as a novelist. His selection and arrangement of the "facts" and his emphasis on certain scenes over others lend a power to his account not commonly found in journalism. Yet the preparation for *In Cold Blood* began much earlier with the narrative techniques Capote had experimented with in magazine articles that clearly anticipated the new journalism of the sixties.

I

While it is less well known, Capote's development as a reporter, local colorist, and screenwriter has steadily paralleled his growth as a novelist. Prior to *In Cold Blood* he wrote three books of nonfiction and travel sketches, *Local Color* (1950), *The Muses Are Heard* (1956), *Observations* (1959) with photographer Richard Avedon,

ımber of shorter pieces for various magazines now collected
....ed Writings (1963). Two works in particular—*The Muses
Are Heard*, an account of the Russian tour of an American opera
company, and "The Duke in His Domain," a biographical sketch of
actor Marlon Brando—figure prominently in the development of
the techniques of the nonfiction novel.

Although *Muses* and "The Duke" were written in the first person,
Capote clearly strove for the kind of objectivity that became his
goal in *In Cold Blood*. Both articles began as journalistic assign-
ments, but under Capote's artistic hand, became "something more."
Capote used such fictional techniques as "scenic" reconstruction,
flashbacks, foreshadowing, and the heightening of dialogue for
dramatic effect. The initial form of these articles developed in the
New Yorker's "Profiles" section, where the pioneering work of
Joseph Mitchell, A. J. Liebling, and Lillian Ross often appeared.
Comparing the profiles of the forties and fifties with today's new
journalism, one reviewer wrote that "Capote and Lillian Ross have
virtually invented in the pages of *The New Yorker* a new 'school' of
reportage built upon a sensitive ear for the incongruous and depending in the correct measure on attentive eavesdropping."[7]

Capote demonstrated with *The Muses Are Heard* that attentive-
ness to the facts and an ear for ironic detail can produce artistic
results. In a series of reports he chronicled the American production
of Gershwin's "Porgy and Bess" from a 17 December 1955 State
Department briefing in West Germany to the opera's gala premiere
in Leningrad ten days later. While striving for objectivity, Capote
gave the reports a narrative sense that made them read like short
stories.

Working from overheard conversations, diaries and letters of the
actors, and his own observations, he carefully chose scenes and
conversations to create a coherent narrative. The arrogant pride of
director Robert Breen, the charming idiosyncrasies of Mrs. Ira
Gershwin, and the dramatic impact of an all-Negro cast touring
Russia are all captured. Capote occasionally unleashes biting irony
against the Americans as, for example, when Mrs. Gershwin is told
that Soviet authorities have not arranged a proper room for her:
" 'Darling, please. It's not important, not the tiniest bit. If they'll just

put me *somewhere*, I would not dream of moving,' said Mrs. Gershwin, who was destined, in the course of the next few days, to insist on changing her accommodations three times."[8] In a similar way, Capote's descriptions of the superficial personality of New York columnist Leonard Lyons are devastating. In one scene, Lyons is speaking with lead singer Earl Bruce Jackson about his planned Moscow wedding (scheduled as part of the troupe's publicity). Capote shows Lyons's inflated sense of self-importance in the following exchange:

"That's great. Just great, Earl," said Lyons, scribbling away. "Brown tails. Champagne satin lapels. Now—who's going to be your best man?" . . . [Jackson indicates the cast's assistant director.]
"Listen," he said, tapping Jackson on the knee, "did you ever think of asking somebody, well, important? . . . Like *Khrushchev*," said Lyons. "Like *Bulganin*." [SW, p. 311]

Capote achieves truly revealing personality sketches that often rely upon the characterization techniques of the short story. *Muses* confirms throughout what new journalist Joan Didion once wrote in a preface to her work: "People tend to forget that my presence runs counter to their best interest. That is one last thing to remember: *Writers are always selling somebody out*."[9] *Muses* may have begun as a simple journalistic assignment, but it soon grew to its present length of 128 pages in the *Selected Writings*. After the publication of *In Cold Blood*, Capote became fond of referring to *Muses* as a "nonfiction comic novel." For the emotional detachment it displays, as well as for its scenic reconstruction and its ironic heightening, it clearly anticipates the methods Capote was later to use in *In Cold Blood*.

The portrait of Marlon Brando, "The Duke in His Domain," began as a conscious experiment to convert the typical *Photoplay*-type of movie star interview into "something more"—"a sow's ear into a silk purse," Capote once quipped.[10] Capote begins with a brief sketch of the filming of the Warner Brothers' production of *Sayonara* in Kyoto, Japan, and then turns to a reconstruction of Brando's artistic career. All material for the article came from a single evening's interview conducted in Brando's hotel suite, yet Capote manages to explore the actor's powerful *essence* as a film artist. Like the scene-setting and dramatic dialogue of *Muses*, the techniques of "The Duke" closely resemble those employed in *In Cold Blood*.

Capote first pays close attention to the physical setting of Brando's suite, which almost comes to symbolize the actor's personality: "Brando seemed unwilling to make use of the apartment's storage space, concealed behind sliding paper doors. All that he owned seemed to be out in the open. Shirts, ready for the laundry; socks, too; shoes and sweaters and jackets and hats and ties, flung around like the costume of a dismantled scarecrow" (*SW*, p. 407). Capote then engages the actor in a long monologue on his ambitions, his aspirations, and his fears of failure. Significant biographical details are interspersed with the monologue to provide, in the end, a full summary of his career. In an outstanding scene, Capote juxtaposes a flashback of the young Brando he had met on the set of *A Streetcar Named Desire* with the fleshier and more famous actor sitting before him. "Watching him now, with his eyes closed, his unlined white face under an overhead light, I felt as if the moment of my initial encounter with him were being recreated" (*SW*, p. 411). Capote continually swings back and forth between Brando then and now, reflecting on the actor's artistic achievements as well as on his public image.

The piece ends with the description of a huge picture of Brando that Capote sees on a movie marquee while walking back to his own hotel. This tableau anticipates several of the scenic endings of individual sections in *In Cold Blood*. In it, Capote brings together two thematic elements that dominate the entire portrait: Brando as talented actor; Brando as cinematic idol. Looking up, Capote sees:

Sixty feet tall, with a head as huge as the greatest Buddha's, there he was, in comic-paper colors, on a sign above a theatre that advertised *The Teahouse of the August Moon*. Rather Buddha-like, too, was his pose, for he was depicted in a squatting position, a serene smile on a face that glistened in the rain and the light of a street lamp. A deity, yes; but, more than that, really, just a young man sitting on a pile of candy. [*SW*, p. 444]

Capote's transformation of a standard magazine formula—the star interview—to an artistic portrait is typical of all his work, both fiction and nonfiction. He once told an interviewer: "My work must be held together by a narrative line. Even the Brando piece was narrative."[11]

Capote's artistic career has never been limited to a single medium; his work for films and the theater also contributed to his nonfiction novel. He has written screenplays for two feature-length Hollywood movies and has adapted several of his stories for the stage. In 1954, he collaborated with John Huston on the screenplay for the United Artists' production of *Beat the Devil*, a spy spoof starring Humphrey Bogart, Jennifer Jones, and Robert Morley. His screen adaptation of Henry James's *The Turn of the Screw* appeared as *The Innocents* in 1961. Capote told an interviewer for the *Paris Review*: "I think most of the younger writers have learned and borrowed from the visual, structural side of movie technique. I have."[12]

The structural relationship between film technique and *In Cold Blood* is most apparent in the parallel narratives of the opening sections. Two narratives—one of the Clutters' last day alive, the other of the preparations of Hickock and Smith—are made to appear simultaneous, yet causally unrelated stories. Steinbeck used a similar technique of "crosscutting" in *The Grapes of Wrath*. Gradually, Capote tightens the trajectory of two independent narratives until they converge in Holcomb on the night of the murders. Film critics Stanley Kauffmann and Dwight Macdonald both noted that Capote's method, especially in these early sequences, owes much to film.[13] Kauffmann explained in the *New Republic* that "Capote's structural method can be called cinematic: he uses intercutting of different story strands, intense close ups, flashbacks, traveling shots, background detail, all as if he were fleshing out a scenario." Capote's experimentation in a variety of artistic media all contributed to the narrative devices that make *In Cold Blood* such a compelling book.

2

Critics who have praised the book, placing it astraddle the literary no-man's-land between fact and fiction, have focused upon Capote's technical virtuosity. Unlike most traditional journalism, *In Cold*

Blood possesses a tremendous power to involve the reader. This immediacy, this spellbinding "you-are-there" effect, comes less from the sensational facts (which are underplayed) than from the "fictive" techniques Capote employs. The narrative reads "like a novel" largely because of the use of scene-by-scene reconstruction instead of historical narration, the ironic heightening of dialogue, and the skillful manipulation of point of view.

Capote began his research with stacks of documents, public records, and interviews with Holcomb residents close to the case. In a number of interviews at the time of the publication of *In Cold Blood*, Capote repeatedly insisted upon the factual accuracy of his work. He explains in an acknowledgment that "all material in this book not derived from my own observation is either taken from official records or is the result of interviews with persons directly concerned, more often than not, numerous interviews over a considerable period of time." Yet, in effect, Capote wanted it both ways: the impeccable accuracy of fact *and* the emotional impact found only in fiction. In order to reconstruct conversations by the deceased family, he elicited and tirelessly double-checked the recollections of neighbors who were present. After overcoming the initial skepticism of the killers, he eventually gained access to their confessions, diaries, letters, and special narrative accounts written especially for his use. All of these materials permitted Capote to reconstruct as closely as possible the scenes and situations prior to the murders, even before his arrival in Holcomb.

Like a biographer working from documentary materials, he constructed a final narrative that includes events and incidents at which he was not present. At his own expense, he even retraced every mile of the killers' zig-zag path in flight from the scene of the murders to Florida, to Mexico, and eventually, back to Kansas. Unlike the typical historical account, however, dramatic events are foreshadowed and dialogue takes on hidden meaning not apparent in its original context. Because the novelist must inevitably select materials from the flow of real life, Capote had to impose a form—a narrative structure—upon the experiences he had so carefully documented.

He began writing with "six thousand pages of notes and an accumulation of boxed and filed documents bulky enough to fill a small room."[14] Despite the documentary ambitions he had for the nonfiction novel, he clearly recognized the need to select and arrange his materials for maximum emotional impact. The final story line is as spare as that of Greek drama or a film scenario. "I've often thought of the book as being like something reduced to seed," Capote recalled. "Instead of presenting the reader with a full plant, with all the foliage, a seed is planted in the foliage of his mind."[15]

Capote's skill and experience as a novelist are everywhere evident in the final product. He could not, of course, record all of the events of the Clutters' lives, nor did he dwell on each minute detail concerning the killers. Instead, he chose the scenes and conversations with the most powerful dramatic appeal. He selected what French critic Jean Mouton has called *des temps forts*—the significant moments. Mouton compared Capote's selection of scenes and dialogue to that of a classical dramatist, who chooses only those scenes that contribute cumulatively to his dramatic purposes: "There is obviously a certain artifice in selecting significant moments [*des temps forts*], the same artifice as in the classical theater where one only represents a crisis isolated from its antecedents; because of these significant moments with which the dramatist satisfies himself to accomplish his action, numerous events of an interior order, which unfold themselves between the scenes, remain hidden."[16] It is precisely Capote's ability to capitalize on the hidden meanings of these significant moments that contributes to the narrative impact of the book. The conversations of close friends of the Clutters, of the chief detectives, and even of the killers themselves are powerfully rendered. A comment dropped innocently by a neighbor or a casual remark made by an investigator to his wife takes on meanings in the context of the murders that were not apparent in the original context.

For example, on the day before Herbert Clutter's death, Capote shows a neighbor commending him for the "courage" he displayed in an impromptu speech to a local booster club: "I can't imagine you afraid. No matter what happened, you'd talk your way out of it" (*CB*, p. 36). This comment, made originally in the flow of everyday life, takes on hidden meaning in light of the brutality that the reader knows is soon to descend on River Valley Farm. Or, in another incident, Hickock and Smith had planned to kill and rob a motorist who gave them a ride during their cross-country flight from the scene of the crime. Capote records Dick telling "Mr. Bell" an innocent joke, the punchline to which is "When you gotta go, you gotta go" (*CB*, p. 174). Little does Bell know that Perry Smith is hidden in the back seat with a huge rock ready to take his life. This killing is averted by the miraculous appearance of a third hitchhiker for whom Bell pulls over, but this use of dialogue for ironic effect is typical of Capote's method. Throughout *In Cold Blood*, a silent alliance is maintained between the narrator and the reader as Capote presents hidden meanings not apparent to the speakers.

In addition to the use of dialogue to underscore his themes and to heighten suspense, Capote manipulates with the skill of the novelist the point of view from which events are perceived. His choice of third person, omniscient narration promotes "objectivity" and suggests, at the same time, a complex pattern of cause-and-effect relationships surrounding the crime. Capote shapes our perceptions of the criminals by using various spokesmen—Holcomb's postmistress, chief detective Alvin Dewey, Hickock and Smith themselves—to avoid direct authorial comment. Melvin J. Friedman contends that this progression of vantage points for reviewing events recalls Henry James's theory of "reflectors": "One of Capote's procedures for giving this effect [of complexity] is his skilled manipulation of point of view. He tries to present the events through as many eyes as possible. He sets up, as James said in his Preface to *Wings of the Dove*, 'successive centers,' who manipulate the point of view."[17] This technique allowed Capote to maintain the illusion of objectivity, since he scrupulously avoided direct comment or evaluation in his own speaking voice. Each major section of the narrative is told from what James called "the successive windows of other people's interest."

In Cold Blood is organized by the "scenic" construction of the novel rather than by the historical or chronological summary common to history and journalism. There are eighty-five individual scenes, ranging from two paragraphs to twenty-five pages, with most running about ten pages. In turn, these scenes are grouped into four major sections. In the first section, "The Last to See Them Alive," the reader meets the Clutters and comes to understand their stature in the community, primarily from the viewpoint of the Holcomb townspeople. In section two, "Persons Unknown," Capote explores the bewilderment and hysteria the seemingly motiveless crime stirs up among the town leaders and neighbors closest to the Clutters. Chief detective Alvin Dewey's perspective, that of a confused investigator chasing down dead-end clues, predominates in the third section—"Answer."[18] In the final section, "The Corner" (named for Kansas State Penitentiary's death row), we view the killers directly through their recollections about the crime and their conversations with other condemned criminals.

Despite Capote's insistence on objectivity, many critics have seen his sophisticated use of point of view as a mask for submerged authorial judgment. His reluctance to speak in his own voice conceals his strong personal involvement in the case and his skillful manipulation of the reader's reactions. Tony Tanner explains that for this reason *In Cold Blood* nourishes "an illusion of art laying down its tools as helpless and irrelevant in front of the horrors and mysteries of life itself." "Facts" never speak for themselves, however, since the writer's selection and arrangement inevitably impose a design—a fiction—not apparent in life itself:

I find something just a shade suspicious in this maintained illusion of objective factual presentation. Certainly it is in the American grain—"pleads for itself the fact," said Emerson. But facts do not "sing themselves," as Emerson maintained. Facts are silent as Conrad said, and any singing they do depends on their orchestration by a human arranger.[19]

Tanner's statement underscores the necessity of the "human arranger's" hand in any account, fictional or nonfictional. Narratives abstracted and reduced from the chaotic flow of experience itself acquire a structure and a meaning from the necessary choices the writer must make. Wayne Booth points out in *The Rhetoric of Fiction* that "the author cannot choose whether to use rhetorical heightening. His only choice is of the kind of rhetoric he will use."[20] Capote's heightening of dialogue and his selection of significant moments to depict suggest that every detail, every fact, is fraught with meaning. Yet the narrator refrains from supplying easy morals. Capote says merely: all this *happened*, these facts *exist*. When he does, at times, come close to moralizing or offering an interpretation of the terrible events, he quickly retreats again to simple narration.

Although Capote does his best to minimize direct commentary, the ideal of perfect neutrality, as Wayne Booth suggests, is impossible. The sequence in which events are presented is another form of heightening. In an exchange between two reporters at Smith and Hickock's trial, for example, Capote gets in the last word. The first reporter expresses sympathy for Smith's "rotten life." But the second counters by saying: "Many a man can match sob stories with that little bastard, me included. Maybe I drink too much, but I sure as hell never killed four people in cold blood." The first speaker's final comment shows that Capote's title is a twin-edged sword: "Yeah, and how about hanging the bastard? That's pretty goddamn cold-blooded too" (*CB*, p. 306). Capote clearly strives for balance and impartiality, but the author's viewpoint is hinted at even in the arrangement of such dialogue. In similar scenes throughout the book, Capote makes clear the cold-blooded nature of society's demand for the death penalty.

Capote must have realized that the final narrative presents only *one version* of the facts. *In Cold Blood*, despite its scrupulous adherence to verifiable events, suggests the impossibility of any "objective" history, since any attempt to write a narrative account implies establishing a "fiction" that best fits the facts as they are known. Capote admitted as much when he said:

I could have added a lot of opinions [on the motives of the killers, on the psychiatric reports, etc.]. But that would have confused the issue, and indeed the book. I had to make up my mind, and move towards one view, always. You can say that the reportage is incomplete. But then it has to be. It's a question of selection, you wouldn't get anywhere if it wasn't for that. . . . I make my comment by what I choose to tell and how I choose to tell it.[21]

His final interpretation of the facts gradually emerges as the reader begins to see Hickock and Smith, as one reviewer put it, not as "illiterate, cold-blooded murderers" but as "literate, psychopathic heroes."[22]

3

The main dramatic interest of the book—Capote's greatest accomplishment—is his portrayal of Perry Smith. More than the social critic's indictment of injustice, or the crime writer's concern for a "whodunit" plot, the novelist's concern for character analysis and moral ambiguity dominates *In Cold Blood*. A detailed examination of the portrayal of Perry Smith will reveal three things about the nature of this nonfiction novel: (1) the affinity of Smith's character to the characters of Capote's fiction; (2) the methods of heightening dialogue and scenes; and (3) the legitimacy of Capote's claims that *In Cold Blood* should be considered literature rather than journalism.

Although Capote was proud of the prodigious research and legwork that contributed to *In Cold Blood*, his themes as a novelist intrude themselves upon the observable facts collected by the journalist. Capote's twenty years of experience as a writer of fiction had considerable impact on the final form and style of *In Cold Blood*. Just as Mailer *saw* in the 1967 march on the Pentagon many of the obsessive themes that dominate his fiction, so Capote perceived in the Kansas murders some of the preoccupations of his stories and novels.

Like the protagonist of a Capote gothic story or novel, Perry Smith is a loner, a psychic cripple, almost from birth an outcast from society. Capote's sympathy for such characters echoes back to Joel Knox of *Other Voices, Other Rooms* (1948), to Collin Fenwick and Dolly Talbo of *The Grass Harp* (1951), and even to Holly Golightly, the "wild thing" portrayed in *Breakfast at Tiffany's* (1959). William L. Nance has noted in *The Worlds of Truman Capote* (1970) that much of Capote's fiction can be seen as an attempt to vindicate the abnormal or unusual person. Alluding to such early Capote stories as "Shut a Final Door" (1947), "The Headless Hawk" (1948), and "Master Misery" (1948), Nance shows that Capote has always been interested in such characters. "One of the main purposes of his writing," Nance argues, "[has been] to safeguard the unique individual's freedom from such slighting classifications as 'abnormal.' "[23]

Capote enlists the reader's sympathy for Perry Smith from the outset, frequently by comparing him to wounded animals. In fact, Smith is more often described as a frightened "creature" than as a human being responsible for his actions. A description of Perry's appearance at his trial begins: "Only Perry Smith, who owned neither jacket nor tie, seemed sartorially misplaced. Wearing an open-necked shirt (borrowed from Mr. Meier) and blue jeans rolled at the cuffs, he looked as lonely and inappropriate as a seagull in a wheatfield" (CB, p. 222). This portrait evokes the reader's sympathy for Smith, while at the same time establishing the viewpoint that the defendant is an outsider, an outcast from society, like so many of Capote's characters.

Capote's presentation also shows that Perry has been wronged by society. Although we tend to see Perry ironically because of his self-delusions, we are also provided with the testimony of his prison friend Willie-Jay who sees him as "sensitive" and "artistic." Capote also draws upon Smith's fantasies about get-rich-quick schemes of buried treasure and his fanciful alter-ego as "Perry O'Parsons, singing sensation of stage and screen." These incidental descriptions all contribute to a cumulative and sympathetic portrait. While Smith is waiting for Hickock to return from a spree of writing bad checks at one point, Capote shows him reflecting back on the thefts of his childhood: "Things hadn't changed much. Perry was twenty-odd years older and a hundred pounds heavier, and yet his material situation had improved not at all. He was still (and wasn't it incredible, a person of his intelligence, his talent?)—an urchin dependent, so to say, on stolen coins" (CB, p. 194).

Even without the omniscient narrator's direct comments upon Smith's character, the reader sees him from the favorable viewpoints of protective women. In "The Corner," Perry is frequently presented through the eyes of Mrs. Josie Meier, wife of the Finney County undersheriff. Smith is portrayed as pensive but "artistic," writing endlessly in his journal, taming a pet squirrel, making imaginary friendships with passers-by beyond his cell window. When Mrs. Meier bakes the condemned man's favorite foods, she tells her husband: "We talked some, he was very shy, but after a while he said, 'One thing I really like is Spanish rice.' So I promised to make him some, and he smiled kind of, and I decided—well, he wasn't the worst young man I ever saw" (CB, p. 253).

Such scenes build the reader's sympathy for Perry Smith as they might for the protagonist of a novel. Smith's internal contradictions and the disparity between his personality and his crime begin to haunt the reader. How could this gentle, literate man have slaughtered four innocent people? Capote's fascination with Perry casts suspicion upon his claims of objectivity. For, as Capote told an interviewer, he often worried that he might never finish the book. But about eight months into the project, things suddenly jelled: "Something in the whole material appealed to something that has always been inside me anyway, waiting there. It was Perry that made me decide to do it really. Something about Perry that turned the whole thing, because Perry was a character that was also in my imagination."[24]

Because of the descriptions of Smith draw freely on the resources and obsessions of Capote's fiction, they serve to reveal clearly the imprint of dramatic heightening. Capote's sympathy for both killers as persons, as unique individuals, elevates the nonfiction novel above the pulp detective story. Alfred Kazin contends that while Capote may be concerned with criminal justice and capital punishment,

[his] more urgent relationship is of course with "Perry and Dick." Almost to the end one feels that they might have been saved and their souls repaired. . . . This felt interest in "Perry and Dick" as persons whom Capote knew makes the book too personal for fiction but establishes it as a casebook for our time. The background of the tale is entirely one of damaged persons who wreak worse havoc on others.[25]

When Donald Cullivan, Smith's one close friend who had known him in the army, visits him in jail, he cannot reconcile the jovial soldier he once knew with the accused murderer of four sitting before him. The reader, with Cullivan, must ask at this point: "What went wrong?" Ultimately, Capote raises without answering the important questions of how a man can be so riddled with contradictions and how our society could have produced such a man.

Beyond these techniques of characterization, *In Cold Blood* lies closer to fiction than to journalism on what might be called a symbolic level. Capote's treatment of the "facts" creates a context of meaning beyond these particular killers, this particular crime. He weaves the facts of the case into a pattern that resonates with the violence of an entire decade of American life. And yet, how, exactly, does the book achieve this suggestive power? How does it become universal in a way that most reportage is not?

4

Robert K. Morris suggests in a provocative essay on Capote's imagery that the selective repetition of certain images, landscapes, and atmospheric details creates a cumulative impact. As in Capote's fiction, Morris explains, the environments of *In Cold Blood* are "the 'lonesome areas' of 'out there' where people are isolated, muted, rarely able to vent their cry of loneliness or anger or impotence or fear, and perhaps never heard when they do."[26] This austere, remote atmosphere is established from the opening paragraphs:

The village of Holcomb stands on the high wheat plains of western Kansas, a lonesome area that other Kansans call "out there." . . . After rain, or when snowfalls thaw, the streets, unnamed, unshaded, unpaved, turn from the thickest dust into the direst mud. At one end of the town stands a stark old stucco structure, the roof of which supports an electric sign—DANCE—but the dancing has ceased and the advertisement has been dark for several years. [*CB*, pp. 3–4]

Melvin J. Friedman contends that Capote's exploitation of these remote, almost uninhabitable environments allies him with French experiments in the *nouveau roman*, notably the work of Alain Robbe-Grillet. Such antinovels as Robbe-Grillet's *Les gommes*, Michel Butor's *L'Emploi du temps*, and Nathalie Sarrault's *Portrait d'un inconnu*, Friedman explains, rely upon three common assumptions and techniques: (1) the use of a mock-detective motif that "parodies the novel of quest"; (2) the repetition of certain objects and images; and (3) a philosophic reluctance to impose human meanings on the nature of things in the phenomenological world.[27]

The most striking similarity between *In Cold Blood* and such new novels as *Les gommes* or *Portrait d'un inconnu* is the technique of repeating certain landscapes and inanimate objects. As Friedman observes, these repetitions serve "as almost musical reminders and help to enrich the texture of the prose." Capote returns again and again to patterns of physical objects, such as the elm trees glowing in the moonlight along the Clutters' driveway or the sunlight reflected from young Kenyon Clutter's eyeglasses. Even the snow, which is late in coming to western Kansas that year, appears to have a will of its own: it waits to fall until the killers are apprehended.[28] In the *nouveau roman*, this attention to physical objects, which are strategically repeated in the narrative, is founded on a phenomenological assumption that the world as portrayed in the conventional novel is too orderly and too vulnerable to human interpretation. In the *nouveau roman*, critic David Lodge has pointed out, "what is purged is not so much a matter of invented characters and actions as a philosophic 'fiction,' or fallacy, which the traditional novel encourages—namely, that the universe is susceptible of human interpretation."[29] Capote's position in *In Cold Blood* is not nearly so radical as that of the French new novelists, but he shows a similar predisposition to present landscapes, environments, and objects in repeated patterns. He leaves to the reader the attribution of value and the responsibility of moral interpretation. He resists the temptation to impose meaning or to moralize upon fundamentally inexplicable events.

Yet, despite Capote's relentless care to present only the facts and his reluctance to impose a too easy moral, his story achieves in the end a kind of mythic significance. The destiny of an archetypal American family crosses paths with warped killers whose vengeance is portrayed more as the result of fate than of human motivation. For Tony Tanner, Capote's creation of myth from a passionless presentation of "facts" recalls a statement Thoreau made in *Walden*:

Thoreau wrote: "I would so state facts that they shall be significant, shall be myths or mythologic" and Capote is in something of an old American tradition when he tries to get at the "mythic" significance of the facts by simply stating them. . . . It is a tradition based on the belief that "if men would steadily observe realities only" they would discover "that reality is fabulous."[30]

This mythic dimension of Capote's story dawns on the reader gradually and subtly. First of all, the Clutter family is shown to typify all of the traditional American values. Herbert Clutter is a man whose prosperity is built upon hard work, endurance, and faith in God. He is a pillar of the community, a local booster, and a successful farmer—a man who has played hard by the rules and won.

In the eyes of Holcomb's people, Herbert Clutter and his family represent the American Dream come true. Capote's selection of dialogue strongly reinforces this viewpoint, especially in the early sections of *In Cold Blood*. Surveying his land, Mr. Clutter comments: "An inch more rain and this country would be paradise—Eden on earth" (*CB*, p. 12). Next we see Mr. Clutter working eighteen hours a day, converting his small farm into the sprawling enterprise it has become by the time of his death. Even the Clutter children complement this pattern. Nancy and Kenyon are members of the local 4-H Club and smart in school; they are independent and resourceful teenagers. Nancy especially shows the all-American character of her family. She is popular and pretty, the recent star of her school play. And on the day before her death, she teaches a neighbor youngster to bake cherry pie "her special way."

Once this mythic dimension of the Clutters is established, we see that their inexplicable deaths profoundly disrupt Holcomb's ethical universe. For by all the conventional values of our society, and most of our ready notions of good and evil, such murders are incomprehensible. Alfred Kazin remarks that "death in round numbers is by definition the death of strangers, and this is one of the outrages to the human imagination, the killing after killing which we 'know all about' and to which we cannot respond."[31]

Capote gives us a local schoolteacher's comments as representative of the community's collective disbelief:

"Feeling wouldn't run half so high if this had happened to anyone *except* the Clutters. Anyone *less* admired. Prosperous. Secure. But that family represents everything people hereabouts really value and respect, and that such a thing could happen to them—well, it's like being told there is no God. It makes life seem pointless." [*CB*, p. 88]

While these are the teacher's actual words, Capote obviously chose an especially articulate spokesman to express the impact of the murders in Holcomb.

At another point, Capote depicts Mr. Clutter's lifetime friend Andy Erhart gazing at the burning debris in a bonfire at River Valley Farm. Capote shows him, too, pondering the meaninglessness of Herb Clutter's death:

"He was a modest man but a proud man, as he had a right to be. He raised a fine family. He made something of his life." But that life, and what he'd made of it—how could it happen, Erhart wondered as he watched the bonfire catch. How was it possible that such effort, such plain virtue, could overnight be reduced to this?—smoke, thinning as it rose and was received by the big, annihilating sky? [CB, p. 79]

As the passage shows, the first words are a direct quotation, but in the wings is the novelist who underscores the significance and moral implications of the scene.

Capote also stresses the impact of the murders by recording the dreams and fantasies of principals in the case. Mrs. Alvin Dewey, the wife of the chief detective investigating the murders, sees an apparition of Bonnie Clutter in her kitchen. In this dream, the slain Mrs. Clutter screams: "To be murdered. To be murdered. No. No. There's nothing worse. Nothing worse than that. Nothing" (CB, p. 154). In another scene, Capote shows Alvin Dewey and several detectives sipping coffee in a Holcomb diner. Two men resembling Hickock and Smith suddenly get up, and seeing the detectives in pursuit, crash through a huge glass window to escape. Only several paragraphs later does the reader realize that this is all a fantasy, the product of Dewey's sleepless exhaustion and his obsessive search for the killers. Such scenes, which recur throughout the book, contribute to the reader's perception of the crime's symbolic force.

If the Clutters are portrayed as representatives of the American Dream, Hickock and Smith are shown to be agents of fate rather than morally culpable human beings. The reader is asked to view Perry Smith's crime as the product of a "brain explosion"—a "mental eclipse"—rather than an act for which he is responsible. The role of fate in shaping Smith's personality gradually emerges as

Capote recounts his family background. Capote summarizes at length the thoughts of Smith's successful, middle-class sister (referred to as Mrs. Johnson) in a particularly revealing way. All the sons and daughters of Tex John Smith seem doomed by fate, except for Barbara Johnson whose marriage and children assure her of a "normal" and "respectable" life. When she learns that the FBI has set a dragnet for Perry, however, she broods about the destiny of her family and fears her criminal brother. The narrator presents her thoughts in an interior monologue when he has her ask herself:

... but was it simply Perry she feared, or was it a configuration of which he was part—the terrible destinies that seemed promised the four children of Florence Buckskin and Tex John Smith? The eldest, the brother she loved, had shot himself; Fern had fallen out of a window, or jumped; and Perry was committed to violence, a criminal. So, in a sense, she was the only survivor; and what tormented her was the thought that in time she, too, would be overwhelmed: go mad, or contract an incurable disease, or in a fire lose all she valued—home, husband, children. [CB, p. 183]

In such scenes, *In Cold Blood* becomes more than merely a documentary. It is almost a moral allegory of an innocent family struck down by killers who are themselves victims of fate. The Clutters stand for everything in life that Perry Smith found unattainable: sustaining love, economic security, an orderly existence based on simple virtue. The "mental eclipse" that prompts Perry's vengeance against them can only be understood, if at all, in this light. In his confession, Smith says in effect that Mr. Clutter was the scapegoat for the collected wrongs of his life. "It wasn't because of anything the Clutters did. They never hurt me. Like other people have all my life. Maybe it's just that the Clutters were the ones who had to pay for it" (CB, p. 290).

5

In the beginning of this chapter I briefly alluded to the most perplexing problem critics of *In Cold Blood* have faced: Is it a "serious new art form"? Most critics have been skeptical of Capote's claims, and in refuting them, they have pointed to a distinguished literary tradition of books based on actual crimes. In another sense, however, the difficulty of placing *In Cold Blood* generically brings into clear focus a long-standing criticial problem. How do we distinguish fiction from nonfiction? What are the basic differences between *literature* and *mere* journalism? Such special cases as *In Cold Blood* and *The Armies of the Night*—which have been labeled "nonfiction novels," "novels-as-history," "the literature of fact"—serve to illuminate the problems of generic classification.

First we might ask what a novel is. In *Anatomy of Criticism* Northrop Frye concludes that "any literary work in a radically continuous form, which almost means any work of art in prose," might be considered a novel. Second, Frye declares that a novel must be "made for its own sake," that is, for intrinsically aesthetic rather than didactic purposes. By both these criteria, then, *In Cold Blood* would qualify. Frye further shows the difficulty of classification, when he asks: "Shifting the ground to fiction, then, is *Sartor Resartus* fiction? If not, why not? If it is, is *The Anatomy of Melancholy* fiction? Is it a literary form or only a work of 'nonfiction' with 'style'?"[32]

Perhaps because it was written by a novelist, many reviewers have considered *In Cold Blood* on aesthetic rather than didactic grounds—as they would a novel. Yet in the Library of Congress system it is placed under nonfiction, in a category of "social pathology" including murder case histories.[33] Meyer Levin's *Compulsion* (1956), a remarkably similar book about the sensational Leopold-Loeb murder case of the twenties, is placed in the cataloging system under fiction. These discrepancies merely demonstrate our critical problems in classifying certain works. In the end, attempts to place a work like *In Cold Blood* definitely in a generic category appear doomed. For as F. W. Dupee contends in his review of Capote's work, "Certain of anyone's favorite books—*A Sentimental Journey*, *Walden*,—are, *sui generis*."[34] Perhaps a more manageable problem than whether Capote has established a new literary form is to examine why he might have made such extravagant claims.

As we have seen, Capote's role as a literary promoter is foremost. His rhetoric of originality neglects to mention a whole tradition of true crime books he found it convenient to ignore. The author's tactic of imposing a polemical definition of his work, however, is a familiar one. In the eighteenth century, Fielding called *Joseph Andrews* "a comic epic poem in prose." Like Fielding, Capote wanted to appropriate for himself the prestige of his era's dominant literary form and, in part, to shape the critical standards for judging his work. Capote wanted to define a virgin territory of literature where he could be the sole inhabitant. He explained to George Plimpton in an interview:

The nonfiction novel should not be confused with documentary novels—a popular and interesting but impure genre, which allows all the latitude of the fiction writer, but usually contains neither the persuasiveness of fact nor the poetic altitude fiction is capable of reaching. The author lets his imagination run riot over the facts! If I seem querulous or arrogant about this, it's not that I have to protect my child, but that I truly don't believe anything like it exists in the history of journalism.[35]

Capote's insistence upon the sanctity of his *new genre*, however, reflects an impossibility, a romantic yearning for more than the form he chose will allow. For while *In Cold Blood* is an extremely well-documented and dramatically satisfying account of a case history, it follows in a well-established tradition. Stendhal's *The Red and the Black*, Dostoevski's *Crime and Punishment*, and Dreiser's *An American Tragedy* were all drawn from actual case materials. Perhaps the most recent example of the genre, and the closest to *In Cold Blood*, is Levin's *Compulsion*, which the author calls a "documentary novel." Like Capote, Levin relied heavily upon documentary evidence, newspaper accounts, and hundreds of interviews with the principals of the case. Levin addresses the problem of genre in his preface, but he is more forthright than Capote by acknowledging the poetic license he found indispensable:

If I have followed an actual case, are these, then, actual persons? Here I would avoid the modern novelist's conventional disclaimer, which no one fully believes in any case. I follow known events. Some scenes are, however, total interpolations, and some of my personages have no correspondence to persons in the case in question. This will be recognized as the method of the historical novel. I suppose *Compulsion* may be called a contemporary historical novel or a documentary novel.[36]

If a precise generic classification must be made in the case of *In Cold Blood*, it belongs to the class Levin describes. Although Capote did not allow himself the degree of latitude of interpolation that Levin chose, we have seen that he has heightened the dramatic effect of actual events to make for a good story. I am inclined to agree with the assessment of William Nance who states that "the book he finally wrote, failing to attain the charmed circle in which fact and fiction would blend, falls back into a category which may as well be labeled 'documentary novel.' "[37]

Although Capote's scrupulously factual account represents no new literary genre, it is a work of literature because it is clearly the product of an artist's imagination. Capote shaped the "facts" and manipulated our responses to the characters and events he described. In the most eloquent defense of the book, William Weigand observed that what separates literature from reporting "is not the imagined, or fictional, character of the material, . . . but the suggesting and extending capacity all art forms share." Arguing in a similar vein, Tony Tanner compared *In Cold Blood* with *Crime and Punishment* and *The Red and the Black*. What Capote has done, he argued, is what the best authors have always done. "By making their works frankly 'fictions,' [Dostoevski and Stendhal] tacitly assumed that to explore the latent significance of the grim, silent facts, the most valuable aid is the human imagination. I cannot see that Capote goes anywhere near to proving them wrong."[38]

Through his use of fictional plotting techniques and through his selection and arrangement of significant moments, Capote has equaled the "suggesting and extending" power common to literature. In a fascinating speculation in the foreword to *Compulsion*, Meyer Levin suggests that certain crimes come to typify the eras in which they occur. Thus *Crime and Punishment* arises from the "feverish soul-searching" of Dostoevski's Russia and *An American Tragedy* arises from the "sociological thinking" of Dreiser's era in America. In a similar way, *In Cold Blood* exemplifies the seemingly random, meaningless crime that became symptomatic of America in the sixties. For implicit in the story of the Kansas killings are larger questions about the social dislocations of the sixties and the failure of conventional morality to explain away the senseless violence we read about daily in the newspaper. Ultimately, Capote's story of Perry and Dick and the Clutter family transcends the here and now, the merely local and particular that are the hallmarks of journalism.

His account invites us to see the fates of the Clutters, like the destinies of Smith and Hickock, as a contemporary tragedy about which we know so little and over which we have so little control. The particular case radiates outward to a decade of political assassinations, to the random slaughter of the Vietnamese, to the systematic starvation of the Ibo, to the shooting of college students by National Guardsmen. Perhaps it is this view of the book Alfred Kazin had in mind when he called *In Cold Blood* "an emblematic situation for our time."[39]

5

MAILER'S VISION: "HISTORY AS A NOVEL, THE NOVEL AS HISTORY"

> *I am imprisoned with a perception which will settle for nothing less than making a revolution in the consciousness of our time.* –NORMAN MAILER, Advertisements for Myself

> *The other kind of writer can be better or worse, but the writings always have a touch of the grandiose, even the megalomaniacal: the reason may be that the writings are parts of a continuing and more or less comprehensive vision of existence into which everything must fit.* –NORMAN MAILER, Cannibals and Christians

IT IS DIFFICULT to take Norman Mailer seriously. Too profoundly influenced by Mailer the man—the angry young novelist who alienated his early admirers, the "existentialist" who stabbed his wife, the dreamer who ran for mayor of New York on a secessionist ticket—it is hard for us to validate whatever claims he might have as a major American writer. And yet, while posing defiantly in the public eye, and formulating in private a mystical vision of the nation's fate, Mailer has implanted himself memorably in our consciousness.

Consider Mailer's problem as a man of twenty-five with an enormously successful first novel, *The Naked and the Dead* (1948). Then an arrogant young leftist, he railed at his critics and rebuffed his admirers alike. He was lionized as part of what John Aldridge has called "the literary establishment." In a defiant testament to his own powers and ambitions, *Advertisements for Myself* (1959), Mailer demanded: "Had this first published novel been all of my talent? . . . Was I to write about Brooklyn streets . . . or another war novel (*The Naked and the Dead Go To Japan*) . . . ?"[1] Throughout his career Mailer has been concerned with how to shape a literary career, how to meet the critical expectations placed upon him, how to win and maintain a loyal public. How, in short, to become a *great* American writer.

From Hemingway and Fitzgerald before him, Mailer inherited a literary tradition in which the writer's public image—the man and his ability to capture the public's imagination—may easily overshadow his talents as a literary artist. Although it is impossible to single out a Mailer novel as a masterpiece, criticism must now concede the cumulative brilliance of his career. For more than a quarter of a century Mailer has been hammering away at his own obsessions and concocting his own mystical remedies for national ills. Each novel, story, and political article contributes to the cumulative effect. Mailer's work from *The Naked and the Dead* to experiments with film to *Marilyn*, one critic has suggested, is the greatest *roman fleuve* of recent literary memory.[2]

Mailer's nonfiction of the sixties, and his relationship to the new journalism, stems directly from this career that embraces the writer as artist and as public man. Mailer's three major nonfiction works of the sixties, *The Armies of the Night* (1968), *Miami and the Siege of Chicago* (1968), and *Of A Fire on the Moon* (1970), develop from his unique sense of the artist's role in society. Mailer sees the writing of books as a competition—the Great American Novel race—as did Hemingway and Fitzgerald before him. From the outset of his career, Mailer has seen literary art not only as intrinsically valuable but also as a vehicle, a way of mattering in our national life.

Richard Gilman, in a persuasive essay called "Norman Mailer: Art as Life, Life as Art,"[3] explains that Mailer is a novelist primarily because novelists command the largest audiences. His more profound ambition, Gilman contends, is to be a kind of psychic president, a moral leader, the country's savior. Elsewhere Gilman explains that it is this moralistic aspect of Mailer's sensibility that led to *The Armies of the Night*:

I don't think anyone who is more purely an artist than Mailer could have brought this [*Armies*] off; but neither could any kind of journalist, no matter how superior. This is the conjunction of Mailer's special nature— part artist, part activist, part inventor, part borrower—with what the times required: an end, for certain purposes, of literary aloofness on the one hand, and of the myth of "objective" description on the other.[4]

Clearly Gilman is right in understanding that Mailer's view of the novel and its social premises is directly opposed to the *purer*, more strictly literary stance of most of his contemporaries. Saul Bellow, Philip Roth, John Updike, Bernard Malamud, William Styron—to name only a few important contemporaries—are often better novelists in a formal sense than Mailer. Yet these writers, for all their stylistic and technical accomplishments, have not struggled to *matter* in our culture as Mailer has. He tends to see his own life, as Norman Podhoretz once put it, as "a battleground of history."[5] And *The Armies of the Night*, his protest against the Vietnam War, blends art and life, journalism and the novel, and most importantly, Mailer the man and Mailer the would-be prophet.

By applying the fictional techniques of the novel to real events in *Armies*, Mailer rekindled the critical debates about "a higher journalism" that Capote had started with *In Cold Blood*. As a "true history" of the author's experiences in a protest march at the Pentagon, Mailer's book, like Capote's, raised important questions about changes in journalistic conventions and the directions of American writing. If Capote began with a specific artistic premise "that journalism, reportage, could be forced to yield a serious new art form,"[6] it was clear that Mailer too wanted to appropriate the prestige of the novelist for his nonfiction work. But Mailer has always been serious about his journalism. He told an interviewer in 1964 that although "one wouldn't want to be caught justifying journalism as a major activity, . . . if what you write is a reflection of your own consciousness, then even journalism can become interesting."[7]

Mailer's journalism, like Capote's documentary treatment of the Clutter murders, strives for freedom from the formulas and "objectivity" of conventional reporting. The writer's subjectivity, his personal opinions, his sense of his own experience are crucial to Mailer's three nonfiction novels. Together these books comprise a kind of impressionistic history of the sixties seen through the distorting lens of a participant-observer. Mailer's gifts as a novelist, his powers of social observation, his eye for minute details, his ability to convey the subjective atmosphere of an experience make these narratives read more like novels than like nonfiction.

In the bewildering social change of the late sixties, Mailer's journalistic approach proved a uniquely appropriate one. "Probably the main reason for the profound relevance of this approach," wrote one reviewer of *Armies*, "is its combination of the objectivity of journalism and the intimacy of a memoir, both of which satisfy our present need to make sense of a kaleidoscopic world, always more astonishing than the wildest fiction, and at the same time, to establish contact with at least one rational person within it."[8] In his nonfiction novels, Mailer creates fictional structures using the sophisticated techniques of the novel without the need to invent plot and character.

I

In Cold Blood began when Capote read about the Clutter case in the *New York Times*. Mailer's account of the 1967 Pentagon march started with a phone call inviting him to participate in a demonstration that might lead to civil disobedience and arrest. As Mailer's moral indignation against American involvement in Vietnam grew, so did his desire to record his experiences as a "revolutionary-for-a-weekend." He approached his writer's task, however, in an entirely different way from Capote. In describing the Clutter murders, Capote had kept the narrator out of sight, by allowing the "facts" to speak for themselves. Capote's denial of the artist's role gave his narrative a powerful documentary, "you-are-there" immediacy. For Mailer, who almost always writes autobiographically in both fiction and nonfiction, the aesthetic was different. Writing at lightning speed to fulfill a contract for *Harper's*,[9] Mailer wrote instinctively, groping his way toward the truth, without Capote's scrupulousness for verifying the facts.

Like *In Cold Blood*, however, *Armies* relies heavily on the story-telling strategies and the form of the novel. Rather than recording events in simple chronological order, Mailer, like Capote, constructed a plot that presents each event in a sequence that heightens its dramatic impact. Such novelistic techniques as foreshadowing, flashbacks, scene-by-scene presentation, and extensive dialogue make *Armies* a brilliant interplay of narrator and event, of history and memoir. Mailer's work conforms to Capote's definition of the nonfiction novel as a blending of novelistic and journalistic forms.

Mailer divided *Armies* into two main parts. Part I, subtitled "History as a Novel," chronicles more or less faithfully Mailer's personal involvement in the speeches and parties, the mass rallies, and the long march from the Lincoln Memorial into Virginia, culminating with the confrontations with federal marshals that led to Mailer's arrest. The narrative obeys novelistic conventions in what Mailer calls "history in the guise or dress or manifest of a novel" (a definition to which I shall return). The shorter Part II, "The Novel as History," relies heavily on secondary sources, news clippings, and New Left pamphlets to provide a historical distance that contrasts with the personal quality of Part I. Alan Trachtenberg observes in a *Nation* review that "the two sections effectively complement each other and produce a unified, encompassing point of view toward the March and its symbolic meaning . . . . Book Two is . . . a muted coda, adding information but not really extending the insights and feeling of Book One."[10]

At the heart of Mailer's assumptions is the viewpoint that any complicated, multiplex event cannot be accurately reported. His main premise is that "there is no history without nuance," a point he feels is often missed by the mass media. Mailer begins by juxtaposing his own account of his exploits (drunkenness, boisterous shouting of obscenities) against a *Time* magazine report. But "let us leave *Time* in order to find out what happened" (*AN*, p. 14), he quips. Similarly, Part I ends with a newspaper account of Mailer's speech upon his release from jail; here he manages artfully to show the distortions of a daily press, which interprets his antics only in the light of his past reputation for public display and misses the sincerity of his statement.[11] Clearly Mailer intends *Armies* as an antidote to the inevitable distortions of the traditional press, especially in its coverage of New Left politics and mass demonstrations. Like so much of the new journalism, Mailer's book is an explicit attack on the "objectivity" and impersonality of the conventional media.

Despite the journalistic conventions used throughout *Armies*, Mailer sees his role as a "novelist posing as the Historian." Since objective history cannot be written, Mailer argues, one should celebrate the superiority of the novelist's intuitive and speculative insights into social history:

The mystery of the events at the Pentagon cannot be developed by the methods of history—only by the instincts of the novelist. The reasons are several but reduce to one ... the novel must replace history at precisely that point where experience is sufficiently emotional, spiritual, psychical, moral, existential, or supernatural to expose the fact that the historian in pursuing the experience would be obliged to quit the clearly demarcated limits of historic inquiry. [*AN*, p. 284]

Despite its documentary ambitions, *Armies* reads like the fictional account of a well-known novelist playing at revolutionary-for-a-weekend against the symbol of America's industrial-military complex. Instead of writing in the first person, Mailer views events and his own involvement ironically by creating a participant-observer, almost a fictional character, called "Mailer." Another Mailer, the omniscient narrator, mocks and exaggerates the foibles of the protagonist "Mailer" (also called the Novelist and the Historian) by pulling the strings within a verbal construct. The complexity of this narrative strategy, because of the varieties of ironic distance it allows, is crucial to the technique of self-presentation and the key to the book's success.

Mailer justifies his mock-epic protagonist, explaining that "Mailer's" personality is representative of the ambiguity of the march itself. "It is fitting that any ambiguous comic hero of such history should be not only off very much to the side of the history, but that he should be an egotist of the most startling misproportions, outrageously and often unhappily self-assertive, yet in command of detachment classic in severity. . . . Once History inhabits a crazy house, egotism may be the last tool left to History" (AN, p. 68). The Historian approaches "the crazy house of history" much like Henry Adams did in his *Education*. Standing before the Vietnam demonstrators, like Adams confronting the Dynamo and the Virgin, Mailer "discovers an aptness between his own posture in the world and the crazy configurations of the world itself."[12] For humility and self-parody, Mailer's creation of a comic-epic protagonist in *Armies* marks a significant watershed in his career. Since *Advertisements for Myself*, he had written earnestly of his literary ambitions. In *Armies*, for the first time, he establishes an ironic distance between himself and the world, which tempers his exuberant self-assertions with a new sense of modesty. "The most striking thing about Mailer's protagonist," writes Barry Leeds, "is a new sense of modesty and personal limitation. He is often frightened and weak, uncertain of how he will react in the face of moral confrontation or physical danger."[13]

Despite the sincerity of his opposition to the Vietnam War, Mailer is often playful. *Armies* begins with vignettes of "Mailer" missing the urinal at the Ambassador Theatre and embarrassing fellow-dignitaries Robert Lowell and Dwight Macdonald with his attempts at public speaking, which serve to undercut his otherwise grandiose proclamations. Although inept during the actual event, Mailer can be brilliant in the reconstruction. He recreates his mood, his attitudes, and what he would have *liked* to have said rather than what he actually said. This interplay of description and post-mortem analysis, of Mailer-the-narrator and Mailer-the-protagonist, neatly balances the serious politics of *Armies*.

At times, Mailer resorts to the narrative devices of the eighteenth-century novelists. At one point, echoing Fielding's style in *Tom Jones*, he writes: "Mailer did not know, but he had already unwitting to himself metamorphosed into the Beast. Wait and see!" (AN, p. 42). Periodically, he digresses at length or calls self-conscious attention to his narrative strategies, as in his arrest by federal marshals:

One of the oldest devices of the novelist—some would call it a vice—is to bring his narrative (after many an excursion) to a pitch of excitement when the reader no matter how cultivated is reduced to a beast who can pant no faster than to ask, "And then what? Then what happens?" . . .

This, of course, was Victorian practice. Modern audiences, accustomed to superhighways, put aside their reading at the first annoyance and turn to the television set. [AN, p. 152]

By hectoring the reader, Mailer defines the rules by which his book shall be read. At another point, he emphasizes his novel-like strategy with a quip: "Of course, if this were a novel, Mailer would spend the rest of the night with a lady. But it is History, and so the novelist is for once blissfully removed from any description of the hump-your-backs of sex. Rather he can leave such matters to the happy or unhappy imagination of the reader" (AN, p. 52).

The loose, episodic structure of the narrative recalls Dos Passos's *U.S.A.* because of the freedom and artistic flexibility the form allows. The narrator can follow "the Novelist" as he blunders through events, or departing from him for a time, can provide panoramic descriptions of the crowd, observations on the politics of the march, or long digressions on the hierarchy of the New Left, on technology, frozen foods, obscenity, or the ineffectiveness of political jargon. Barry Leeds has explained that "as his own narrator/protagonist, Mailer is free to present any perception or attitude without fictional disguise. And because *Armies* is a novel as well as a history, the author is freed from the obligation to create the ostensible mood of objectivity sought by most 'factual' reporting."[14]

In addition to Mailer's playfulness with novelistic conventions, *Armies* is a tour de force for its variety of writing styles and rhetorical guises. Mailer's various styles, his range of narrative voices, provide powerful contrasts to the conventional reporting that he so strongly objects to. Paradoxically, however, Mailer *can* at times be an excellent "objective" reporter. His talent for social observation and his passion for understanding the sources of political power contribute to his effectiveness. One hallmark of Mailer's technique inherited from Dos Passos is the panoramic, camera-eye sweep of a crowd. At the Lincoln Memorial, for example, Mailer uses the vivid costuming of demonstrators to suggest that the Pentagon march is symbolically "an intersection of history":

The hippies were there in great number, perambulating down the hill, many dressed like the legions of Sgt. Pepper's Band, some were gotten up like Arab shieks [sic], or in Park Avenue's doormen's greatcoats, others like Rogers and Clark of the West, Wyatt Earp, Kit Carson, Daniel Boone in buckskin, some had grown mustaches to look like *Have Gun Will Travel*—Paladin's surrogate was here!—and wild Indians with feathers, a hippie gotten up like Batman, another like Claude Rains in *The Invisible Man*—. . . . A host of these troops wore capes, beat-up khaki capes, slept on, used as blankets, towels, improvised duffle bags; . . . there were Martians and Moon-men and a knight unhorsed who stalked about in the weight of real armor. There were to be seen a hundred soldiers in Confederate gray, and maybe there were two or three hundred hippies in officer's coats of Union dark-blue. They had picked up their costumes where they could, in surplus stores, and Blow-your-mind shops, Digger free emporiums, and psychedelic caches of Hindu junk. There were soldiers in Foreign Legion uniforms, and tropical bush jackets, San Quentin and Chino, California striped shirts and pants, British copies of Eisenhower jackets, hippies dressed like Turkish shepherds and Roman senators, gurus, and samurai in dirty smocks. They were close to being *assembled from all the intersections between history and the comic books, between legend and television, the Biblical archetypes and the movies.* [italics mine, AN, pp. 108-9]

His considerable gifts for social observation fully in display, Mailer here creates a metaphorical and historical context beyond this time and this event. Like a great processional—perhaps a Last Judgment—the marchers are a blend of high and low culture, of the past and the future. By suggesting more than he asserts, Mailer amplifies this specific demonstration into a watershed in American history.

Mailer's personal feelings, changes in attitude, and large and small emotions make *Armies* a revealing document. He admires Robert Lowell's stern Yankee moral character and openly confesses his professional envy for the poet:

Mailer discovered he was jealous. Not of the talent. Lowell's talent was very large, but then Mailer was a bulldog about the value of his own talent. No,

Mailer was jealous because he had worked for this audience, and Lowell without effort seemed to have stolen them: Mailer did not know if he was contemptuous of Lowell for playing *grand maitre*, or admiring of his ability to do it. [*AN*, p. 58]

In addition to his multiple roles as comic figure and march "dignitary," Mailer also sees himself at times as a patriot and representative citizen. He conveys convincingly his ambivalence toward an America that can simultaneously engage in a brutal war in Asia yet allow its citizens the right to demonstrate openly and massively against that war. Although Mailer believes in American innocence, he sees it as contradicting an all-pervasive corruption:

Mailer felt a confirmation of the contests of his own life on this March to the eye of the oppressor, greedy stingy dumb valve of the worst of the Wasp heart, chalice and anus of corporation land, smug, enclosed, morally blind Pentagon, destroying the future of its own nation with each day it augmented in strength, and the Novelist induced on the consequence some dim un-awakened knowledge of the mysteries of America buried in these liberties to dissent—What a mysterious country it was. The older he became, the more interesting he found her. Awful deadening programmatic inhuman dowager of a nation, corporation, and press—tender mysterious bitch whom no one would ever know, not even her future unfeeling Communist doctors if she died of the disease of her dowager, deadly pompous dowager who had trapped the sweet bitch. [*AN*, pp. 132–33]

Like Capote's reconstruction of the Clutter murders, Mailer's nonfiction novel strives for a wider metaphorical and symbolic context than does conventional journalism. Like *In Cold Blood*, Mailer's account of the Pentagon demonstration transcends the surface event being described. Like many American writers—Mark Twain in *Roughing It* or Stephen Crane in his sketches of Manhattan, for example—Mailer interprets events imaginatively and metaphorically, relying upon the themes that dominate his fiction. Mailer's true role is that of mystic prophet who would read in the tea leaves of daily events portents for the future of the American enterprise. At the heart of *Armies* lies his deep concern for the individual in a society increasingly governed by bureaucratic and totalitarian impulses that threaten personal responsibility. Although for Mailer America's destiny remains an open question, his dialectic of opposed principles (the sweet bitch and the dowager) foreshadows, on the one hand, utopian hopefulness, and on the other, utter doom both for the individual and for the state.

Mailer's preoccupation with man's diminishing role in a centralized society has been a consistent theme since his first novel. In *The Naked and the Dead*, the antagonists Hearn and General Cummings represent the dual sides of man's nature—saintliness and beastliness—the tendencies toward Christian-humanism and toward totalitarian lust. Mailer's first portrait of men-at-war is intended, on one level, as a microcosm of the human struggle for individuality against increasing governmental control. Although Mailer's general is often repressive in his lust for power, he sees man as capable of sainthood. Man-the-saint and man-the-beast, the angel and the devil, lie at the heart of Mailer's vision of existence.

This fundamental duality in man's nature deeply colors *Armies* as well. "Mailer" exhibits both qualities simultaneously. His drunken exhibitionism at the Ambassador Theater represents "the Beast" within him, a Hyde-like counterpart to the more responsible "Historian": " . . . the modest every day fellow in his daily rounds was servant to a wild man in himself, while troublesome, the wild one, was indispensable, however, and Mailer was even fond of him for the wild man was witty in his own wild way and absolutely fearless—once at the edge of paralysis he had been ready to engage Sonny Liston" (*AN* p. 24).

The war between opposing forces in his own ego becomes a microcosm for the larger struggle in the national psyche of which the Pentagon march becomes the emblem. The Pentagon building itself and the federal marshals who must guard it come to represent "the schizophrenia in the land." Gazing over row on row of armed marshals, Mailer sees superimposed upon them the faces of the raw recruits of the Texas brigade with whom he had served in World War II. Brooding on the intervening experience of twenty years, he writes that the marshals "emitted a collective spirit which, to his mind, spoke of little which was good, for their eyes were blank and dull, that familiar small town cast of eye which speaks of apathy rising to fanaticism only to subside in apathy again" (*AN*, p. 171). They are representatives of the "schizophrenia" in America. They become a human residue left behind in the wake of technological progress. For Mailer, they are the characters "from the pages of a hundred American novels, from *The Day of the Locust* to *Naked Lunch* and *The Magic Christian*" (*AN*, p. 172).

In contrast, despite his mistrust of their psychedelic drugs and banal jargon, Mailer wants to embrace the radical youth of America as the embodiment of a new hope. Continually throughout the book, he depicts students, hippies, yippies, and anarchists in Civil War metaphors. He views them as a kind of Christian army—a Child's Crusade—against the oppressiveness of the military machine. At their best, their spontaneity, their rejection of the old leftist "logic-of-the-next-step" makes of them

a generation of the American young [that] had come along different from five previous generations of the middle class. The new generation believed in technology more than any before it, but the generation also believed in LSD, in witches, in tribal knowledge, in orgy, and revolution. . . . belief was reserved for the revelatory mystery of *the happening where you did not know what was going to happen next*; that was what was good about it. [italics mine, *AN*, p. 103]

The coalition of middle-class youth, old leftists, and writers and professors inspires in Mailer the faint hope of what America might become if the best impulses can be actualized and the "madness" suppressed.

Mailer fears and predicts, however, that the opposed forces of the youthful protesters and the marshals may generate "a civil war that might go on for twenty years." Surging forward to the Pentagon, he sees the same submerged "schizophrenia" he has written about in all his books rising to the surface. As early as *The Presidential Papers* (1963) Mailer had warned:

Americans have been leading a double life, and our history has moved on two rivers, one visible, the other underground; there has been the history of politics which is concrete, factual, practical and unbelievably dull if not for the consequences of the actions of some of these men; and there is a subterranean river of untapped, ferocious, lonely and romantic desires, that concentration of ecstasy and violence which is the dream life of the nation.[15]

In *Armies*, American involvement in Vietnam becomes merely the most recent manifestation of the "underground river" of violence.

Sensing that this thesis may be too weighty to be credited on its own merits, Mailer writes a scene to dramatize this suppressed violence and the contradictions in American life. He portrays an old woman with dyed orange hair playing the slot machines in Las Vegas:

If one could find the irredeemable madness of America . . . it was in those late afternoon race track faces coming into the neon lights of the parimutuel windows, or those early morning hollows in the eye of the soul in places like Vegas where the fevers of America go livid in the hum of the night, and Grandmother, the church-goer, orange hair burning bright now crooned over the One-Arm Bandit, pocketbook open, driving those half-dollars home, home to the slot.

"Madame, we are burning children in Vietnam."

"Boy, you just go get yourself lost. Grandma's about ready for a kiss from the jackpot."

The burned child is brought into the gaming hall on her hospital bed.

"Madame, regard our act in Vietnam."

"I hit! I hit! Hot deedy, I hit. Why, you poor burned child—you just brought me luck. Here, honey, here's a lucky half-dollar in reward. And listen sugar, tell the nurse to change your sheets. Those sheets sure do stink. I hope you ain't got gangrene. Hee, hee, hee, hee. I get a supreme pleasure mixing with gooks in Vegas." [AN, p. 172]

In this bitterly ironic sketch, Mailer summarizes his interpretation of American violence established in his novel, *Why Are We in Vietnam?* (1967). If technology and modern progress have demolished the small town, Mailer concludes, then "one had to find [the lust and the madness] wherever fever, force, and machines could come together, in Vegas, at the race track, in pro football, race riots for the Negro, suburban orgies—none of it was enough—one had to find it in Vietnam; that was where the small town had gone to get its kicks" (AN, p. 174).

The metaphorical and philosophical context Mailer creates is much richer than the typical journalistic account of a protest demonstration. While the risks of speculation are great, typically he finds in isolated, discrete events the larger issues that harken back to the basic metaphors of all his work. Richard Poirier observes that Mailer's excessive repetitiveness and his tireless use of Manichean oppositions serve an important narrative function:

It is very much to the point that he inveterately translates the journalistic issues of the day into metaphors that have long since dominated his mind and his work: technology, fascism, dialectics, apocalypse, being, cancer, obscenity, dread, existentialism, drugs, violence, totalitarianism, . . . God and the Devil, . . . At some point any subject in Mailer manages to get linked metaphorically to one or more of these terms which are of course complexly linked among themselves. This is one reason why he is best read as the author of a large work in progress.[16]

Armies thus provides a fuller answer to the question raised in the title of *Why Are We in Vietnam?*, his novel about big-game hunting in Alaska. Mailer's analysis of American violence is as old at least as D. H. Lawrence's view of Cooper's Natty Bumppo: "A man who turns his back on white society. A man who keeps his moral integrity hard and intact. An isolate, almost selfless, stoic, enduring man, who lives by death, by killing. This is the very intrinsic-most American."[17] Mailer's treatment of the Pentagon march becomes an extension of the apocalyptic "vision of existence" that he has been formulating for twenty-five years. All of the opposed forces—totalitarianism and democracy, age and youth, technology and humanism, the Devil's curse and God's grace—come together on a weekend in October 1967. Although Mailer fears a twenty-year civil war, he forecasts in the end two alternate versions of America's future. Echoing Yeats's poem "The Second Coming," he ends the book:

Brood on that country who expresses our will. She is America, once a beauty of magnificence unparalleled, now a beauty with a leprous skin. She is heavy with child—no one knows if legitimate—and languishes in a dungeon whose walls are never seen. Now the first contractions of her fearsome labor begin—it will go on: no doctor exists to tell the hour. It is only known that false labor is not likely on her now, no, she will probably give birth, and to what?—the most fearsome totalitarianism the world has ever known? or can she, poor giant, tormented lovely girl, deliver a babe of a new world brave and tender, artful and wild? [AN, p. 320]

Despite his comic sequences, his self-parody, and his playful use of novelistic devices, Mailer concludes with characteristic prophecy.

For he is quintessentially American and quintessentially a moralist. Although he fears the dominance of totalitarianism represented by the Pentagon, Mailer offers simultaneously the hope of a new American Eden populated by the youthful ranks of his Christian army.

The Armies of the Night, like *In Cold Blood*, demonstrates the power of fusing the journalistic idiom with the techniques of the novel. By applying the imaginative resources of fiction to contemporary history, Mailer transcends the clichés and formulas of conventional reportage. The nonfiction novel is a synthesis of diverse tendencies in his public life and his literary career. Mailer recreated an emblematic event in a bewildering period of American life, and by doing so, helped to clarify the meaning of one significant moment in a kaleidoscopic decade. His history "in the form of a novel" transforms an isolated event into a significant reflection of the social climate of the sixties. As Conor Cruise O'Brien suggests in his review of *Armies*, perhaps Mailer in 1968 was still interested in fundamental questions that have now become unfashionable in fiction. If that is true, then Mr. O'Brien is correct in saying that no one of Mailer's power "will ever write again about America in this vein. Insofar as the word 'America' implied a freshness and righteous confidence which had been lost to Europe, then Mr. Mailer's autobiography—in which we may hope 'The Steps of the Pentagon' is but a chapter—will constitute the Confessions of the Last American."[18]

2

Mailer's second nonfiction novel of the sixties, *Miami and the Siege of Chicago* (1968),[19] was modeled upon his previous political journalism. He had written two earlier reports on political conventions: "In the Red Light," an account of the 1964 Republican convention, and "Superman Comes to the Supermarket," an analysis of John Kennedy's climb to the presidency in 1960.[20] Throughout his career, Mailer has written as a journalist, contributing articles to such periodicals as *Esquire*, *Harper's*, *Dissent*, *Commentary*, the

New York Review of Books, and the *Village Voice* (which he helped to establish).

Like *Armies*, Mailer's report on the 1968 political conventions employs various "fictive" elements that distinguish it from conventional reportage. Instead of "the Historian," here Mailer becomes "the Reporter." He says, in effect: "I am a typical reporter on the scene, getting the 'story,' meeting my deadlines. Although I'll try to remain objective, I will also let you in on what a typical news story cannot tell: my own reactions, omissions, and errors that underscore the impossibility of ever *really* knowing what happened."

Despite the similarities between Mailer's multifaceted role in *Armies* and his persona in *Miami and Chicago*, the playful exhibitionism of the former book becomes muted in the latter. In Chicago, especially, Mailer seems more serious about his task and attempts to be more prudent in his judgments. He reveals his own convictions and political beliefs, especially when violence breaks out between the demonstrators and the police in Chicago. He broods on his own lack of physical courage, on his ambivalence toward the New Left, and on his fears for the country's future. Peter Shaw wrote in *Commentary* that *Miami and Chicago* is characterized by "a new kind of reasonableness for Mailer which I find an achievement larger than that of his last book."[21]

Again Mailer counters the distortions of the conventional press with what he calls "history with nuance." He demonstrates his point in the *Miami* section by reprinting a *New York Times* account of a black demonstration at Governor Reagan's headquarters. Probing the omissions and inadequacies of the *Times* story, Mailer demands: "Were the Reagan girls livid or triumphant? Were the Negro demonstrators dignified or raucous or self-satisfied? The *Times* was not ready," he concludes, "to encourage its reporters in the thought that there is no history without nuance" (*MC*, p. 56).

Instead of the stories that make headlines, Mailer is interested in the *ambiance* of the convention—the smells in the air, the makeup and costuming of delegates—what he calls "the outriggers of their activity." In the Miami section, for example, he tests the hypothesis of a "new" Nixon, not by examining the candidate himself, but by observing a performing elephant sent to Nixon by admirers. Mailer's subjective method accumulates these seemingly unimportant details to "better comprehend the subterranean character of what he saw on the surface" (MC, p. 51). A successful dancing elephant becomes Mailer's

first clue to the notion that there was a new Nixon. He could have read a dozen articles which said the same thing and paid no mind, for the men who wrote them were experts and so were wrong in their predictions as often as they were right. Experts he would disregard—so far as he was able—but Ana [a gift from Nixon supporters in Anaheim, California] had been happy doing her handstand: that was an unexpected fact he would have to absorb into the first freshets of his brooding. Of course a reporter had once decided (using similar methods) that Barry Goldwater could win the 1964 election. [MC, p. 18]

Mailer relishes his nonexpert status and often ironically undercuts his own methods when they fail. For Mailer reporters should be subjective readers of omens and portents.

The use of "the Reporter" as the protagonist serves conveniently as a rhetorical strategy for masking Mailer's errors and omissions. Missing the story can be attributed to the human foibles of the Reporter, not to all-knowing, famous novelist Norman Mailer. When the Reporter fails to discover an important behind-the-scenes political deal, Mailer writes:

If he had been more of a reporter (or less of one) he would have known that the Reagan forces were pushing an all-out attack . . . to steal Southern delegates from Nixon, and that Nixon forces were responding with a counter-offensive . . . but the reporter worked like a General who was far from the front—if he could not hear the sound of cannon, he assumed the battle was never high. [MC, p. 57]

At times, the Reporter becomes comically involved in the hijinks itself. At one point, like a character in a picaresque novel, he crashes the Republican Gala Ball by posing as a plainclothes security guard:

It was assumed by the people who gave way to the Governor [Reagan] that the reporter must be one of the plainclothesmen assigned to His Excellency's rear, and with a frown here, judicious tightening of his mouth there, look of concern for the Governor's welfare squeezed onto his map, offering a security officer's look superior to the absence of any ticket, he went right in through the ticket-takers. [MC, pp. 31–32]

Mailer's use of such comic scenes provides some diverting relief from the rather dull politics in Miami, since a Nixon victory was seldom in doubt. In contrast, the Reporter's involvement in the Democratic convention in Chicago becomes more earnest as Mailer's exuberance is subdued.

The techniques for heightening narrative suspense are similar to those of *The Armies of the Night*. Instead of describing the conventions in chronological order, Mailer filters the reader's awareness of events through the changing perceptions of his protagonist. Mailer presents his political hypotheses as revelations. The Reporter *realizes*, for example, that Richard Nixon will be president: "So the reporter stood in the center of the American Scene . . . and realized he was going through no more than the rearrangement of some intellectual luggage (which indeed every good citizen might be supposed to perform) during these worthy operations of the democratic soul when getting ready to vote" (*MC* pp. 63–64).

As his fascination with Kennedy in *The Presidential Papers* shows, Mailer's approach to politics is often more personal than ideological. Like Emerson, he believes that to know an era is to study its representative men. His dedication to defining the personal style of a politician often leads to more subjective judgments than the depersonalized "straight news" story permits. Consider this portrait of Richard Nixon conducting a press briefing:

Now [Nixon] tried to use slang, put quotes around it with a touching, almost pathetic, reminder of Nice-Nellyism, the inhibition of the good clean church upbringing of his youth insisting on exhibiting itself, as if he were saying with a YMCA slick snicker, "After we break into slang, there's always the danger of the party getting *rough*." . . . So, now he talked self-consciously of how the members of his staff, counting delegates, were "playing what we call 'the strong game.'" SMILE said his brain. FLASH went the teeth. But his voice seemed to give away that, whatever they called it, they probably didn't call it "the strong game," or if they did, *he* didn't. So he framed little phrases. Like "a leg-up." Or "my intuition, my 'gut feelings,' so to speak." Deferential air followed by SMILE—FLASH. [*MC*, p. 47]

Mailer's irreverence and his lack of charity have met with strong objections by his critics. But his arrogant sketches often capture more of the essence of a political style than the typically gray prose of the newspaper column.

Although Mailer is ruthless in describing Nixon, he spares few Democrats. He portrays Eugene McCarthy as unwilling or unable to play "politics-as-property," Mailer's dominant metaphor throughout the book for traditional American politics: "McCarthy was proceeding on the logic of the saint . . . : God would judge the importance of the event, not man, and God would give the tongue to speak, if tongue was the organ to be manifested. He would be good when the Lord chose him to be good" (MC, pp. 119–20). Mailer's portrait of Hubert Humphrey on the night of his acceptance speech for the Democratic nomination is a cruel, but nonetheless telling, picture. As few conventional journalists would dare, Mailer compares Humphrey to the small-town American sales manager with all the usual foibles. Ascending to the podium,

Humphrey had had a face which was as dependent upon cosmetics as the protagonist of a coffin. . . . [He possessed] the shaky put-together look of a sales manager in a small corporation who takes a drink to get up in the morning, and another drink after he has made his intercom calls. . . . He goes to the john and throws a sen-sen down his throat. All day he exudes odors all over; sen-sen, limewater, pomade, bay rum, deodorant, talcum, garlic, a whiff of the medicinal, the odor of Scotch on a nervous tum, rubbing alcohol! [MC, p. 208]

Mailer can move from the individual politician to a panoramic sweep of a crowd with equal skill. Joan Didion once observed that Mailer shares with Fitzgerald an "instinct of the essence of things, that great social eye. It is not the eye for the brand name, not at all the eye of a Mary McCarthy or a Philip Roth. It is rather some fascination with the heart of the structure, some deep feeling for the mysteries of power."[22] At one point in Miami, for example, Mailer visits a small reception for Nixon's most devoted supporters. It is this kind of social observation that distinguishes *Miami and Chicago* from most journalistic accounts:

. . . [It began with] a parade of wives and children and men who owned hardware stores or were druggists . . . [a] local lawyer, [a] retired doctor, a widow on tidy income, . . . minor executives from minor corporations, . . . the editor of a small-town paper, [a] professor from [a] Baptist teachers' college . . . —the stable and the established, the middle-aged and the old, a sprinkling of the young . . . [from] quiet respectable cities of the Midwest and the Far West and the border states were out to pay their homage to their own true candidate. [MC, p. 59]

Mailer analyzes the Republicans' return to power in 1968 as a reaffirmation of basic American values, echoing back to Puritan and Calvinist ancestors. In a threatening period characterized by the existence of such splinter groups as "cosmopolitans, one-worlders, trade-unionists, black militants, New Leftists, acid-heads, . . . families of the Mafia, . . . fixers, [and] swingers" (MC, p. 33), Mailer sees Nixon's success as a desire for an older, simpler version of America. In *Miami and Chicago*, as he was to in *Of a Fire on the Moon*, Mailer sees this reaffirmation of white WASP values inspired by radical changes in society and the decline of fundamental virtues. In the latter, Mailer was to find the successful space flight a triumph of technology and progress over the social upheaval at work in the nation.

Unlike an "objective" reporter, Mailer openly engages in political auguries. His prediction of a Republican disaster, made in 1968, rings true as prophecy today in the light of Watergate and Richard Nixon's subsequent fate. Mailer's forecast for the Republicans reads:

One could predict: their budgeting would prove insane, their righteousness would prove insane, their love for order and clear-thinking would be twisted through many a wry neck, the intellectual foundations of their anti-Communism would split into its separate parts. And the small-town faith in small free enterprise would run smash into the corporate juggernauts of technology land; their love of polite culture would collide with the mad aesthetics of the new America; their livid passion for military superiority would smash its nose on the impossibility of having such superiority without more government spending; their love of nature would have to take up arms against the despoiling foe, themselves, their own greed, their own big business. [MC, p. 63]

Mailer concludes the Miami section (one-third of the book) with a final portrait of Richard Nixon. Despite all the political differences between the two men, the characterization recalls an earlier sketch of John Kennedy. Mailer likes to see politicians as "existential" heroes, capable of either massive good or uncontrolled evil. Knowing that the Democrats must lose, the Reporter closes the Miami section with two opposing viewpoints on the "new" Nixon: " . . . [the Reporter] did not know if he was ready to like Nixon, or detested him for his resolutely non-poetic binary system, his computer's brain, did not know if the candidate were real as a man, or whole as a machine, lonely in his mad eminence or megalomaniacal, humble enough to feel the real wounds of the country or sufficiently narcissistic to dream the tyrant's dream" (*MC*, pp. 81–82).

In Part II, "The Siege of Chicago," we are immediately aware of Mailer's gifts as a novelist. He begins with a powerful description of the city, focusing on the stockyards as a central metaphor. If Mailer had found the plastic materialism in Miami representative of Republican thought, he describes Chicago richly as *the* Great American City. Like Dreiser, Mailer evokes "the beast" in man to serve as backdrop to the activities and people of the city:

Watching the animals be slaughtered, one knows the human case—no matter how close to angel we may come, the butcher is equally there. . . . Yes, Chicago was a town where nobody could ever forget how the money was made. It was picked up from floors still slippery with blood. . . . So something of the entrails and the secrets of the gut got into the faces of native Chicagoans . . . It was the last of the great American cities, and people had great faces, carnal as blood, greedy, direct, too impatient for hypocrisy, in love with honest plunder. [*MC*, pp. 89–90]

Even when Mailer gets his facts wrong (since Chicago has now replaced the primitive slaughtering methods he describes with modern practices), metaphorically he is right. Peter Shaw explained in *Commentary*: "Mailer is right . . . in the long introductory section on Chicago's stockyards with their primitive slaughtering methods, which he makes into epitomes of the hardness of the city. The smell of the yards hovers over the rest of the narrative, reminding us that the beatings of the demonstrators and the strong-arm methods at the convention taking place right in the stockyards are both versions of Chicago violence."[23]

Mailer views the convention delegates as representatives of the physical decay and "honest plunder" depicted in his portrait of the city. Unlike Miami, "there was *bottom* to this convention: some of the finest and some of the most corrupt faces in America were on the floor. Cancer jostled elbows with acromegaly, obesity with

edema, arthritis with alcoholism, bad livers sent curses to bronchi-
acs, and quivering jowls beamed bad cess to puffed-out paunches"
(MC, p. 176). This depiction of the delegates suggests the initial
portrait of Chicago and creates a metaphorical unity uncommon in
journalism. The final lines recall Yeats's line in "The Second Coming": "The best lack all conviction, while the worst/Are full of
passionate intensity." For Mailer such political rituals as conventions
become microcosms of society.

Although Mailer writes on a literal and metaphorical level simultaneously, at times he is content to play the "straight" political
reporter. The action on the convention floor, such as scenes demonstrating Mayor Daley's strong-arm tactics, proves more interesting
than the banalities of Miami Beach. The Doves had been anxious to
prolong debate on the Vietnam plank, while the Hawks (recogniz-
ing the detriment to their cause of prime time television exposure)
are eager to stifle discussion:

So a signal was passed to Daley by a [Johnson] Administration spokesman
who drew his finger across his throat, an unmistakable sign to cut off
conversation for the night. Daley, looking like he had just been stuffed with
a catfish, stood up, got the floor, made a move to adjourn. Immediately
recognized by Carl Albert. The little Chairman was now sufficiently excited
to start to say Mayor Daley of the Great State of Chicago. He recovered
quickly, however, quick enough to rap his gavel, and declare that the Chair
accepted the motion, snapping it through with a slick haste, as if it had
been his idea all along! The debate was postponed. [MC, p. 161]

Mailer captures at once the influence of Daley's power, Albert's
damaged pride, and the significance of live television coverage.

As in Miami, Mailer's politics are those of personality, although
he does analyze the impotence of the Democrats in a somewhat
detached manner. As he was later to do in Of a Fire on the Moon,
Mailer sees in the decay of the party a larger disintegration of
American values and attitudes. Nixon's success in Miami, coupled
with Humphrey's dominance in Chicago, inspire nausea in the
Reporter. The final portrait of Humphrey's victory for the party's
nomination echoes the politics-as-property motif that dominates
Mailer's analysis:

The twenty years in Washington had become this night property to harvest; politicians who didn't even like him, could think fondly of Hubert at this instant, he was part of their memory of genteel glamour at Washington parties, part of the dividend of having done their exercise in politics with him for twenty years. . . . The grand Establishment of the Democratic Party and its society life in Washington would soon be shattered—the world was shattering it. So they rose to cheer Humphrey. He was the end of the line. [MC, p. 209]

In Humphrey's predictable defeat in November, Mailer sees the end of the hopeful era with the politican cast as romantic hero that he had first written about in "Superman Comes to the Supermarket."

Although the Chicago section begins with accounts of the action on the floor, Mailer's objectives soon become confused. The brutal confrontations between war protesters and police in the streets and parks of Chicago cast a shadow over the events in the amphitheater. Sharing a reporter's dilemma with the reader, Mailer announces a change in tactics:

We have been present until now at an account of the Democratic Convention of 1968. It has not, however, been a description of the event. The event was a convention which took place during a continuing five-day battle in the streets and parks of Chicago between some of the minions of the high established, and some of the nihilistic of the young. But if we had begun with a description of this superb battle, it might not have been automatic to transfer interest to the convention, since the greatest excitement in the Amphitheatre was often a reflection of the war without. [MC, p.131]

In effect, Mailer is also asking: "Should the Reporter leave the Convention when the main news is happening in the streets?" Mailer decides to shift his focus and beautifully integrates the "war within and without," by showing the effects of the street violence upon the action on the floor. Significantly, Mailer pauses to explain the Reporter's motives. He shares with the reader the dilemma of how the story should be covered. Such admissions, normally omitted from the objective and depersonalized formulas of daily newspapers, distinguish Mailer's frankly subjective approach.

When Mailer turns to the violent demonstrations in Chicago, he does his best writing. The Reporter mingles with the protesters to provide long panoramic shots of the crowds, close-ups of police brutality, and a feeling for the boring hours of speeches. In a well-drawn scene, Mailer depicts protesters shouting slogans near the Chicago Hilton, where most Democratic delegates are lodged for the night. Later, he describes almost surrealistically the most brutal of all the police attacks, from his nineteenth-floor hotel room. Imagining himself a general surveying his troops, Mailer gains an aesthetic distance. He interprets the havoc on Michigan Avenue as one battle in a larger war:

. . . the marchers, who now, several thousand compressed in this one place, filled the intersection of Michigan Avenue and Balbo. There, dammed by police on three sides, and cut off from the wagons of the Poor People's March, there, right beneath the windows of the Hilton which looked down on Grant Park and Michigan Avenue, the stationary march was abruptly attacked. The police attacked with tear gas, with Mace, and with clubs, they attacked like a chain saw cutting into wood, the teeth of the saw the edge of their clubs, they attacked like a scythe through grass, lines of twenty and thirty policemen striking out in an arc. . . . Watching it from a window on the nineteenth floor, there was something of the detachment of studying a storm at evening through a glass, the light was a lovely gray-blue, the police had uniforms of sky-blue, even the ferocity had an abstract elemental play of forces of nature at battle with other forces, as if sheets of tropical rain were driving across the street in patterns, in curving patterns which curved upon each other again. [MC, p. 169]

Mailer's abstraction of the violence and his fascination with the "elemental play of forces" gives the reader an entirely different perspective from what was reported in the daily press. The passage could easily be a scene from *The Naked and the Dead*. Later, Mailer will see the street battle as part of the "twenty-year war" he had predicted in *Armies*. Pitching his metaphors to the brink of the apocalypse, the self-styled general of the legions in the streets

felt a sense of calm and beauty, void even of the desire to be down there, as if in years to come there would be beatings enough, some chosen, some from nowhere, but it was as if the war had finally begun, and this was therefore a great and solemn moment, as if indeed even the gods of history had come together, . . . as if the military spine of a great liberal party had finally separated itself from the skin, as if, no metaphor large enough to suffice, the Democratic Party had here broken in two before the eyes of a nation like Melville's whale charging right out of the sea. [MC, p. 172]

Each of Mailer's nonfiction novels of the sixties relies upon the apocalyptic metaphors of his fictional vision to provide a larger context for specific events. To write well, Mailer must fit disparate experiences into a larger pattern of interlocking metaphors. His allusion here to Melville demonstrates his desire to evoke the most grandiose metaphor possible to reinforce his assertions. If the confrontation on Michigan Avenue is a sign of America's future, then its chronicler becomes doubly important. Mailer allows his impulse for drama to dominate his thoughts in order to render the subjective experience of what it must have been like to be stationed at the Chicago Hilton in August of 1968.

Mailer soon switches, however, from the brutality on the street to the convention floor to show its impact upon the delegates. A moral showdown develops between Mayor Daley's forces, who rule the convention and the streets, and the genuinely outraged delegates. One speaker Mailer reports, "wanted the convention moved to some city far away, because of the 'surrounding violence' and 'pandemonium' in the hall" (MC, p. 177). Mailer then describes Daley's attempts to stifle the outraged liberals in images that recall the long introductory passage about the stockyards:

Before a mighty roar could even get off the ground, the Chair had passed to other business, and nominations were in order and so declared to a round of boos heavy as a swell of filthy oil. The sense of riot would not calm. Delegates kept leaving the floor to watch films on TV of the violence. . . . That was the mood which hung over the hall, a revel of banquetry, huzzah and horror, a breath of gluttony, a smell of blood. [MC, p. 177]

An unspoken assumption, Mailer reports, was "the real panic of wondering: was this how it felt with the Nazis when first they came in?" (MC, p. 178).

Yet his portrayal of the demonstrations in Chicago involves Mailer personally much less than his depiction of the march did in The Armies of the Night. The civil disobedience, speeches, and rallies of New Left youth, hippies, yippies, and college students raise for Mailer, however, the same moral dilemmas he recognized during the Pentagon march. He finds himself "once again in those endless ledgers he kept of the balance between honor and shame" (MC, p. 212). He is, he confesses, a paid professional writer under contract to a national magazine, but is also a public figure whose adrenalin flows at the sight of speaker's stands, mass rallies, and opportunities for public display.

In confessional passages, Mailer shares his ambivalence about aligning himself politically with groups that can endorse a live pig as a presidential candidate; his shame upon seeing friends Allen Ginsberg, William Burroughs, and Jean Genet[24] entering into a demonstration from which he is fleeing; his bungled attempts to organize a silent vigil; his fear for his own safety. After debating if he should drop his journalistic assignment and participate actively, Mailer has the Reporter conclude: "So one could protest with one's body, one could be tear-gassed . . . and one could take a crack on the head with a policeman's stick . . . [but] the reporter had an aversion to this" (MC, p. 145). He decides that his duty as a professional writer is to write well rather than to participate. These introspective passages, for the most part, enhance rather than detract from the narrative. Mailer reveals his changing commitment, his ethical dilemmas, and his ambivalent motives in a candid way. As a gloss on his career, such statements show his gradual evolution from the young firebrand of *Barbary Shore* to a middle-aged man with the hint of a paunch.

As a counterpart to *Armies*, the convention report creates another installment in Mailer's informal history of the decade. By creating a hybrid form of journalistic writing and fiction, he explores many of the themes of his novels. In Chicago, toward the end of the convention, the Reporter openly muses that "the plague he had written about for years seemed to be coming in—he would understand its social phenomena more quickly than the rest" (MC, p. 187). Although the Reporter confesses that his visions of perpetual social disruption are "large thoughts for a reporter to have," Mailer finds in national rituals like political conventions the signs of the plague he has feared since *The Naked and the Dead*. By not being bound to reporting the facts alone, Mailer was able to speculate freely and to create a vivid picture of the nation's mood in the late summer of 1968.

3

After the success of his convention reports, and the winning of both a National Book Award and a Pulitzer Prize for *The Armies of the Night*, Mailer turned his attention to nonliterary pursuits. He ran unsuccessfully for mayor of New York and financed two films that he directed and starred in himself.[25] Then, in 1969, he accepted a *Life* contract for a series of articles about the American space program. Three long articles, entitled "Of a Fire on the Moon," "The Psychology of Astronauts," and "A Dream of the Future's Face" chronicle the space program from early suborbital flights through the Apollo 11 mission.[26] Later published in book form, *Of a Fire on the Moon* is a well-written journalistic work that provides a general audience with a good understanding of space technology and the political background of the Apollo flights. Compendious, difficult in parts, it is Mailer's third nonfiction novel, a final installment in his informal history of America in the sixties.

Of a Fire on the Moon is a book with flashes of brilliance. In structure and narrative technique, it is similar to *Armies* and the convention reports, but it lacks the special blend of Mailer's art and life that made *The Armies of the Night* so successful. Again, Mailer creates an alter ego for himself, analogous to "The Novelist" and "The Reporter" of the previous books. Here he becomes Aquarius, since "born January 31, he is entitled to the name" (*FM*, p. 10). Unlike *Armies* and *Miami and Chicago*, however, *Fire* required a vast technical vocabulary and a mass of engineeering data that stand between the narrator and the event. Uncomfortable with the technical material, and ill-at-ease with the bland personalities of the astronauts, Mailer opens with a disclaimer: He is a literary "detective" who will attempt to assemble the facts about the moonshot into a coherent vision, but now that we "enter the Age of Aquarius, he has never had less sense of possessing the age" (*FM*, p. 10).

Aquarius suffers from a "loss of ego," and so provides more of a straight report than in Mailer's previous high flights of metaphor. Having seen himself for more than two decades as the battleground of history, Mailer finally meets his match—an event that he cannot appropriate for his own purposes. Without the symbolic wounding of the Pentagon or the brutality of the Chicago convention, Mailer has great difficulty finding the grandiose metaphors that enable him to write so much and, at times, so well.

Of a Fire on the Moon has been reviewed less favorably than has either *Miami and Chicago* or *Armies*. Although written in the loosely episodic structure of the nonfiction novel, *Fire* shows major differences from Mailer's two previous excursions. The success of both previous history-narratives was based on the direct involvement of the narrator-participant in the events. In *Fire* we are keenly aware, however, of Mailer's need to reconstruct from secondary materials, from NASA manuals and transcripts, from interviews and television. Mailer laments that "Aquarius was in no Command Module preparing to go around the limb of the moon, burn his rocket motors and brake into orbit, no, Aquarius was installed in the act of writing about the efforts of other men" (*FM*, p. 260).

The exuberant, boisterous tone of the narrator in *Armies* and the sometimes whimsical reporter of *Miami and Chicago* yield to a more serious and emotionally depressed speaking voice. As Morris Dickstein wrote in the *New York Times*, "The famous persona of *The Armies of the Night* and *Miami and the Siege of Chicago*, the man who imagines to himself at moments that he led the troops against the Pentagon and Mayor Daley, cuts no ice at Cape Kennedy or at the Manned Space Center outside Houston."[27]

The great variety and unevenness of the writing makes *Fire* difficult to assess. To make his report as complete as possible, Mailer includes lengthy verbal transcripts of astronaut talk, a day-by-day chronology of the flight, and a series of impromptu lectures on basic engineering. Aquarius lectures the reader: "Orbits are not difficult to comprehend" (*FM*, p. 199), he intones. Mailer the existential novelist is at times overwhelmed by Mailer the amateur savant of astrophysics and psychology. *Fire*, at its worst, reads like a science textbook for general audiences. Roger Sale observed that Mailer seems insecure, that he "will be content for a while to report straightforwardly, but then as if he feels he were being paid to be Norman Mailer, he lurches out: Is the trip to the moon a fulfillment or a failing of God's will?"[28] Yet Mailer does, at times, break away for a daring series of insights and perceptions that places the entire space effort in new perspective.

Fire has three main parts. In the first, entitled "Aquarius," Mailer tells of his sense of woe standing before the finely tuned machines and faceless men of NASA. He visits the Manned Space Center in Houston and provides political background on the personalities behind the American space program. He writes compellingly at times of NASA executives, offers some interesting insights into the nuts and bolts of rocketry, and informs the reader of differences between science and engineering. The most interesting section is a long chapter called "The Psychology of Astronauts," in which Mailer invents a "new" psychology appropriate to the men who must face dread and venture into the future. Since "they were either the end of the old or the first of the new men, . . . one would have nothing to measure them by until the lines of the new psychology had begun to be drawn" (*FM*, p. 49). Next we move to a journalistic examination of the Cape Kennedy installation and the festive activities of NASA men and members of the press on the eve of the launch.

In Part II, "Apollo," Mailer doubles back on his subject and retells the story of the launch and the landing on the moon in a detailed narrative told from the point of view of the astronauts. Aquarius, gadfly and reporter, all but disappears. Mailer speculates upon the astronauts' experience in the hollows of space, with Aquarius tagging along at a safe distance as a wonder-struck admirer of technology. Aquarius digresses on lunar orbits, rocket parts, and the happy wedding of engineering and technology. Mailer's engineering background at Harvard gives him a relish for technical mastery.

Part III, "The Age of Aquarius," contains some of the best writing in *Fire*. Mailer explores the implications of the moonshot for America's future and speculates that it may mean the end of heroism. He blends these weighty musings with recollections about his own disintegrating marriage, the Sharon Tate murders in Los Angeles, and the latest Kennedy tragedy off Chappaquiddick Bridge. Effectively, Mailer-as-Aquarius broods upon his own depression at the decade's close and the loss he feels from the suicides of Hemingway and Marilyn Monroe, which he sees as early warnings of his present gloom. He suggests that Apollo's success spells the end of romantic idealism. With the astronauts' victory over space, Aquarius envisions the supremacy of WASP culture and the domination of the computer's binary language over the literary language of metaphor. In Part III, Mailer achieves a measure of the interplay between events and his own ideas, between personal and social history, that helped *Armies* succeed.

As in *Armies* and *Miami and Chicago*, Mailer organizes closely observed facts and public events as parts of a larger design. He creates his speculative history of the Apollo flight, too, with the themes of his fictional vision. Like "the Reporter" of *Miami and Chicago*, Aquarius has "large thoughts": he wonders "whether the space program was the noblest expression of the Twentieth Century or the quintessence of our fundamental insanity." Unable to make contact with the men and events at NASA, Aquarius fears an irreparable gulf between the "two cultures" originally described by C. P. Snow.

Aquarius views himself as the "old breed" of man standing in "the face of the future" that he neither comprehends nor desires. Mailer creates a myth of the growing obsolescence of language, and by extension, the death of literature itself:

It was as if the more natural forms of English had not been built for the computer: Latin maybe, but not simple Anglo-Saxon. That was too primitive a language—only the general sense could be conveyed by words. . . . Computerese preferred to phase out such options. The message had to be locked into a form which could be transmitted by pulse or by lack of pulse, one binary digit at a time. . . . You could not break through computerese. [*FM*, p. 41]

In a similar vein, Aquarius says of his fellow journalists: "One of the cess-filled horrors on the Twentieth Century slowly seeping in on the journalists was that they were becoming obsolete. Events were developing a style and structure which made them almost impossible to write about" (*FM*, p. 82).

Abandoning the logic of computers, Mailer attempts to understand man's reach for the stars metaphorically and intuitively. He has always believed in a national destiny, and in *Fire*, he feels the

Twentieth Century (always capitalized) coming to a close. He fears that the rigid logic of technology will suppress magic, voodoo, and poetry. But without the immediately observable events, without the opportunities for self-display that sustained him in *The Armies of the Night*, Mailer must wrench the scenario of the Apollo flight to fit the metaphorical and philosophical schemes of his other books. The now-familiar Mailer dualities that dominate his novels are evident: the Hip vs. the Square, the Human Body vs. Machines, Language vs. Computerese, and, most fundamentally, God vs. the Devil. These basic antitheses are often sprinkled in casually in a variety of odd contexts.

For example, Mailer writes of the "psychology" of machines:

For if machines have psychology, then technology is not quits with magic—technology is founded on the confidence that magic does not exist. [*FM*, p. 147]

He describes computer language as follows:

The heart of astronaut talk, like the heart of all bureaucratic talk, was a jargon which could be easily converted to . . . [a] language like Fortran or Cobol. [*FM*, p. 29]

Deodorants become an analogy for "engineering":

. . . a male perfume is concocted to alter the husband's armpit: it blends, alters, nay *diverts* his natural odor over to one end of the wife's spectrum of acceptance. . . . That's when engineering is happy. [*FM*, p. 162]

God and the Devil will decide if man should reach the stars:

What if God wrestled for the soul of man in some greased arena with the Devil, who was now fortified by every emanation from baleful stars beyond the sun—could that be so? What if God . . . was in a combat just so crude . . . ? [*FM*, p. 411]

Richard Poirier explains that these dialectical oppositions are "best understood and made altogether less debilitating, I suspect, if the reader takes them less as part of the substance of the book [*Of a Fire on the Moon*] than as its necessary fuel, its lubricant even. They get him moving, get him involved and boosted to a level of intensity where he will then be able to produce the masterful straight stuff in the book."[29]

On a more basic level than that of Mailer's verbal-philosophical shorthand, however, his reporting of the moonshot becomes linked with the romantic vision inherent in his fiction. As in *An American Dream*, Mailer evokes memories of the deaths of President Kennedy, Hemingway, and Marilyn Monroe as cultural symbols in *Fire*. He sees their romanticism defeated by the faceless, logical astronauts. He wrote that Hemingway's

death would put secret cheer in every bureaucrat's heart for they would be stronger now. . . . Hemingway constituted the walls of the fort: Hemingway had given the power to believe you could still shout down the corridor of the hospital, live next to the breath of the beast, accept your portion of dread each day. Now the greatest living romantic was dead. Dread was loose. The giant had not paid his dues, and something awful was in the air. Technology would fill the pause. [*FM*, p. 10]

In the void left by the deaths of romantic figures, the astronauts seem unlikely prospects to generate a new kind of heroism. Try as he may, Aquarius cannot make Neil Armstrong, Buzz Aldrin, and Michael Collins into heroic figures. At a press conference, the astronauts speak of their potential deaths in space as part of one "scenario." "Even as the Nazis and the Communists had used to speak of mass murder as liquidation, so the astronauts spoke of possible personal disasters as 'contingency' " (*FM*, p. 29). The romantic heroes of former eras had mastered metaphorical language, but Aquarius reports that Armstrong spoke "a style of language that all the astronauts had learned. There were speeches where you could not tell who was putting the words together—the phrases were impersonal, interlocking. One man could have finished a sentence for another" (*FM*, p. 35).

With difficulty, Mailer struggles valiantly to transform the astronauts into mythic heroes. In the long section entitled "The Psychology of Astronauts," he recalls Neil Armstrong's boyhood dream "in which he would hold his breath and rise from the ground and hover" (*FM*, p. 49). With Armstrong's dream as a beginning premise, Mailer constructs his "new psychology," arguing that

astronauts have learned not only to live with opposites, but it was conceivable that the contradictions in their nature were so located in the very impetus of the age that their personality might begin to speak, for better or

worse, of some new psychological constitution to man. For it was true—
astronauts had come to live with adventures in space so vast one thought
of the infinities of a dream, yet their time on the ground was conventional,
practical, technical, hardworking, and in the center of the suburban middle
class. . . . The century would create death, devastation and pollution as
never before. Yet the century was now attached to the idea that man must
take his conception of life out to the stars. It was the most soul-destroying
and apocalyptic of centuries. So in their turn the astronauts had personalities
of unequaled banality and apocalyptic dignity. So they suggested in their
contradictions the power of the century to live with its own incredible
contradictions and yet release some of the untold energies of the earth. . . .
Aquarius, who had been reconnoitering for months through many a new
thought (new at the very least to him) on the architecture and function and
presence of the dream, would build his theory, on Armstrong's dream
would Aquarius commit himself. Any notes toward a new psychology
could take their departure from here. [FM, pp. 47–49]

After developing this thesis that astronauts, like blacks, may generate a "new psychology" because they embody a schizophrenia
apparent in the nation and in the century, Mailer begins to apologize
for, to renege upon, his own speculations. He begins to wonder "if
the glints and notes of these cosmic, if barely sketched, hypotheses
about earth, moon, life, death, the dream and the psychology of
astronauts would be offered the ghost of a correlative" (FM, p.
38). This search for a "correlative"—an objective fact to anchor
his speculations—is illustrative of Mailer's general method. As in
his novels, Mailer-the-reporter concocts his theories *first* and then
searches desperately for the empirical facts on which to ground his
flights of fancy.

   Mailer's myth of the obsolescence of humanism and heroism
heightens the narrative suspense of *Fire*. If the struggle between
technology and humanism can be seen as war, then as in all of
Mailer's wars, the dread-inducing forces that victimize the individual
appear to be winning. Mailer sees in the supremacy of WASP
technology that led to Apollo's success the final defeat of "the
hipster" and the "existential" criminal he has celebrated since
Advertisements for Myself. Richard Poirier observes that for Mailer,
"The Wasps have won by default. . . . They are coming into control
of evolution, and the literary imagination, with all the odors and
obscenities that nourish it, is at last obsolete with this book itself as

one of its final records."[30] Mailer must continually create wars, oppositions, major battles. In *Fire*, Aquarius views himself as the final "defender of the faith" of romanticism. The book is intended, at least in part, as an anthropological artifact to be sealed in a time capsule to be uncovered only in the distant future by unborn generations. In a time when media prophet Marshall McLuhan has predicted the growing irrelevance of print, Mailer confesses that he too must struggle "to capture the language again." Even in the dawning era of technological domination that he envisions, Mailer implicitly asserts that man's story must be told with words.

Morris Dickstein has called *Fire* "partly [Mailer's] revenge, a quest for the human and magical side of the fact, and an effort to steal back the Moon from NASA and the astronauts and reclaim it (and them) for existential psychology."[31] Mailer laments at one point that NASA's technologese "had been so complete that the word 'spook' probably did not appear in twenty million words of NASA prose" (*FM*, p. 120). He deliberately seeks to *mystify* science again by introducing a "new science of smell," by positing "a psychology of machines," and by speculating upon a "psychology of astronauts." He does not want to repudiate science. Rather, as Dickstein explains, "his aim is rather to leap over and back [between the 'two cultures'], to reclaim the event for mystery and romance, and human dread, to retrieve it in the shape of the book." For Mailer the moon has always conjured up magic and witchcraft. In *An American Dream*, his hero Rojack bounces mystic messages off the moon and, at times, the lunar surface beckons to him with invitations to suicide.

One paradox of each of Mailer's nonfiction novels is that despite their ostensible everyday realism, they frequently lead him to find mythic patterns of experience. Capote's *In Cold Blood* can be read, as we have seen, as the confrontation of the American dream of success with killers as mysterious as the forces of fate, analogous to those of Greek tragedy. Like Capote, Mailer tends to see contemporary events in more elemental patterns of experience. Mailer wants the flight of Apollo 11 to be an emblem of America's fundamental quest. Throughout *Of a Fire on the Moon* he repeatedly evokes images of *Moby Dick* in order to conjure up a profoundly American analogue of the quest pattern. Melville's influence on Mailer is considerable. As we recall, at the height of the action in the streets of Chicago, Mailer had seen the splitting of the Democratic party symbolized by the erupting violence on Michigan Avenue: "As if, no metaphor large enough to suffice, the Democratic Party had broken in two before the eyes of the nation like Melville's whale charging right out of the sea" (MC, p. 172). In *The Naked and the Dead*, Mailer's protagonist writes his college honors thesis on "The Cosmic Urge in the Novels of Herman Melville." As much for Melville's literary reputation as for the magnitude of his themes, Mailer's attraction to the creator of *Moby Dick* is apparent throughout *Fire*.

John Sisk has pointed out the many parallels between Melville's novel and Mailer's account of the moonshot. He first compares Mailer's doubts about man's ability to reach the stars to Ishmael's ambivalence toward Captain Ahab: "Ishmael, who faces a similar structural question—whether Ahab's furious pursuit of the diabolized whale is heroic absolutism or appalling madness—is in the end, I believe, less confused in his choices, perhaps because he had learned to contemplate the mighty opponent with what . . . he calls the 'equal eye.' "[32] Paralleling Ishmael's fundamental uncertainties, Aquarius wonders "whether the space program was the noblest expression of the Twentieth Century or the quintessence of our fundamental insanity" (FM, p. 20). Mailer makes clear that the metaphorical leap from the sea to outer space is a short hop for a man of his bent of mind. He quotes President Kennedy's inaugural address: "The nation, Kennedy decided, 'should commit itself to achieving the goal, before this decade is out, of landing a man on the moon and returning him safely to the earth. . . . This is a new ocean, and I believe the United States must sail upon it' "(FM, pp. 10–11).

Mailer's reliance on Melville is evident even in casual descriptions of the apparatus of Cape Kennedy. Sisk shows, for example, that the "memory of the greatest reporter of American moonshots" obviously colors Mailer's portrait of the Vehicle Assembly Building: "Aquarius' inspection of the Vehicle Assembly Building and his observation that seeing the interior of a Saturn V rocket 'was like

looking into the abdominal cavity of a submarine or a whale'
recalls Ishmael's inspection of the skeleton of the mighty whale as
he finds it embowered on a South Pacific island."[33] Seen in the
context of *Moby Dick*, even Mailer's long and sometimes boring
transcripts of astronaut talk, his reproduction of technical manuals,
and his minute examination of the machinery of the Saturn V
rocket make perfect sense. Like Melville's ship and whaling catalogs,
such passages serve to balance with concrete, knowable realities the
philosophical and metaphorical intensity of the quest. Mailer, writing more than a century after Melville, leaves no "fact" unexplored.
His main intention seems to be to write for future generations a
complete account of America's exploration of space.

Although *Of a Fire on the Moon* is primarily a journalistic
account of a contemporary event, Mailer shares Melville's basic
assumptions about the mystery of the universe and the impossibility
of knowing God's intent. And Melville would have understood
Mailer's desire to recreate the astronauts as heroes and to replace
their computer technology with metaphor. Like Ishmael, Sisk tells
us, Aquarius knows that "the true gestalt of an event is available
only to the charged up imagination acting as co-creator of reality in
a universe adapted more to metaphor than to the computer."[34]

In the closing pages of *Fire*, Mailer regains some measure of
optimism by imagining for himself a trip to the outer reaches of
space. He hopes that sending technicians now will be the first stage
of a necessary progression. In the end Mailer casts off his previous
ambivalence toward the space shot, and decides that

the hour of happiness would be here when men who spoke like Shakespeare
rode the ships: how many eons was that away! Yes, he had come to believe
by the end of this long summer that probably we had to explore into outer
space, for technology had penetrated the modern mind to such a depth that
voyages in space might have become the last way to discover the metaphys-
ical pits of that world of technique which choked the pores of modern
consciousness—yes, we might have to go out into space until the mystery
of new discovery would force us to regard the world once again as poets,
behold it as savages who knew that if the universe was a lock, its key was
metaphor rather than measure. (*FM*, pp. 412–13)

Critics who have attacked *Of a Fire on the Moon* most sharply
have often done so for the wrong reasons. Raymond A. Schroth, for

example, expected a political analysis of budgeting priorities and how all that money might have better been spent. Schroth complains that "Mailer the political journalist is sucked in by Mailer the philosopher of technology. He is diverted from his real subject—human motivation and political responsibility—into worrying over what is essentially a secondary issue, the relationship of man and machines."[35] Sisk, arguing from slightly different grounds, objects to Mailer's forcing all of the facts into his apocalyptic vision. "Why may not the Space Program," he asks, "be imagined as producing the usual mixed bag, failing no less to satisfy the hopes of Pelagian technologists than the fears of Manichean novelists?"[36]

Mailer's achievement, however, must finally be assessed on aesthetic rather than didactic grounds. The flight of Apollo 11 becomes, for Mailer, a quest generated by man's innermost search for mystery and adventure, not a question of who signed which bills or which German scientists promoted which booster rockets. As in all his novels, Mailer has created a "fiction," but in this nonfiction novel, that fiction transcends the known facts compiled in thousands of NASA documents. Mailer's various roles as fact-gatherer, work-a-day journalist, and reader of "many a technical manual" are subservient to that of mystic prophet. The Mailer who stands behind *Of a Fire on the Moon* is the social novelist whose fascination with the sources of our national fate leads him to an analysis of the current manifestations of that destiny. Like many modern writers, Mailer has relied upon the apocalyptic myth, as explained by Frank Kermode in *The Sense of an Ending*. To make sense of man's experience, Kermode argues, writers have frequently made use of the myth of apocalypse, of the world's violent end or, more optimistically, the millennial utopia that emerges from it. In modern literature, many writers have employed versions of the apocalypse to explain contemporary social disruptions. For Mailer the trip to the moon becomes just such an apocalyptic experience as the end of the decade becomes associated in his mind with the century's end. In the final pages of *Fire* he writes that

a species of apocalypse was upon us. This was, after all, the year in which a couple had fornicated on the stage and we had landed on the moon, this was the decade in which we had probed through space, and who knew which belts of protection had been voided and what precisely they had protected. A revolution was in the air which could overthrow every living establishment, an organization of society was also building which might march men daily through aisles monitored by computer probes, there to measure the individual deviations and developments of the night. That was equally on its way. We had contracted for a lunar program in 1961 and what a decade had followed! [FM, pp. 400–401]

In an earlier version of the End of Days, a 1962 story called "The Last Night," Mailer depicts an American president abandoning the earth to eventual destruction. Mailer's president addresses the doomed populace left on earth, while he streaks away in a spaceship: " 'Pray for us,' says the President to them, speaking into his microphone on that rocket ship one million miles away. 'Pray that we are true and not false. Pray that it is part of our mission to bring the life we know to other stars.' And in his ears he hears the voice of his wife, saying through her pain, 'You will end by destroying everything.' "[37] Like *The Armies of the Night*, *Fire* portrays an ambivalent vision of the End of Days. Mailer presents simultaneously the possibility of millennial utopia, and alternatively, the destruction of human life. Typically, he has no final answer but holds both possibilities in balance.

Mailer concludes *Fire* by dramatizing Aquarius's personal ambivalence toward the Apollo flight. In the book's final pages, Aquarius broods on the personal costs of the decade, on the loss of all his romantic heroes of the past, on his own impulse for self-destruction, and on his disintegrating marriage: "Aquarius was in a depression which would not lift for the rest of the summer, a curious depression full of fevers, forebodings, and a general sense that the century was done—it had ended in the summer of 1969" (FM, p. 381). Reviewing the careers of his friends, artists and bohemians of the fifties now middle-aged, Mailer finds their exploration of experience with art and drugs defeated by the progress-oriented WASP mentality. They were "an army of outrageously spoiled children who cooked with piss and vomit while the Wasps were quietly moving from command of the world to command of the moon" (FM, p. 386).

Roger Sale has summarized Mailer's final viewpoint in *Fire* and Doris Lessing's in *Four-Gated City* in a review of both books. "Not since the Victorians," Sale writes, "have so many very good writers been so completely in earnest as they feel themselves become watch-men of the night." He concludes:

Both Mailer and Lessing are great and incorrigibly egotistical writers obsessed with the urge to tell us who we are and where the world is headed; both seem to have to write much too much in order to write anything good at all, and we can treasure both not for their books, but for those passages that turn, snap, explode, only to turn and explode again, and again. Giddy with contemplating their grandeur or the world's doom, the brain of each seared with excess of perception, surely it is only in years when we *want* others to tell us who we are and where we are going that such writers appear, become famous, and feel needed, in a way mere literary types are not, indeed because they are.[38]

Needed or not, Mailer has in these three books told us more about the American experience during the sixties than have many novelists. His imaginative treatment of the Pentagon march, his convention reports, and finally, his examination of the space effort have treated significant events of the decade. Too rapidly written, these books are at times verbose, egotistical, even boring. Yet in a time when few novelists appeared able or willing to capture the tenor of contemporary life, writers of nonfiction novels managed to convey what Tom Wolfe calls "the subjective experience" of the period. Mailer attempted to counter journalistic objectivity by re-flecting on events with impressionistic freedom. Read as imaginative literature, these books embody many of the major themes of his fiction. Mailer has reaffirmed that reality is mysterious and finally unknowable: to state the facts is to have created a fiction. Whether his nonfiction novels will be read in the future with the enthusiasm shown by readers in the sixties is an open question, but clearly they will be seen as important works in Mailer's literary career and as rich chronicles of these years.

6

LIFE IN EDGE CITY: WOLFE'S NEW JOURNALISM

Because always comes the moment when it's time to take the Prankster circus further on toward Edge City. –TOM WOLFE, The Electric Kool-Aid Acid Test

DESPITE THE CONTRIBUTIONS of such novelists as Capote and Mailer to the new form of nonfiction, the writer whose name has become almost synonymous with the term *new journalism* is Tom Wolfe. His outlandish electric-blue suits and his flamboyant style, incorporating "every device known to prose," have placed him at the eye of the storm as the new journalism's best-known writer and chief promoter. Since the early sixties when his articles about radio "deejays," underground movie queens, topless dancers, celebrities, and social climbers first began appearing in the *New York Herald Tribune*, critics have either praised his genius or dismissed his unorthodox journalism as the product of our decadent age.

When his first collection of articles, *The Kandy-Kolored Tangerine-Flake Streamline Baby*, shocked New York literary circles in 1965, a reviewer wrote in *Newsweek*:

Wolfe's prose is as outrageous as his clothes. For the who-what-where-when-why of traditional journalism he has substituted what he calls "the wowie!" Wolfe's wowie is a seemingly anarchic barrage of metaphor, exclamations ("I love exclamation points!"), neologisms, hip phrases, nonsense words, ellipses, onomatopoeia, learned references to Greek myths and the Pre-Raphaelites, and architectural, medical, and comic-strip allusions.[1]

Dwight Macdonald attacked Wolfe in the *New York Review of Books* by labeling his style "parajournalism, a bastard form, having it both ways, exploiting the factual authority of journalism and the atmospheric license of fiction." But in a 1966 *Atlantic* article, Dan Wakefield compared Wolfe's writing with Capote's and argued that together the two writers had created a new synthesis of reporting and fiction. This personal form of reportage, Wakefield continued, combined the empirical virtues of journalism with the imaginative insights of the novel.[2]

After his initial success with *Streamline Baby*, Wolfe published three books. His articles for *New York* (which splintered from the *New York Herald Tribune* to become an independent magazine in 1967), *Esquire*, and the *London Weekend Telegraph* were gathered in *The Pump House Gang* (1968). Two long satiric pieces on the embrace of radical causes by New York's elite and on federal poverty-program hijinks appeared as *Radical Chic and Mau-Mauing the Flak Catchers* (1970). A full-length nonfiction novel, *The Electric Kool-Aid Acid Test* (1968), chronicles the experimental lifestyle of novelist Ken Kesey and his band of Merry Pranksters.

A native of Virginia, Wolfe graduated cum laude from Washington and Lee University, where he had majored in English, served as sports editor of the campus newspaper, and starred on the baseball team. After graduating in 1951, he tried out unsuccessfully as a pitcher with the old New York Giants. Abandoning his hopes for a professional baseball career, he enrolled in graduate school in American Studies at Yale University. Wolfe received his doctorate in 1957, but was by that time disenchanted with academic life and set out instead to earn his living as a reporter. *Current Biography* reports that he found the idea of newspaper work exciting: "After five years in graduate school, . . . I very much wanted to break away from academic life and went into the only field where I thought I could make a living—newspaper work. To tell the truth, I found it immediately glamorous."[3]

Wolfe began as a general assignment reporter for the *Springfield* (Massachusetts) *Union*, before moving on to the *Washington Post* in June 1959. While at the *Post* he wrote local feature stories and reported on Latin America, winning Washington Newspaper Guild awards in both categories. In April 1962 he joined the staff of the *New York Herald Tribune*, where he began writing colorful feature stories for *New York*, then the newspaper's Sunday magazine. His sketches of the lives of mafiosi, fighter Cassius Clay, New York celebrities, and other topics on the popular culture also appeared in *Harper's Bazaar*, *Confidential*, and *Esquire*. In his personal account of the rise of the new journalism, Wolfe confesses that many New York feature writers in the early sixties were dreaming the novelist's dream of instant success:

The idea was to get a job on a newspaper, keep body and soul together, pay the rent, get to know "the world," accumulate "experience," perhaps work some of the fat off your style—then, at some point, quit cold, say goodbye to journalism, move into a shack somewhere, work night and day for six months, and light up the sky with the final triumph. The final triumph was known as The Novel.[4]

Like Mailer, Wolfe idolized the literary figures of the twenties and thirties—Hemingway, Fitzgerald, Thomas Wolfe, James T. Farrell—who had parlayed literary talent into fame and financial success. The thought of writing the "great novel," Wolfe reminisces, "was like a spiritual calling."[5]

His literary ambitions, combined with financial pressures to help build the circulation of a faltering newspaper, led Wolfe to experiment with the narrative techniques and plotting devices of the short story and the novel. His now infamous, idiosyncratic style developed in part, too, from rebellion against the formulas and "pale beige tone" of traditional journalism. Of his early career on the *Tribune*, Wolfe told an interviewer:

I thought, Goddamnit. I've got to think of ways to get people reading, to create an atmosphere right away that would absorb them. I just had to grab them by the lapels—and just *hold* them there. I had visions of foldouts and drawings in them, but no magazine publisher would ever put those damn fold-outs in. So I started developing a style that could capture the spontaneity of thought, not just speech.[6]

A major stylistic breakthrough came with his unorthodox approach in covering a hot rod and custom-car show for *Esquire*
during the long New York newspaper strike of 1963. He had gone
to California and spent months researching the strange creations of
California's cult of custom-car artists who rigged conventional
Detroit products with souped-up motors, extra chrome and tail
fins, and wildly sculptured bodies. The subject did not lend itself to
the who-what-where-when-why tradition of journalism that Wolfe
had been trained in. "The thing was, I knew I had another story all
the time, a bona fide story, the real story of the Hot Rod & Custom
Car Show, but I didn't know what to do with it. It was outside the
system of ideas I was used to working with."[7] Under editorial
pressure to file the story, Wolfe fired off a forty-page memo addressed
to *Esquire* editor Byron Dobell:

I told Byron Dobell, the managing editor at *Esquire*, that I couldn't pull
the thing together. O.K., he tells me, just type out my notes and send them
over and he will get somebody else to write it. So about 8 o'clock that night
I started typing the notes out in the form of a memorandum that began,
"Dear Byron." I started typing away, starting right with the first time I saw
any custom cars in California. . . . And inside a couple of hours, typing
along like a madman, I could tell that something was beginning to happen. . . . [Dobell] told me they were striking out the "Dear Byron" at the
top of the memorandum and running the rest of it in the magazine. That
was the story, "The Kandy-Kolored Tangerine-Flake Streamline Baby."[8]

After the initial success of his two collections of magazine articles
had made him a social critic to be admired and feared, Wolfe
attacked New York's "beautiful people" for their sudden interest in
radical politics in an article called "Radical Chic: That Party at
Lenny's" in a June 1970 issue of *New York*. His subject was a party
given by conductor and well-known liberal Leonard Bernstein for
the Black Panthers that had attracted some of New York's wealthiest
celebrities. Wolfe's satiric portrait of the elite's sudden embrace of
urban guerillas is permeated with close attention to "status details"
of dress, styles, and dialogue. Like Capote's method in *The Muses
Are Heard*, Wolfe's selective eavesdropping brilliantly counterpoints
the discrepancies between two completely different social worlds.
Consider this snapshot of Panthers and socialites munching hors
d'oeuvres:

Mmmmmmmmmmmmmmmmm. These are nice. Little Roquefort cheese morsels rolled in crushed nuts. Very tasty. Very subtle. It's the way the dry sackiness of the nuts tiptoes up against the dour savor of the cheese that is so nice, so subtle. Wonder what the Black Panthers eat here on the hors d'oeuvre trail? Do the Panthers like little Roquefort cheese morsels rolled in crushed nuts this way, and asparagus tips in mayonnaise dabs, and *meatballs petites au Coq Hardi*, all of which are at this very moment being offered to them on gadrooned silver platters by maids in black uniforms with hand-ironed white aprons. [...] Deny it if you wish to, but such are the *pensées metaphysiques* that rush through one's head on these Radical Chic evenings just now in New York.[9]*

The companion piece in the same volume, "Mau-Mauing the Flak Catchers," is an irreverent exposé of the strategies devised by militant groups in the late sixties to maximize their benefits from the poverty programs. According to Wolfe, militant groups would gather together about fifteen to twenty of their members and then descend upon the local Office of Economic Opportunity. Generally, this would lead to a confrontation with a second-level bureaucrat (a flak catcher) in a necessary ritual before the funds could be granted:

They [the poverty program administrators] sat back and waited for you to come rolling in with your certified angry militants, your guaranteed frustrated ghetto youth, looking like a bunch of wild men. Then you had your test confrontation. If you were outrageous enough, if you could shake up the bureaucrats so bad that their eyes froze into iceballs and their mouths twisted up into smiles of sheer physical panic, into shit-eating grins, so to speak—then they knew you were the real goods. They knew you were the right studs to give the poverty grants and community organizing jobs to. Otherwise they wouldn't know.[10]

Despite Wolfe's popular success, some critics have attacked his brand of the new journalism, not because of his ideas but because of the outward manifestations of his style. Festooned with elaborate repetitions and unorthodox punctuations, his prose flagrantly violates nearly all the rules of standard usage. Critics of his work charge that he makes up his dialogue and that he freely ignores the conven-

---

*Because of Wolfe's unconventional use of ellipsis marks, it is necessary to distinguish his writing from the author's editing. Hence, bracketed ellipsis marks represent editing; all others appear in the original text.

tional journalistic virtues of objectivity and balance. Wolfe's defenders, however, find his style an appropriate medium to explore the excesses of a period in which differences between fact and fiction are increasingly difficult to defend. Robert Scholes has labeled Mailer and Wolfe "hystorians" because they chronicle the hysteria of contemporary life:

The so-called stylistic excesses of such men as Norman Mailer and Tom Wolfe are in my view no more than the indispensable equipment they must employ in doing justice to our times. This is not to say that one must himself be hysterical to chronicle hysteria, but to suggest that hysteria cannot be assimilated and conveyed by one who is totally aloof. Mailer and Wolfe are not hysterical but they manage to remain more open to the contemporary scene than most reporters or commentators. They are more involved in what they report than a journalist would be, and they bring to their reporting a more efficient intellectual apparatus, a richer framework of ideas and attitudes, a perspective more historical than journalistic.[11]

I

Wolfe's main contribution to the nonfiction novel, *The Electric Kool-Aid Acid Test*, explores the drug-inspired life-style of novelist Ken Kesey and his group called the Merry Pranksters. The book takes its title from the practice in the early sixties of spiking vats of Kool-Aid punch with large doses of LSD. Like *In Cold Blood* and *The Armies of the Night*, Wolfe's book applies the techniques of fiction to true events.

Wolfe carefully documents his work with supporting interviews, tape recordings, films, letters, and diaries. He blends these materials, which the Kesey group had fortunately preserved in the Prankster "archives," into a continuous and suspenseful narrative that reads more like a novel than like journalism or biography. Just as Capote depicted the Kansas murders through the eyes of Perry Smith, so Wolfe visualizes the beginnings of the "hippie movement" from the participants' point of view. In a more prominent way than Capote, however, Wolfe presents his own emotions in the minor role of participant-observer. Like Mailer, Wolfe is particularly adept at sensing meanings beneath surface details. Michael L. Johnson contends that Wolfe's writing frequently resembles that of Norman Mailer in its quick cadences and rapid-fire illuminations, . . . [and] like Mailer, [Wolfe] has an uncanny ability to respond to the hidden and less obvious forces of events and phenomena, to see madness beneath the surface of accepted behavior, and to discern the allegorical and ritual significance, or the desperate absurdity, of human activity, whether it be everyday or extraordinary.[12]

The Electric Kool-Aid Acid Test is an updating of the Beat Generation saga chronicled in Kerouac's *On the Road*. Neal Cassady, the model for Kerouac's protagonist Dean Moriarty, was in fact part of the nucleus of Kesey's group. Unlike Wolfe's satiric attitude toward most of his subjects, his approach is enormously sympathetic to the Prankster experience. Comparing Wolfe with Kerouac, Michael Johnson observes that Wolfe "is more willing to see comedy and absurdity than Kerouac was, but both books have a vision of the tragedy of their respective cultures and are closely attuned through style to the feverishness of people living out new and sometimes desperate life-experiments in order to transcend the sickness of their age."[13]

Rather than rejecting the materialism and technology of American society as did the Beat Generation, however, Kesey's Pranksters attempted to blend psychedelic drugs, futuristic technology, and fantasies drawn from comic books. Unlike the introverted bohemians of the fifties who had rejected middle-class materialism, the Pranksters were "going to try it right down the main highway, eight lanes wide, heron-neck arc lamps rising up as far as the eye can see, and they will broadcast on all frequencies, waving American flags, turning up the Day-Glo and the neon of 1960s electro-pastel America, wired up and amplified, 327,000 horsepower, a fantasy bus in a science-fiction movie, welcoming all on board."[14] Although Wolfe's sympathy toward the Pranksters is apparent, he achieves what Robert Scholes calls a double perspective, a viewpoint at once inside and outside the group's experience: "Wolfe also has the double vision it takes to see Kesey as a genuine religious leader and a projection of a comic-book fantasy—both Buddha and Captain Marvel. Keeping his own cool, Wolfe ranges from strong empathy with Kesey's group to detached skepticism. This double perspective, simultaneously inside and outside the object of his investigation, is typical of his method."[15]

Wolfe begins his account by admitting his initial, rather shallow journalistic motives. Kesey, the much-celebrated novelist of *One Flew Over the Cuckoo's Nest* (1962), had fled from California authorities following a second drug arrest and was rumored to be in hiding in Mexico. Wolfe's too simplistic "totem story," he mockingly tells us, was supposed to be called "Promising Novelist Real-Life Fugitive." But like Capote in Kansas and Mailer at the Pentagon, Wolfe found himself involved in "another story"—a far more engaging one. Like *In Cold Blood* and *The Armies of the Night*, *Acid Test* developed from the writer's intense personal involvement with people and events; it conveys his conviction that a creative response to the facts was required.

The book begins with a first-person account of the reporter's initial meeting with Kesey and several Pranksters. Wolfe had gone to California to gather only enough material to write a brief magazine article. When he met Kesey, however, then jailed in San Francisco, he became fascinated with the novelist and the more bizarre aspects of his group. Kesey told Wolfe of his plans to deliver a warning to the entire Bay Area about the dangers of LSD. Drugs, Kesey explained, can open the doors of perception, but one must go "beyond acid." After this *in medias res* beginning, Wolfe stops the present narrative and shifts to an extended flashback, taking the Pranksters from their beginnings in the early sixties to the time of Kesey's arrest. In early chapters Wolfe briefly sketches in Kesey's family background, his role in the bohemian community at Stanford University, and his early success as a novelist.

The Prankster saga proper comprises the book's second and major section. Wolfe colorfully documents the $103,000 cross-country bus trip to visit Timothy Leary's League for Spiritual Discovery, the group's musical influence on such Bay-area rock groups as the Grateful Dead, an uneasy alliance with the Hell's Angels, and finally, a series of "acid tests" in which large doses of LSD were administered to mass audiences in huge vats of Kool-Aid punch. These collective LSD trips, accompanied by rock music and stroboscopic light shows, became the prototypes for the activities of the hippie community that was then gathering in San Francisco's Haight-Ashbury district. The final third of Wolfe's account provides the details of Kesey's second marijuana charge that led to his self-imposed exile in Mexico. The nonfiction novel closes by returning to present time—to Kesey's return to and capture in San Francisco and the "beyond acid" speech only barely sketched in the first few pages. The saga ends with the eventual dissolution of the Pranksters and Kesey's move into seclusion in Oregon.

The narrative techniques that Wolfe uses in *Acid Test* closely resemble those of fiction rather than the usual devices of journalism. Wolfe's nonfiction novel recreates the milieu in which events occur and reflects the attitudes and behavior of the characters rather than mere facts. His desire is to capture what he calls "the subjective reality of the Prankster experience." His use of language immediately distinguishes *Acid Test* from what he calls the "totem stories" of the traditional press. His style ranges from short essay-like passages to the elaborate explosions of words and letters that have become his trademark as a new journalist. While he can write short concise passages with simple sentences, he also creates passages several pages long that are as syntactically and semantically complex as prose poems.

One of Wolfe's most effective techniques for immersing the reader gradually into the Prankster world is his adoption of the specialized cant and argot of the drug culture. Early in his account, Wolfe introduces Prankster terms and phrases into the narrative and never fully returns to standard English. In *Future Shock*, Alvin Toffler argued that American society had been fragmenting into subcultures that deviate markedly from dominant middle-class values. Toffler thinks that soon the values, attitudes, and languages of these groups will require what he calls "transcultural translators" to interpret one group to another.[16]

Wolfe might be called such a translator for the Kesey group since he interprets and explains their deviant life-style to middle-class readers. Like the speaking voice that Mark Twain adopts in such books as *Roughing It* and *Life on the Mississippi*, Wolfe's voice is that of a tour guide who introduces to the reader exotic manners and values quite alien to his own. A great deal of travel literature has fulfilled this function, and for societies as a whole it has been the special province of the novel. In an essay on the function of the nineteenth-century novel, Lionel Trilling explains that the British novelist's major achievement has been to portray

a culture's hum and buzz of implication . . . the whole evanescent context in which its explicit statements are made. It is that part of a culture which is made up of half-uttered or unutterable expressions of value. They are hinted at by small actions, sometimes by the arts of dress or decoration, sometimes by tone, gesture, emphasis or rhythm, sometimes by the words that are used with a special frequency or special meaning. They are the things that for good or bad draw the people of one culture together and that separate them from the people of another culture.[17]

But if Toffler's theory of social fragmentation is correct, then the kind of social cohesiveness that Trilling ascribes to the function of the novel is no longer possible. What Wolfe does is to accomplish this novelistic function with reference to a specialized subculture instead of to a culture as a whole. By tuning in upon the Pranksters' special words, as well as their gestures and forms of expression, Wolfe successfully captures the "hum and buzz of implication" that surrounds their subculture and separates them from the American mainstream.

   Wolfe's presentation of Prankster language is a blend of the "hip talk" of the Beats of the fifties, drug-related jargon, and imagery drawn from comic books like "Captain Marvel." Each of the group's projected activities, large or small, is referred to as "the current fantasy" or "the movie." These phrases imply a radically different conception of "reality," of time and space, and of cause and effect. The Pranksters view life as a Bergsonian flow, a "movie," rather than as something that occurs in discrete time-units all of which are related to one another by causality. Wolfe frequently adopts the metaphorical shorthand used by the group. Suburban families, whose values the Pranksters hold in contempt, are referred to mockingly as "Mom & Dad & Buddy & Sis." The Prankster ethos is founded upon what Wolfe calls "the unspoken thing," an unac- knowledged hero-worship of Kesey as guru. Other phrases that have now gained wide currency because of the broadening of the counterculture are used throughout. If Cassady gets pleasure from tossing a sledgehammer around the warehouse, he is "doing his thing" or "his freak." Expressing feelings openly is being "out front." More specialized Prankster language is also adopted at times. Those who share in the life-style are "on the bus"; dropouts get names like "Dismount." Wolfe relies almost entirely on the colorful nicknames the Pranksters had adopted to abandon their middle-class identities: Mountain Girl, Doris Delay, the Hermit, Hassler, Fetchin' Gretchen, Zonker.

Although Wolfe's reliance upon this specialized subjective language deviates from conventional journalistic practice, it allows him to explore the Pranksters' perceptions of their experiences. In contrast, most ostensibly "objective" press reports about "hippies" or the "youth culture" unconsciously accepted the standards of the law enforcement authorities whose viewpoints implied social pathology: How many people used illegal drugs? How many persons were arrested? What socially and sexually unacceptable practices did the group engage in? Like Mailer's credo of "history as nuance," however, Wolfe's commitment is to inform more deeply than do the television film crews whose superficial and distorting lenses comb Haight-Ashbury in search of "hippies."

Wolfe's idiosyncratic prose style melds perfectly with the Day-Glo reality of Prankster life—their brightly dappled suits, their highly amplified rock music, their psychedelic visions. Wolfe's unorthodox spellings, his repetition of words and syllables, his use of onomatopoeia, all contribute to the total evocation of the group's experience. Wolfe's opening portrait of the Prankster bus wired for amplified sound quickly establishes this "subjective reality":

And they went with the flow, the whole goddamn flow of America. The bus barrels into the super-highway toll stations and the microphones on top of the bus pick up all the clacking and ringing and the mumbling by the toll-station attendant and the brakes squeaking and the gears shifting, all the sounds of the true America that are screened out everywhere else, it all came amplified back inside the bus. [...]Barreling across America with the microphones picking it all up, the whole roar, and microphone up top gets eerie in a great rush and *skakkkkkkkkkkkkkk* it is ripping and roaring over asphalt and *thok* it's gone, no sound at all. The microphone has somehow ripped loose on top of the bus and hit the roadway and dragged along until it snapped off entirely— [...] They are all rapping and grokking over the sound it made—"Wowwwwwwwwww! Did you—wow-wwwwww"—as if they had synched into a never-before-heard thing, a unique thing, the sound of an object, a microphone, hitting the American asphalt, the open road at 70 miles an hour. [*AT*, pp. 75–76]

Wolfe can, however, shift rapidly from raucous description to subtle judgment. He focuses on the human anguish of a drug experience gone awry when he reports the "freak-out" of a woman called Stark Naked gone insane from an LSD overdose:

oooooooooooooooooooooooooo—Stark Naked waxing weirder and weirder, huddled in the black blanket shivering, then out, bobbing wraith, her little deep red aureola bobbing in the crazed vibrations—finally they pull into Houston. [. . .] And there, amid the peaceful Houston elms on Quenby Road, it dawned on them all that this woman—which one of us even knows her?—had completed her trip. She had gone with the flow. She had gone stark raving mad. [AT, pp. 76–77]

Occasionally assuming his role as Ph.D. in American Studies, Wolfe will digress to lecture the reader, as Mailer does in *Of a Fire on the Moon*. The Pranksters' mystical experience on LSD is the key to the group's cohesiveness, a religious unity that they share with many groups throughout history. "Countless philosophers, prophets, early scientists, not to mention alchemists and occultists," Wolfe tells us,

had tried to present the same idea in the past, Plotinus, Lao-tse, Pico della Mirandola, Agrippa, Kepler, Leibniz. [. . .] And *then*—some visionary, through some accident—[. . .]—through some quirk of metabolism, through some *drug* perhaps, has his doors of perception opened for an instant and he almost sees—*presque vue*!—the entire being and he knows for the first time that there is a whole...*other pattern* here...Each moment in his life is only minutely related to the cause-and-effect chain within his little molecular world. Each moment, if he could only analyze it, reveals the entire pattern of the motion of the giant being, and his life is minutely synched in with it—[AT, p. 126]

[handwritten margin note: Not ambiguous but besides the point]

Whether Wolfe himself took LSD remains ambiguous, but he describes events *as if* he were present as the drug experiences unfolded. For example, at a Beatles concert in San Francisco, Wolfe writes about the rock group's impact on a large teenage audience as if he were experiencing it through Kesey's eyes:

[handwritten margin note: through research, he presents the scene as if we the reader are there present tense]

Ghhhhhhooooooooooowwwwww, it is like the whole thing has snapped, and the whole front section of the arena becomes a writhing, seething mass of little girls waving their arms in the air, this mass of pink arms, it is all you can see, it is like a single colonial animal with a thousand waving pink tentacles,—vibrating poison madness and filling the universe with the teeny agony torn out of them. It dawns on Kesey: it is *one being*. They have all been transformed into one being [. . .] and Kesey sees it. [. . .]
    Control—it is perfectly obvious—[the Beatles] have brought the whole

mass of human beings to the point where they are one, out of their skulls, one psyche, and they have utter control over them. [*AT*, p. 182]

Although Wolfe strives to present the perceptions of Kesey and the Pranksters whenever possible, he intervenes at times in his role as transcultural interpreter. He occasionally pauses in his narrative to explain arcane practices of the group much like a wonder-struck anthropologist just discovering some new exotic lore. He lectures, for example, on the importance of "light shows" to the drug-oriented milieu of the Pranksters:

The strobe! The strobe, or stroboscope, was originally an instrument for studying motion, like the way a man's legs move when he is running. In a darkened chamber, for example, you aim a bright light, flashing on and off, at the runner's legs as he runs. The light flashes on and off very rapidly, maybe three times as fast as a normal heartbeat. Every time the light flashes on, you see a new stage in the movement of the runner's legs. The successive images tend to freeze in your mind, because the light flashes off before the usual optical blur of motion can hit you. The strobe has certain magical properties in the world of the acid heads. At certain speeds stroboscopic lights are so synched in with the pattern of brain waves that they can throw epileptics into a seizure. Heads discovered that strobes could project them into many of the sensations of an LSD experience without taking LSD. *The strobe!* [*AT*, p. 214]

Brilliantly at times, Wolfe's stream-of-consciousness technique presents Kesey's thoughts and actions as they might have occurred. Interior monologue dominates his account of Kesey's self-imposed exile in Mexico. Working from Kesey's recollections months later and from letters he wrote to novelist Larry McMurtry at the time,[18] Wolfe enters Kesey's mind like a Joyce or a Virginia Woolf might have. Gorham Munson explains in *Style and Form in American Prose* that "the aim of imaginative literature is to create an *as if*. . . . In other words, the writer of fiction with nothing personally at stake must by the sheer power of his imagination write as if everything were in question. Only thus can he fully compel the reader to share in his imaginary experience, to feel throughout his being, as if he also were actually present."[19] Like Perry Smith in *In Cold Blood*, Kesey emerges not so much as a criminal but as a hero in the pattern of the rebel-victim described by Ihab Hassan in

Radical Innocence. With the narrator of *Acid Test*, the reader roots for the hero to evade the Mexican Federales who have tracked him to a sequestered village:

Haul ass, Kesey. Move. *Scram. Split flee hide vanish disintegrate*. Like *run*.

Rrrrrrrrrrrrrrrrrrrrrev revrevrevrevrevrevrevrevrev or are we gonna have just a late Mexican re-run of the scene on the rooftop in San Francisco and sit here with the motor spinning and watch with fascination while the cops they climb up once again to *come git you*—[. . .]

[. . .] COME ON, MAN, DO YOU NEED A COPY OF THE SCRIPT TO SEE HOW THIS MOVIE GOES? YOU HAVE MAYBE 40 SECONDS LEFT BEFORE THEY COME GET YOU

—a Volkswagen has been cruising up and down the street for no earthly reason at all, except that they are obviously working with the fake telephone linesmen outside the window who whistle—

THERE THEY GO AGAIN [. . .]

[. . .]MORE TELEFONO TRUCKS! TWO LOUD WHISTLES THIS TIME—FOR NO EARTHLY REASON EXCEPT TO COME GIT YOU. YOU HAVE MAYBE 35 SECONDS LEFT

—Kesey has Cornel Wilde Running Jacket ready hanging on the wall, a jungle-jim corduroy jacket stashed with fishing line, a knife, money, DDT, tablet, ball-points, flashlight, and grass. Has it timed by test runs that he can be out the window, down through a hole in the roof below, down a drain pipe, over a wall and into the thickest jungle in 45 seconds— [*AT*, pp. 256–57]

Wolfe's use of the stream-of-consciousness technique heightens the suspense in chapters 21 and 23, since Kesey's paranoid thoughts are subtly interspersed with the narrator's comments on the action. Sophisticated shifts in point of view occur: the italicized portions are Kesey's actual words excerpted from Kesey's letters to McMurtry; the capitalized imperatives are messages from Kesey's drug-crazed brain that Wolfe has arranged in a countdown sequence concluding with a dash to the jungle at the zero-second mark; in passages introduced by dashes, the narrator supplies needed circumstantial background; finally, words characteristic of Kesey's speech patterns such as "telefono" (his adopted Spanish) and "come git you" (echoing his Oregon drawl) are interspersed throughout. Significantly, just as in *In Cold Blood*, the reader becomes captivated by the *as if* sensation of a novel. He wonders, Will Kesey be caught? The reader identifies with the fugitive-hero—*as if*—he too were down in the Mexican ratlands wondering just when and how the

[handwritten margin notes: "May be from letters but here operates as interior thought"]

[handwritten margin notes: "H. Girl! not KK"]

Federales would close in on him, tap him on the shoulder, and say: "Gotcha!"

Another narrative technique Wolfe employs is what has been called "substitutionary narration."[20] Rather than reporting a character's direct speech, the narrator imitates or even parodies those speech cadences and inflections that often reveal a character's values and attitudes. If used to excess, this technique can lead to burlesque, which is what frequently happens when Wolfe wants to show the reactions of outsiders to the Pranksters. For example, Wolfe assumes the voice of a typical cop trying to grapple with the "hippie phenomenon":

Sergeant, they're lollygagging up against the storefronts on Haight Street up near that Psychedelic Shop like somebody hocked a bunch of T. B. lungers up against windows and they've oozed down to the sidewalks, staring at you with these huge zombie eyes, just staring. And a lot of weird American Indian and Indian from India shit, beaded headbands and donkey beads and temple bells—[. . .] *The cops!*—oh, how it messed up their minds. The cops knew drunks and junkies by heart, and they knew *about* LSD, but this *thing* that was going on...[*AT*, p. 315]

Wolfe's parody of a "typical cop's" reaction to hippies creates an ironic distance between the understanding reflected by the policeman's comments and the reader's inside knowledge. At other points, he parodies quite effectively the reactions of shocked citizens who encounter Kesey's crazies bouncing across the countryside in the Prankster bus. Unlike most conventional reporters, Wolfe filters the events and characters he depicts through the voices and thought patterns of those both inside and outside the group.

2

Wolfe's complex use of point of view has led some critics to conclude that he does not judge or evaluate what he reports. Michael Wood argues in a review of Wolfe's new journalism anthology that "what characterizes the new journalism, at least as it is represented in this book, is first, a certain elusiveness on the part of the writer . . . because he has made it his job to hide his opinions, or to hint at them only indirectly, or perhaps even to have none."[21]

Although Wood's statement correctly characterizes the work of certain new journalists nothing could be more inaccurate of *Acid Test*. Wolfe comments and evaluates, directly and indirectly, throughout the book.

Wolfe often uses what he has called the "hectoring narrator." When he wishes to suggest, for example, certain similarities between the ritualistic practices of the drug cultists and orthodox Christianity, he describes two Pranksters "guiding" a teenager's first LSD trip:

To the little girl it's her first glimpse of Heaven itself, zonked as she is on LSD, her first capsule—

"I'm—getting the picture! we're all he-e-e-e-e-ere and we can do anything we want!"

—revealing all this to Doris Delay and Zonker. Doris, like a good old helpful hand, says, "That's right. We're all here and everything's all right and you're fine."

The little bud sinks into a folding chair beside Doris's and gives her a look. "I should be suspicious of you..."

"The paranoid stage," Doris says to Zonker. *I love to tell the story—*

"...because I'm stoned."

"I know," says Doris. *To tell the old, old story*—love and glory now playing in your neighborhood for the first run. [italics mine, *AT*, p. 363]

While the dialogue of Pranksters Doris and Zonker is accurately recorded, Wolfe's "hectoring narrator" is singing Sunday-school lyrics in the background to suggest the parallels between this exchange and church ritual, with the two Pranksters as high priests. Even without direct commentary Wolfe makes his point effectively.

In addition to the use of substitutionary narration and the hectoring narrator, Wolfe writes occasionally in the first person. His persona as inquiring reporter is actually like that of the *histor*, a speaking voice familiar from the time of ancient historians and rhetoricians. In *The Nature of Narrative*, Scholes and Kellogg define the *histor* as follows:

The *histor* is the narrator as inquirer, constructing a narrative on the basis of such evidence as he has been able to accumulate. The *histor* is not a character in narrative, but he is not exactly the author, either. He is a person, a projection of the author's empirical virtues. Since Herodotus and Thucydides the *histor* has been concerned to establish himself with the reader as a repository of fact, a tireless investigator and sorter, a sober and impartial judge—a man, in short, of authority, who is entitled not only to present the facts as he has established them but to comment on them, to draw parallels, to moralize, to generalize.[22]

Wolfe's role as *histor*, like Mailer's alter-ego Aquarius in *Of a Fire on the Moon*, permits him to evaluate and to present his changing perceptions of events and personalities as new discoveries—as revelations. At one point, Wolfe tells the reader of his bewilderment in *discovering* that despite all the psychedelic trappings, the Pranksters are essentially a religious cult:

I remember puzzling over this. There was something so...*religious* in the air, in the very atmosphere of the Prankster life, and yet one couldn't put one's finger on it. On the face of it there was just a group of people who shared an unusual psychological state, the LSD experience—But exactly! The *experience*—that was the word! and it began to fall into place. In fact, none of the great founded religions, Christianity, Buddhism, Islam, Jainism, Judaism, Zoroastrianism, Hinduism, none of them began with a philosophical framework or even a main idea. They all began with an overwhelming *new experience*, what Joachim Wach called "the experience of the holy," and Max Weber, "possession of the deity," the sense of being a vessel of the divine, of the All-one. I remember I never truly understood what they were talking about when I first read of such things. [. . .]—After I got to know the Pranksters, I went back and read Joachim Wach's paradigm of the way religions are founded, written in 1944, and it was almost like a piece of occult precognition for me if I played it off against what I knew about the Pranksters. [*AT*, pp. 113–14]

Wolfe frequently evaluates, too, by intruding himself in the narrative in order to modify, to extend, and to judge. Although he does not speak in his own voice exactly, Wolfe often heightens the contradictions of Prankster life by juxtaposing its espoused values to its actual social practices. In principle, Kesey's group has no philosophy: Kesey is the "non-navigator"; all feelings are "out front"; the group is governed by a simultaneously felt "group mind." Yet, at one point, Wolfe depicts a group member speaking of a "Prankster hierarchy," to which Wolfe adds ironically:

Prankster hierarchy? There wasn't supposed to *be* any Prankster hierarchy. Even Kesey was supposed to be the non-navigator and the non-teacher. Certainly everybody else was an equal in the brotherhood, for there was no competition, there were no games [. . .] but sometimes it seemed like the old *personality* game...looks, and all the old *aggressive, outgoing* charm, even athletic ability—it won out here like everywhere else...[*AT*, p. 295]

In addition to the *histor's* voice, Wolfe uses a slightly different "I" voice in the opening chapters of *Acid Test*. Here he adopts the persona of a condescending New York journalist visiting California to write a quick story on the "freaks" and jet back to the East. "All I knew about Kesey at that time point was that he was a highly regarded 31-year-old novelist and in a lot of trouble over drugs.[...] I got the idea of going to Mexico and trying to find him and do a story" (*AT*, pp. 3–5). But just as Mailer had found at the 1968 conventions, part of the real "story" became the reporter's own changing awareness of the events. Wolfe quickly retreats from this slick journalist's pose and invites the reader to share in that ineffable "something more" that lies beneath the surface.

Although Wolfe is at times critical of the Pranksters, his final viewpoint reflects the "double perspective" that Robert Scholes mentioned in his review. Comparing Wolfe with Mailer, Scholes sees Wolfe as more of a satirist concerned with life-styles and manners than is Mailer:

Mailer is engaged, political, ethical. Wolfe is detached, social, esthetic. Mailer has affinities with the activities of the New Left; Wolfe is closer to the hippies and acid heads that are dropping out. Mailer is interested in probing depths, Wolfe in exploring surfaces. Mailer's concern is morals, Wolfe's manners. Mailer's "hystory" has a tragic and apocalyptic dimension; Wolfe's is essentially comic and Epicurean.[23]

Finally, Wolfe's attitude toward the Pranksters shows great sympathy for an experiment that failed. Despite the freak-outs, the occasional power plays for leadership, the jealousies over shared women, Wolfe tells us in the afterword that "the events described in this book were both a group adventure and a personal exploration. Many [Pranksters] achieved great insight on both levels." The book's closing chapter conveys a sense of loss and exhaustion, as well as what was good about the group at its best:

I couldn't figure out what they had to be so exultant about. It beat me. As I look back on it, they were all trying to tell me...Hassler with his discourse on the world full of games and futile oppositioning and how the Pranksters meant to show the world how to live... [. . .] He was trying to give me the whole picture at once. It wasn't about cops and robbers in Mexico, it was about...

Pranksters arriving from far and wide...The old Schism forgotten...Paul Foster back from India, looking emaciated [. . .] Page telling me about huaraches...Mountain Girl, Doris Delay, The Hermit, Freewheeling Frank the Hell's Angel, Cassady flipping his sledgehammer, Babbs, Gretch, George Walker...Zonker coming in with an Arab headdress as Torrence of Arabia... Finally Kesey pulling in, Faye and the kids coming out...The Flag People, the bus glowing, the mystic fog rising...[AT, p. 338]

Despite Wolfe's skepticism throughout the book, he closes with profound empathy for what the group attempted to accomplish— their "we feeling," their collective ethos.

Several other new journalists have written about counterculture experiments, notably Anthony J. Lukas in "The Life and Death of a Hippie" for *Esquire* in 1968 and Robert Christgau in "Beth Ann and Macrobioticism" for the *New York Herald Tribune* in 1966.[24] The most fully developed contrast to Wolfe's book, however, is Joan Didion's *Slouching towards Bethlehem* (1968). Although Didion's exploration of the lives of young people in Haight-Ashbury is close to Wolfe's Prankster saga in its subject, her style reflects a more apocalyptic, moralistic sensibility closer to Mailer's. Didion begins with an explicit reference to Yeats's "The Second Coming":

The center was not holding. It was a country of bankruptcy notices and public-auction announcements and commonplace reports of casual killings and misplaced children and abandoned homes and vandals who misspelled even the four-letter words they scrawled. . . . Adolescents drifted from city to torn city, sloughing off both the past and the future as snakes shed their skins, children who were never taught and never may learn the games that held society together. . . . All that seemed clear was that at some point we had aborted ourselves and butchered the job, and because nothing else seemed so relevant I decided to go to San Francisco. San Francisco was where the social hemorrhaging was showing up. San Francisco was where the missing children were gathering and calling themselves "hippies."[25]

As in her tightly constructed novel *Play It As It Lays* (1970), Didion's spare prose conveys a sense of desperation and generalized irony that underlies specific events. Her concerns are ethical and, like many contemporary writers, she projects an apocalyptic ending upon the sixties by collecting specific occurrences that point toward a general social disintegration. Like Mailer on the steps of the Pentagon, she sees the whole social fabric of America falling apart.

Wolfe's attitude is directly opposed to what he scornfully calls "the apocalypse game." In the preface to *The Pump House Gang* Wolfe predicts instead a "happiness revolution" founded upon the newly acquired affluence of the working class with the leisure and the money to pursue enjoyment in the form of custom cars, motorcycles, and a host of other consumer goods. The desperation and alienation nourished by intellectuals, Wolfe charges, are not really as cataclysmic as some would have us believe: "When the race riots erupted and when the war in Vietnam grew into a good-sized hell—intellectuals welcomed all that with a ghastly embrace, too. War! Poverty! Insurrection! Alienation! O Four Horsemen, you have not deserted us entirely. The game can go on."[26] In contrast to the intellectual necessity of calamity that man has traditionally been conditioned to expect, Wolfe sees the most interesting social trend since World War II to be the increased affluence and leisure available to vast numbers of Americans. He has written elsewhere that the Pranksters were "a forerunner of an Acid Test almost everyone will be facing in the years ahead." The "really scary thing," he explained in an article telling how he came to write *Acid Test*, is the new frontier of life-styles defined neither by social role nor by economic necessity:

The hairy dose in this country now, it seems to me, is neither war nor poverty but the mass wealth that has been building up since World War II. No other nation has ever experienced anything like it. We are barely beginning to understand its psychological impact. [...] I think we are already out on a scarier frontier—where masses of men face the question of what do you do with yourself when you suddenly have the money, time and freedom to extend your ego in almost any direction. The Pranksters went that way, beyond catastrophe and it was strange out there...in Edge City....[27]

And yet despite Wolfe's disavowal of the "apocalypse game," his account of the Prankster saga ends by echoing a theme common to many books of the late sixties. The final scene of his nonfiction novel conveys a sense of hope crushed by nothing so tangible as despair or dread, but rather a muted, inarticulate sadness and loss. In the book's final pages, Wolfe shows Kesey and a few Pranksters sitting around late at night in a cabaret. Kesey and a close friend, guitars in hand, sit facing each other on stage while improvising a talking blues:

"I took some pseulobin and one long diddle..."
"WE BLEW IT!"
"...Ten thousand times or more..."
"WE BLEW IT!"
"...so much we can't keep score..."
"WE BLEW IT!"
"...just when you're beginning to think, 'I'm going to score'..."
"WE BLEW IT!"
"...but there's more in store..."
"WE BLEW IT!"
"...if we can get rid of these trading stamps that get in the way of the merchandise..."
"WE BLEW IT!"
"...Ten million times or more!..."
"WE BLEW IT!"
"...it was perfect, so what do you do?..."
"WE BLEW IT!"
"...perfect!..."
"WE BLEW IT!" [AT, pp. 367–68]

Clearly Wolfe intends this refrain to stand as the epitaph for the Prankster experience as a whole, and by extension, it is a kind of signature for the decade itself.

It is on this note of the failed experiment that the film *Easy Rider* turns, when Peter Fonda's character says this same line to Dennis Hopper's character. And Wolfe's ending anticipates the sense of irrevocable loss Aquarius conveys at the close of *Of a Fire on the Moon*. In so much of the new journalism written late in the decade, rebellion—and the transcendence from society's norms it seems to offer—becomes merely a thwarted alternative. The giant maw of democratizing, leveling America in the end destroys the deviant adventure. For the dropout and the outsider, there appears to be no hope of winning against the system and building a strong, viable, enduring alternative. It is as Chief Broom warns Kesey's hero Randle McMurphy in *One Flew Over the Cuckoo's Nest*: "The Combine had whipped [my father]. It beats everybody. It'll beat you."[28]

7

POSTSCRIPT

*Yet New Journalism's broader legacy
to the print media still resonates. . . .
The future of enterprising new forms of
journalism—be they sociological or
investigative—still looks bright.*
—NEWSWEEK, *31 March 1975*

THE BEST NEW JOURNALISM is a reflection of our unusual self-consciousness about the historical importance of our times. The assumption underlying most of the books of nonfiction I have discussed is that future historians will find these years unique, perhaps even part of a fundamental watershed in human consciousness.[1] The nonfiction novels of Capote, Mailer, and Wolfe are deeply colored with the mood of perpetual crisis that pervaded the sixties. Capote made the Clutter murders seem like symptoms of a society in the process of breaking down. Mailer wrote of the march on the Pentagon as if it were the first battle in a civil war that might continue for twenty years. Wolfe's explorations of new life-styles and manners portrayed them as the surface manifestations of a far broader social transformation. Yet how has the new journalism, so intimately bound to the sixties, fared in the seventies?

In a psychological sense, decades never start or end on time. In terms of symbolic turning points, the mood of perpetual crisis began with John Kennedy's assassination and ended with Richard Nixon's removal from office. This intense period of change and dislocation that inspired the best new journalism now seems behind us. Social problems continue to confront us, but the college campuses are quiet and the Vietnam War is now a subject for historians, not journalists. Perhaps only now can we begin to assimilate the successive shocks to our collective psyche.

The history of Watergate and of the resignation of an American president on the brink of impeachment has been the biggest news story of the seventies—some would say of the century. Yet despite the many fine books on the Watergate tragedy, few have relied on the techniques of the new journalism. Bob Woodward and Carl Bernstein's *All the President's Men* has the narrative force of a suspenseful novel, but the authors' intense involvement in the case makes the vantage point entirely unique. In contrast to the atmospheric license of the new journalism, the day-by-day revelations in the *Washington Post* demanded rigorous and strictly accountable investigative reporting. The corruption of the Nixon administration and the inexorable flow of events leading to impeachment were simply too urgent to permit the fictionalized reconstruction of the new journalism.[2] As a recent television documentary on the Cuban missile crisis illustrates, perhaps news events of such magnitude require the distance of intervening years before dramatization can be effective.

If we look to the future of the nonfiction novel, we see that its close relationship to topical issues poses a threat to its long-range durability. Despite the power and vision of such books as *In Cold Blood* and *The Armies of the Night*, they remain tied to particular events. For this reason, Alfred Kazin believes that the nonfiction novel is already on the decline:

I think that the non-fiction novel is dying, not only because the upheaval story is no longer news, but because non-fiction reporting [and] television reporting . . . suffer from the crisis dying on the writer's hands. It's all too topical, and somehow our whole culture, even with the Nixon crisis and more, recognizes how little journalism has to say, especially, with so many voices all saying the same thing.[3]

Although Kazin is certainly right that old news is no longer news at all, forms of the new journalism have survived into the seventies more successfully than he suggests. The real danger that faces the new journalism, I believe, is that the creative impulses that began in rebellion against journalistic formula may lead to another kind of formula.

This danger is reflected in Norman Mailer's work since *Of a Fire on the Moon*. His recent books include a personal response to the women's liberation movement, a report on the 1972 political conventions, an outrageous "novel-biography" of Marilyn Monroe, and a preface to a collection of photographs of New York subway graffiti.[4] These books illustrate how the siren's song of fame and publicity that the new journalism offers the writer may lead to a repetitious format and books turned out almost on a schedule. Although flashes of insight made *The Armies of the Night* powerful, Mailer's recent books reveal less insight than procedure: queries about which name suits his persona, elaborate apologies, rambling introspection, the usual existential philosophizing, with only scant attention to the events at hand. *The Armies of the Night* succeeded because of the perfect balance between personal and public history, between genuine involvement in events and speculation, between Mailer-the-moralist and Mailer-the-buffoon. Now Mailer's elaborate rhetoric too often seems overblown and inappropriate to the importance of his subjects.[5]

Some of the new journalists have avoided self-parody, however, by embarking on even more ambitious projects than those of the sixties. The emerging trend of the seventies is toward investigative and sociological reporting. Gay Talese is beginning to write what promises to be an interesting study of the impact of the sexual revolution on middle-class morals. His research involves the close scrutiny of prostitution, pornography shops, massage parlors, and the vast cornucopia of carnal services in our society. A recent excerpt that appeared in *Esquire*[6] reflects the careful research and background interviewing that made *Honor Thy Father* and *The Kingdom and the Power* so engaging.

Tom Wolfe's latest book, *The Painted Word*, expands upon his penchant for exploring subcultures and outraging critics. He portrays the celebrity world of modern art with the focus on the rise to popularity of such artists as Jackson Pollock, Willem de Kooning, and Jasper Johns. Wolfe's thesis is that the public's understanding and appreciation of modern art, and even the directions taken by the artists themselves, have been conditioned by the art theories of such critics as Clement Greenberg, Harold Rosenberg, and Leo Steinberg. In Wolfe's view, the verbal has taken precedence over the visual. Although some of the exuberance of *The Kandy-Kolored Tangerine-Flake Streamline Baby* remains, Wolfe has turned to a more academic subject than topless dancers, stock-car drivers, or London teenagers. His depiction of the relationship between the artists and their rich patrons as a refinement of the mating practices of nature—which Wolfe calls "the boho dance"—is fascinating. Yet the idiosyncratic style seems less well suited to the art theories that explain a Pollock or a Johns painting than it was to California surfers or Kesey and the Pranksters.[7]

In the years since *In Cold Blood*, Truman Capote has been conspicuously silent, at least in terms of published work. With the exception of recent personality sketches and a short story, his only published work in the seventies is *The Dogs Bark: Public People and Private Places*, merely a collection of previously published nonfiction. Like Mailer, however, Capote now claims to have returned to fiction. Since 1969 he has reportedly been working on a projected novel of eight hundred pages, tentatively titled *Answered Prayers*, which he describes as a *roman à clef* about many of the famous people he has known.[8]

Although these major figures of the sixties have not published important works in the seventies, the new journalism in general continues to evolve in exciting new ways. The rebellion against formula it represents has already had a significant impact on the standard practices of American journalism. The new spirit of individual freedom can be seen in the increasing number of interpretive and background stories that appear daily in newspapers, in magazines, and in television documentaries. Even the more conservative newspapers now encourage stories with greater detail and atmospheric background than was previously the case. While the power of the new journalism lies in the talent of individual writers, the form can lead to careless or distorted reporting. Some critics fear that young reporters might model themselves on Wolfe or Mailer without having first learned the fundamentals of objective reporting. The historical tradition of objective reporting, they warn, may be eroded by a cult of egotists intent upon imposing personal viewpoints on the public.[9]

In the end, however, the new journalism will remain a vital genre for certain kinds of news events and social trends. The new form of nonfiction cannot, and should not, replace the clear, concise reporting of the day's news. The detailed descriptions, scene-by-scene reconstruction, and fully recorded dialogue are best suited to the reconstruction of particular kinds of events. When the new journalism holds up a mirror to a small portion of the total social fabric—stock-car racers, drug freaks in San Francisco, a political convention—it succeeds best. When the reporter's personal involvement in the story is legitimate, as was Hunter Thompson's ride with the Hell's Angels, it contributes a unique perspective that is unavailable in conventional reporting. When a reporter explores a hidden world or provides an insider's view, and when his writing is supported by careful research, then the new journalist can convey his insights powerfully to a receptive audience.

The new journalism has not replaced the realistic novel, as Wolfe claims, but it remains an alternative to fiction in our continuing period of transition in all the arts. Although the seventies may hold the possibility of a revival of classicism, the forces that engendered the nonfiction novel may give rise to still other blendings of various art forms. Literary critic Ihab Hassan writes in the conclusion to a survey of contemporary literature, "It is more probable that the hybrid forms of the late sixties will continue to evolve, and that in fiction, drama, poetry, essay, and criticism still other experiments will re-create our expectations of literature. New media and new technologies may have a lasting impact on the dispositions of the imagination in culture."[10]

Some critics might argue for the even more radical view that film and television have already replaced written forms of art in our culture. It is more likely, however, that our present period of transition will continue and that experiments in all the arts will proliferate. Whether the journalistic forms I have discussed will

ually replace the novel is, in any case, not really a meaningful
tion. The more important question, I believe, is what new
directions the inventiveness and adaptability of writers will take as
they respond to new pressures and changes in our mutual experience.
For, surely, art will continue to find new ways of imitating life.
More than anything, the new journalism is a testament to the
ability of writers to find new voices and new thresholds of language.
In this way, Truman Capote, Norman Mailer, Tom Wolfe, and
others have done what good writers have always done. They have
rejected the worn conventions of the past to seek forms and language responsive to the dilemmas of their own times. And so
whether or not the new journalism prospers in the years to come,
the best writers in the genre have already begun to convert the
inchoate material of our experience into the meaningful structures
of art. They have given us vivid portraits of American life in these
bewildering years.

NOTES

CHAPTER 1

1. Philip Roth, "Writing American Fiction," p. 224.
2. Norman Mailer, *Advertisements for Myself*, p. 167.
3. Norman Mailer, *Cannibals and Christians*, pp. 95–96.
4. T. S. Eliot, "*Ulysses*, Order, and Myth," pp. 480–83; and José Ortega y Gasset, *The Dehumanization of Art and Notes on the Novel*.
5. Louis D. Rubin, Jr., *The Curious Death of the Novel*, p. 5.
6. Leslie Fiedler, *Waiting for the End*, p. 173.
7. John Barth, "The Literature of Exhaustion," pp. 32–33.
8. Lionel Trilling, *A Gathering of Fugitives*, pp. 85–100; Norman Podhoretz, "The Article as Art," pp. 74–79.
9. Robert Brustein, "Who's Killing the Novel?," pp. 22–24. Another representative article is Eugene Chesnick's, "The Plot against Fiction," pp. 48–67.
10. André Fontaine, *The Art of Writing Nonfiction*, p. 8.
11. Marcus Klein, ed., *The American Novel since World War II*, p. 9.
12. Cited by Alfred Kazin in *Bright Book of Life*, p. 232.
13. Warner Berthoff, *Fictions and Events*, p. 289.
14. Alfred Kazin, "The Literary Sixties," p. 1.
15. Alfred Kazin, personal correspondence with the author, 9 March 1974.
16. Norman Mailer, *Existential Errands*, p. xi.
17. Kazin, *Bright Book of Life*, pp. 218–19.
18. Berthoff, *Fictions and Events*, pp. 288–89.
19. Ihab Hassan, *Contemporary American Literature, 1945–1972*, pp. 173–74.
20. Raymond M. Olderman, *Beyond the Waste Land*, pp. 1–29 passim; and Ihab Hassan, *Radical Innocence*, pp. 61–96 passim.
21. Olderman, *Beyond the Waste Land*, p. 6.
22. Robert Scholes and Robert Kellogg, *The Nature of Narrative*, pp. 3–16 passim.
23. Robert Scholes, *The Fabulators*, pp. 3–31 passim.
24. David Lodge, "The Novelist at the Crossroads," p. 110.
25. For the diagram representing "the spectrum of fiction," I am indebted to Robert Scholes, *Elements of Fiction*, p. 9.

CHAPTER 2

1. *The New Journalism*, ed. Tom Wolfe and E. W. Johnson, p. 23.
2. Michael J. Arlen, "Notes on the New Journalism," pp. 44–45.
3. The term "new journalism" has been defined in a variety of ways by different commentators. Some critics use the term to mean only the experimentation with fictional techniques in reporting, while others include all forms of personal journalism as well as advocacy reporting. The most comprehensive definition is that of Everette E. Dennis and William L. Rivers (*Other Voices*, pp. 1–13) who identify seven different types:

a. *The new nonfiction*—descriptive reporting that employs the techniques of fiction in nonfiction articles by such writers as Wolfe, Breslin, Talese, Mailer, and Capote.

b. *Alternative journalism*—such publications as *Cervi's Rocky Mountain Journal* and the *San Francisco Bay Guardian* that are critical of big business and the powerful vested interests that control the dissemination of the news.

c. *Journalism reviews*—such periodicals as *Columbia Journalism Review* and *Chicago Journalism Review* that developed in the sixties to provide a forum for journalists to "analyze and criticize journalistic performance" as practiced in conventional newspapers, magazines, and the broadcast media.

d. *Advocacy journalism*—the variety of journalism practiced by *Village Voice* reporters Jack Newfield and Nat Hentoff, who openly advocate their political and moral beliefs in their work.

e. *Counterculture journalism*—that practiced in such underground newspapers as the *Los Angeles Free Press* and the *Berkeley Barb*, which are supplied by the two underground wire services, the Liberation News Service and the Underground Press Syndicate.

f. *Alternative broadcasting*—the largely unrealized potential of low-cost cable television as an alternative to the established huge networks that control most television news.

g. *Precision journalism*—which developed in the sixties from the use of social science research tools—census data, opinion polls, survey research techniques—to provide greater background on important social issues (see also Philip Meyer, *Precision Journalism*).

Since my main interest is the relationship between journalism and literary art, I discuss primarily the first category defined by Dennis and Rivers—the new nonfiction. At times, the distinctions between categories blend considerably; the differences between "alternative journalism," "advocacy journalism," and "counterculture journalism" are rather minimal at times. When I refer to the new journalism in this chapter and elsewhere, I am using the term in the restricted sense of the use of fictional narrative techniques applied to nonfiction.

4. Robert Scholes, "Double Perspective on Hysteria," p. 37.
5. Michael J. Arlen, "Notes on the New Journalism," p. 45.
6. Ibid.
7. Tom Wolfe, *The Kandy-Kolored Tangerine-Flake Streamline Baby*, p. xi.
8. Ibid.
9. L. W. Robinson et al., "The New Journalism," p. 32.
10. *The New Journalism*, ed. Wolfe and Johnson, pp. 31–35 passim.

11. Tom Wolfe, *Radical Chic and Mau-Mauing the Flak Catchers*, p. 3.

12. James Mills, "The Detective," pp. 108, 110.

13. *The New Journalism*, ed. Wolfe and Johnson, p. 32.

14. Rex Reed, "Ava: Life in the Afternoon," in *Do You Sleep in the Nude?*, p. 66.

15. Wolfe, "The Last American Hero," in *Kandy-Kolored Baby*, p. 138.

16. Gay Talese, in Robinson et al., "The New Journalism," p. 34.

17. Gay Talese, *The Kingdom and the Power*, p. 353.

18. Gail Sheehy, *Hustling*, pp. 43–44.

19. In a defense of her methods, Sheehy has answered those critics who have challenged "composite characterization" as dishonest: "Every word of the article was true based on police cases, interviews, personal observation and experiences, but the character of 'Redpants' was a composite of several different girls at various stages of their involvement in 'the life' of prostitution. An author's note to that effect was dropped during the printing and the story appeared in *New York* [August 1971] without explanation. Because of this oversight, the technique caused a journalistic controversy. The *Wall Street Journal* fired the first shot, followed by several *New Yorker* writers who blasted out at the 'new journalism.' It was funny in view of the real secret: the composite techniques had been used and celebrated in the past by nonfiction writers for the *New Yorker*, one memorable example being 'Mr. Flood,' a composite character developed by Joe Mitchell to describe the daily life and operations of the Fulton Fish Market" (*Hustling*, p. 16).

20. Sheehy, ibid., pp. 40–41.

21. Actually the close scrutiny of a subject for a personality piece and the use of composite characterization are much older than most new journalists suggest. Freelance journalist Maurice Zolotow explains in a recent handbook for nonfiction writers: "Around 1928, the *New Yorker* pioneered with a new kind of personality piece—the profile. The *New Yorker* profile writer was expected not only to question the subject, but also to pry into the subject's entire life—good and bad—and interview his friends and enemies. In the hands of [Alva] Johnston, Margaret Chase Harriman, Wolcott Gibbs, St. Clair McKelway, Geoffrey Hellman, the profiles became witty, polished, brilliant exercises in human nature" ("Studying a Subject," in *The Writer's Digest Handbook of Article Writing*, ed. Frank A. Dickson, p. 168).

22. The tendency to "fictionalize" a story for dramatic effect can, of course, backfire when the reporter has not been scrupulous to verify the facts. In an appeal case to reach the Supreme Court in December 1974, an invasion of privacy award for $60,000 was upheld against reporter Joe Eszterhas and the *Cleveland Plain Dealer* Sunday magazine. In an August 1968 article for the magazine, Eszterhas had dramatized the impact on a West Virginia family of the father's death in a bridge disaster that took place in December 1967. The story stressed the Cantrell family's poverty and the run-down conditions in which they had lived since Mr. Cantrell's death. According to the Court's ruling, although Mrs. Cantrell was not present while Eszterhas interviewed her children, his story gave the impression that she had been present "wearing the same mask of non-expression she wore (at her husband's) funeral." The Court found that Eszterhas had used "calculated falsehoods" and "had portrayed the Cantrells in a false light through knowing or reckless untruth" (see "Damage Award for Invasion of Privacy by Cleveland Paper is Upheld by Justices," *Wall Street Journal*, 19 December 1974, p. 1).

23. *The New Journalism*, ed. Wolfe and Johnson, pp. 377–78.

24. See, for example, Dwight Macdonald, "Parajournalism, or Tom Wolfe and His Magic Writing Machine," pp. 3–4.

25. Gay Talese, *Fame and Obscurity*, p. vii.

26. *The New Journalism*, ed. Wolfe and Johnson, p. 51.

27. Lester Markel, "Objective Journalism," in *Liberating the Media*, ed. Charles C. Flippen, p. 83.

28. The most frequent charge against the new journalism is that it is not "new," and indeed historical antecedents abound for each of the techniques that Wolfe lists. For discussions of the predecessors of the form see, especially, Harold Hayes, "Editor's Notes," p. 12; Lester Markel, "Objective Journalism," pp. 76–84; and Jack Newfield, "The 'Truth' about Objectivity and the New Journalism," in *Liberating the Media*, ed. Charles C. Flippen, pp. 59–60.

29. Newfield, "The 'Truth' about Objectivity," pp. 59–60.

30. Hazlitt's classic essay, written in 1822, relies on much of the atmospheric detail and vivid description common to the new journalism to describe a bareknuckle struggle between "Gas-Man" Hickman and William Bill Neate, who outweighed his opponent by some thirty pounds. After nearly eighteen rounds of boxing, the smaller and lighter Hickman was "stunned" and could not continue (see "The Fight," in *The Complete Works of William Hazlitt*, ed. P. P. Howe, 17:72–86).

31. Stephen Crane, "In a Park Row Restaurant," and "Mr. Binks' Day Off," in *The Collected Short Stories and Sketches of Stephen Crane*, ed. Thomas A. Gullason, pp. 186–88, 169–75.

32. Talese, in Robinson et al., "The New Journalism," pp. 35, 19.

33. *The New Journalism*, ed. Wolfe and Johnson, p. 6.

34. André Fontaine, *The Art of Writing Nonfiction*, p. 2.

35. Gay Talese, "Joe Louis: The King as a Middle-Aged Man"; reprinted in *Fame and Obscurity*, pp. 155–67.

36. For a brief discussion of the economics of recent magazine publishing, see John W. Tebbel, *The American Magazine*, pp. 249–65, and Roland E. Wolseley, *The Changing Magazine*, pp. 44–61. Professor Wolseley cites the following reasons for the financial difficulties of general magazines in recent years: (1) increased costs of production in terms of printing and paper; (2) increases in second-class mail rates; (3) loss of advertising revenues to television; (4) enormous losses to be absorbed by the managements of large magazines; and (5) the rapid growth of "special interest" magazines that have reduced advertising revenues still further (p. 55).

37. Harold Hayes, in Robinson et al., "The New Journalism," p. 33.

38. Robert J. Glessing, *The Underground Press in America*, pp. 50–69 passim.

39. There are three major anthologies of the new journalism and the four classes have been established from an analysis of the 103 articles they contain. *The New Journalism*, ed. Tom Wolfe and E. W. Johnson (23 articles) is primarily concerned with demonstrating various stylistic approaches to magazine journalism; *Smiling Through the Apocalypse*, ed. Harold Hayes (40 articles) demonstrates clearly the contribution of *Esquire* to the development of new journalism; *The New Journalism*, ed. Nicolaus Mills (40 articles) contains interpretations of contemporary history from the Watts riots of 1965 to the political conventions of 1972.

40. Reed, "Ava: Life in the Afternoon," in *Do You Sleep in the Nude?*, pp. 66–75. Gay Talese, "Frank Sinatra Has a Cold," *Esquire*, April 1966, pp. 89–99, and reprinted in *Fame and Obscurity*, pp. 3–40.

41. John Seelye, "The Shotgun behind the Lens," p. 22.

42. John Gregory Dunne, " 'That's What We Came to Minneapolis For,' Stan Hough Said," in *The Studio*, pp. 187–203; reprinted in *The New Journalism*, ed. Wolfe and Johnson, pp. 281–91.

43. Alvin Toffler, *Future Shock*, pp. 251–84 passim.

44. Robert Christgau, "Beth Ann and Macrobioticism," in *The New Journalism*, ed. Wolfe and Johnson, pp. 331–39; Anthony J. Lukas, "The Life and Death of a Hippie," *Esquire*, May 1968, and in *Smiling Through the Apocalypse*, ed. Harold Hayes, pp. 600–21; Joan Didion, *Slouching towards Bethlehem*.

45. John Sack, M, an excerpt in *The New Journalism*, ed. Wolfe and Johnson, pp. 292–303. Other new journalistic reports on the Vietnam War include Michael Herr, "Khesanh," *Esquire*, September 1969, and Nicholas Tomalin, "The General Goes Zapping Charlie Cong," *Times* (London), 5 June 1966; both are reprinted in *The New Journalism*, ed. Wolfe and Johnson, pp. 85–115 and pp. 197–203, respectively. After his report on motorcycle gangs, Hunter Thompson has gone on to become something of a culture-hero with his columns in *Rolling Stone* and his subsequent books, *Fear and Loathing in Las Vegas* and *Fear and Loathing on the Campaign Trail*.

46. George Plimpton, *Paper Lion*; there is an excerpt in *The New Journalism*, ed. Wolfe and Johnson, pp. 240–58.

47. John Hersey, *The Algiers Motel Incident*. For other reports on the urban riots of the late sixties see Robert Conot, *Rivers of Blood, Years of Darkness*, and Thomas Pynchon, "A Journey into the Mind of Watts"; excerpts of both are reprinted in *The New Journalism*, ed. Mills, pp. 5–21 and pp. 45–54, respectively.

48. Paul Cowan and Geoffrey Cowan, "Three Letters from Mississippi," pp. 105, 106, 190; Garry Wills, "Martin Luther King Is Still on the Case," pp. 89–104, 124–29.

49. *Esquire*'s 1968 Democratic convention issue features four articles by well-known writers on the issues and the background of the convention: Terry Southern, "Grooving in Chi," Jean Genet, "The Members of the Assembly," William Burroughs, "The Coming of the Purple Better One," and John Sack, "In a Pig's Eye," all in *Esquire*, November 1968, pp. 83–94. The last three articles are reprinted in *Smiling Through the Apocalypse*, ed. Hayes, pp. 161–90.

50. Dan Wakefield, "Supernation at Peace and War," *Atlantic*, March 1968, pp. 39–105. It was reprinted in book form by Atlantic Monthly Press in 1968.

51. Macdonald, "Parajournalism," p. 3.

52. Arlen, "Notes on the New Journalism," p. 47.

53. See, especially, ibid.; Hayes, "Editor's Notes"; Macdonald, "Parajournalism"; Lester Markel, "Lester Markel: So What's New?," pp. 1, 7–9; and Jack Newfield, "Is There a New Journalism?," pp. 45–57.

54. Dan Wakefield, "The Personal Voice and the Impersonal Eye," p. 87.

55. Markel, "Objective Journalism," p. 81.

56. *The New Journalism*, ed. Wolfe and Johnson, p. 9.

57. Jay Jensen, "The New Journalism in Historical Perspective," in *Liberating the Media*, ed. Charles C. Flippen, p. 19.

CHAPTER 3

1. Daniel J. Boorstin, *The Image*, pp. 8–9.

2. For an excellent discussion of the role of publicity and promotion in

contemporary literature, see John W. Aldridge, *Time to Murder and Create*, pp. 52–94 passim.

3. *The New Journalism*, ed. Tom Wolfe and E. W. Johnson, p. 4.

4. Tom Wolfe, "The Birth of the New Journalism," p. 36.

5. John Seelye, "The Shotgun behind the Lens," p. 22.

6. *The New Journalism*, ed. Nicolaus Mills, p. xv.

7. Peter Shaw discusses Mailer's public persona in "The Tough-Guy Intellectual," pp. 13–29.

8. Michael J. Arlen, "Notes on the New Journalism," p. 47.

9. Thompson's term "Gonzo journalism" refers to any frantic form of subjective journalism in which the reporter provokes many of the incidents he writes about. The term derives from Thompson's "lawyer" and sidekick on many of his adventures who uses the mysterious pseudonym, "Dr. Gonzo."

10. Steven Selbst, "Journalist Thompson Greets Enthusiastic Campus Following," pp. 1, 8.

11. *The New Journalism*, ed. Wolfe and Johnson, p. 6.

12. Robert J. Glessing, *The Underground Press in America*, p. 144.

13. Morris Dickstein, review of *My Life as a Man* by Philip Roth, p. 1.

14. John Raeburn, "Ernest Hemingway: The Public Writer as Popular Culture," p. 92.

15. Aldridge, *Time to Murder and Create*, p. 66.

16. Jane Howard, "How the 'Smart Rascal' Brought It Off," pp. 75–76.

17. F. W. Dupee, "Truman Capote's Score," pp. 3–5. By one estimate, Capote earned nearly $2,000,000 for the total enterprises connected with the promotion of *In Cold Blood*. Movie rights from Columbia Pictures accounted for an estimated $400,000 to one-half million dollars, and $500,000 was for paperback rights. Figures are from Barbara Long, "In Cold Comfort," p. 126. All of these sums were at that time unprecedented in American publishing for the sale of a nonfiction work.

18. "*In Cold Blood* . . . An American Tragedy," *Newsweek*, 24 January 1966, p. 63.

19. Robert K. Morris, "Capote's Imagery" in *Truman Capote's "In Cold Blood,"* ed. Irving Malin, pp. 176–77.

20. For an entertaining account of the Mailer-Breslin mayoral campaign in New York, see Joe Flaherty, *Managing Mailer*. Reflecting the interchangeable nature of celebrity, former mayor of Cleveland Carl Stokes was for a time a news anchorman with NBC's New York affiliate, and former New York mayor and presidential aspirant John Lindsay has recently embarked on a film and novel-writing career. Increasingly, the celebrity status itself seems to be the only common denominator, since the field in which one's fame was originally achieved has become irrelevant.

21. Aldridge, *Time to Murder and Create*, p. 74.

22. Richard Gilman, "Norman Mailer," in *The Confusion of Realms*, pp. 82–83.

23. For a consideration of the literary merits of nonfiction novels, see: (on Capote and Wolfe) Dan Wakefield, "The Personal Voice and the Impersonal Eye," pp. 86–90; (on Mailer and Wolfe) Robert Scholes, "Double Perspective on Hysteria," p. 37; (on Mailer), Conor Cruise O'Brien, "Confessions of the Last American," pp. 16–18. Discussions of Capote's generic claims for *In Cold Blood* are to be found in Robert Langbaum, "Capote's Nonfiction Novel," pp. 772–80, and

William Weigand, "The Non-Fiction Novel," pp. 243–57. Additional general critical articles may be found by consulting the bibliography, under the sections for Capote, Mailer, and Wolfe.

24. Wakefield, "The Personal Voice and the Impersonal Eye," p. 86.

25. Alfred Kazin, *Bright Book of Life*, p. 209.

26. George Plimpton, "The Story behind a Nonfiction Novel," pp. 1–3.

27. In *The New Journalism*, ed. Wolfe and Johnson, Wolfe writes: "When Truman Capote insisted that *In Cold Blood* was not journalism but a new literary genre he had invented, 'the nonfiction novel,' a flash went through my mind. It was the familiar 'Aha!' flash. In this case: 'Aha! the ever-clever Fielding dodge!' When Henry Fielding published his first novel, *Joseph Andrews* . . . he kept protesting that his book was not a novel—it was a new literary genre he had invented, 'the comic epic poem in prose.' . . . What he was doing, of course—and what Capote would be doing 223 years later—was trying to give his work the cachet of the reigning literary genre of his time, so that literary people would take it seriously" (p. 37).

28. Steven Marcus, "Norman Mailer Interview," in *Writers at Work*, ed. Alfred Kazin, pp. 275–76.

29. Norman Mailer, *Existential Errands*, p. xi.

30. *The New Journalism*, ed. Wolfe and Johnson, p. 46.

31. Ibid., pp. 1–53 passim.

32. Plimpton, "The Story behind a Nonfiction Novel," pp. 2–3.

33. *Smiling Through the Apocalypse*, ed. Harold Hayes, p. xxii.

CHAPTER 4

1. "In Cold Blood: A True Account of a Multiple Murder and Its Consequences," *New Yorker*, 25 September 1965, pp. 57–92; 2 October 1965, pp. 57–175; 9 October 1965, pp. 58–183; 16 October 1965, pp. 62–193 (hereafter cited from *In Cold Blood: A True Account of a Multiple Murder and Its Consequences* [New York: Random House, 1965], and referred to in the text as *CB*).

2. Jackson R. Bryer's "Truman Capote: A Bibliography," which cites over 130 magazine and newspaper reviews of the book, is indicative of the tremendous critical response *In Cold Blood* evoked. The bibliography is included in *Truman Capote's "In Cold Blood": A Critical Handbook*, ed. Irving Malin, pp. 239–69. The Malin handbook also includes twenty-seven background and critical essays and is by far the most useful single source for the student of *In Cold Blood*.

3. George Plimpton, "The Story behind a Nonfiction Novel," p. 2.

4. Ibid.

5. William L. Nance, *The Worlds of Truman Capote*, p. 161.

6. "The Country below the Surface," p. 83; Alfred Kazin, *Bright Book of Life*, p. 209; Granville Hicks, "The Story of an American Tragedy," p. 35; Hamilton Hamish, "Stranger than Fiction," p. 215; and Rebecca West, "A Grave and Reverend Book," p. 114.

7. Melvin J. Friedman, "Towards an Aesthetic: Truman Capote's Other Voices," in *Truman Capote's "In Cold Blood,"* ed. Malin, p. 172.

8. Truman Capote, *The Selected Writings of Truman Capote*, p. 338 (hereafter cited in the text as *SW*).

9. Joan Didion, *Slouching towards Bethlehem*, p. xiv.

10. Truman Capote, *The Dogs Bark*, p. xviii.

11. Barbara Long, "In Cold Comfort," p. 173.

12. Pati Hill, "Truman Capote Interview," in *Writers at Work*, ed. Malcolm Cowley, p. 293; reprinted in *Truman Capote's "In Cold Blood,"* ed. Malin, p. 137.

13. Dwight Macdonald, "Cosa Nostra," pp. 44–48, 58–62; and Stanley Kauffmann, "Capote in Kansas," pp. 19–22.

14. Nance, *Worlds of Truman Capote*, p. 176.

15. Plimpton, "Story behind a Nonfiction Novel," p. 38.

16. Jean Mouton, *Littérature et sang-froid*, p. 157. Translated from the French by the author of this volume.

17. Friedman, "Towards an Aesthetic," p. 175.

18. These section titles, which are drawn from what Capote has called "the verbal matrix" of the case, suggest the simplicity of newspaper headlines. Capote uses them effectively, however, to contrast the simplicity of the daily newspaper accounts of the Clutter murders with the much more sophisticated treatment he has written.

19. Tony Tanner, "Death in Kansas," pp. 331–32; reprinted in *Truman Capote's "In Cold Blood,"* ed. Malin. p. 101.

20. Wayne C. Booth, *The Rhetoric of Fiction*, p. 116.

21. Plimpton, "Story behind a Nonfiction Novel," p. 38.

22. Sol Yurick, "Sob-Sister Gothic," p. 159–60; reprinted in *Truman Capote's "In Cold Blood,"* ed. Malin, p. 80.

23. Nance, *Worlds of Truman Capote*, p. 17.

24. Interview with Nance, ibid., p. 224.

25. Kazin, *Bright Book of Life*, pp. 213–14.

26. Robert K. Morris, "Capote's Imagery," in *Truman Capote's "In Cold Blood,"* ed. Malin, p. 178.

27. Friedman, "Towards an Aesthetic," pp. 163–76 passim.

28. Ibid., pp. 173–74.

29. David Lodge, "The Novelist at the Crossroads," p. 115.

30. Tanner, "Death in Kansas," in *Truman Capote's "In Cold Blood,"* ed. Malin, p. 98.

31. Kazin, *Bright Book of Life*, pp. 218–19.

32. Northrop Frye, *Anatomy of Criticism*, p. 303.

33. Library of Congress classification HV (Social Pathology), from numbers 6251 to 7220 (Crimes and Offenses), includes such recent true crime narratives as Vincent Bugliosi's *Helter Skelter* on the Charles Manson case, Don Moser and Jerry Cohen's *The Pied Piper of Tucson* on the charismatic killer of three young women, *New York Times* editor A. M. Rosenthal's *Thirty-Eight Witnesses* on the well-known case of Catherine Genovese in which thirty-eight persons watched from their apartments while the victim was stabbed, and Joseph Wambaugh's *The Onion Field* on the killing of a Los Angeles police officer. The classification also includes such sociological and psychological studies of murder and the homicidal mind as H. C. Brearley's *Homicide in the United States* (Montclair, N.J.: Patterson Smith, 1969), Albert Ellis and J. M. Gullo's *Murder and Assassination* (New York: Lyle Stuart, 1971), and Colin Wilson's *Encyclopaedia of Murder* (London: A. Barker, 1961).

34. F. W. Dupee, "Truman Capote's Score," p. 3; reprinted in *Truman Capote's "In Cold Blood,"* ed. Malin, p. 71.

35. Plimpton, "Story behind a Nonfiction Novel," p. 3.

36. Meyer Levin, *Compulsion*, p. ix.

37. Nance, *Worlds of Truman Capote*, p. 178.

38. William Weigand, "The Non-Fiction Novel," p. 257; and Tanner, "Death in Kansas," in *Truman Capote's "In Cold Blood,"* ed. Malin, p. 101.

39. Kazin, *Bright Book of Life*, p. 211.

CHAPTER 5

1. Norman Mailer, *Advertisements for Myself*, pp. 86–87.

2. Morris Dickstein, "A Trip to Inner and Outer Space," p. 1.

3. Richard Gilman, "Norman Mailer," in *The Confusion of Realms*, pp. 80–153 passim.

4. Richard Gilman, "What Mailer Has Done," pp. 27–31; reprinted in *Norman Mailer*, ed. Leo Braudy, p. 160.

5. See Norman Podhoretz's discussion in "Norman Mailer: The Embattled Vision," pp. 371–91.

6. George Plimpton, "The Story behind a Nonfiction Novel," p. 2.

7. Steven Marcus, "Norman Mailer Interview," in *Writers at Work*, ed. Alfred Kazin, p. 276.

8. Harry S. Resnick, "Hand on the Pulse of America," p. 25.

9. Appeared originally as "The Steps of the Pentagon," *Harper's*, March 1968, pp. 47–142; and "The Battle of the Pentagon," *Commentary*, April 1968, pp. 33–37. In book form it was published in a paperback edition as *The Armies of the Night: History as a Novel, the Novel as History* (New York: New American Library, 1968), hereafter cited in the text as *AN*.

10. Alan Trachtenberg, "Mailer on the Steps of the Pentagon," p. 701.

11. Throughout *Armies*, Mailer complains of the traditional press's distortion of the actions and words of principals of the March. Writers, he argues, suffer especially in this regard "because every time they did something which got into the papers, the motive for their action was distorted and their words were tortured; since they made their living by trying to put words together well, this was as painful to them as the sight of an ugly photograph of herself on the front page must be to a beauty" (p. 80).

12. Trachtenberg, "Mailer on the Steps of the Pentagon," p. 701.

13. Barry Leeds, *The Structured Vision of Norman Mailer*, p. 250.

14. Ibid., p. 249.

15. Norman Mailer, *The Presidential Papers*, p. 3.

16. Richard Poirier, *Norman Mailer*, p. 58.

17. D. H. Lawrence, *Studies in Classic American Literature*, p. 63.

18. Conor Cruise O'Brien, "Confessions of the Last American," p. 18.

19. Appeared originally as "Miami Beach and Chicago," *Harper's*, November 1968, pp. 41–130. In book form it was published in a paperback edition as *Miami and the Siege of Chicago: An Informal History of the Republican and Democratic Conventions of 1968* (New York: New American Library, 1968), hereafter cited in the text as *MC*.

20. Norman Mailer, "In the Red Light, an Informal History of the Republican Convention, 1964," in *Cannibals and Christians*, pp. 1–45, and "Superman Comes to the Supermarket," *Esquire*, November 1960. The latter is reprinted in *Smiling Through the Apocalypse*, ed. Harold Hayes, pp. 3–30.

21. Peter Shaw, "The Conventions, 1968," p. 96.

22. Joan Didion, "A Social Eye," p. 329.

23. Shaw, "The Conventions, 1968," p. 96.

24. Both Burroughs and Genet were recruited by *Esquire* to write "color stories" on the Democratic convention. Cf. Williams Burroughs, "The Coming of the Purple Better One," and Jean Genet, "The Members of the Assembly," in *Smiling Through the Apocalypse*, ed. Harold Hayes, pp. 168–76 and 161–67.

25. Mailer has directed, starred in, and financed three films. His first improvisational extravaganza was *Wild 90*; *Beyond the Law* is a mock-detective story with Mailer and friends role-playing cops and tough guys; *Maidstone* is a mystery set on a Long Island estate in which Mailer plays Norman T. Kingsley, a presidential candidate who lives in constant fear of assassination.

26. Appeared originally as "A Fire on the Moon," *Life*, 29 August 1969, pp. 24–41; "The Psychology of Astronauts," *Life*, 14 November 1969, pp. 51–63; and "A Dream of the Future's Face," *Life*, 9 January 1970, pp. 57–74. It was issued in book form as *Of a Fire on the Moon* (Boston: Little, Brown & Co., 1970); it was reprinted in a paperback edition (New York: New American Library, 1971), which is hereafter cited in the text as *FM*.

27. Dickstein, "Inner and Outer Space," p. 42.

28. Roger Sale, "Watchman, What of the Night?," p. 13.

29. Richard Poirier, "The Ups and Downs of Mailer," in *Norman Mailer*, ed. Braudy, p. 172.

30. Ibid., p. 174.

31. Dickstein, "Inner and Outer Space," p. 43.

32. John Sisk, "Aquarius Rising," p. 83.

33. Ibid.

34. Ibid., p. 94.

35. Raymond A. Schroth, "Mailer on the Moon," p. 218.

36. Sisk, "Aquarius Rising," p. 84.

37. Norman Mailer, "The Last Night," in *Cannibals and Christians*, p. 396.

38. Sale, "Watchman, What of the Night?," p. 14.

CHAPTER 6

1. "Wowie!" *Newsweek*, 1 February 1965, p. 44.

2. Dwight Macdonald, "Parajournalism," p. 3; Dan Wakefield, "The Personal Voice and the Impersonal Eye," pp. 86–90.

3. *Current Biography*, January 1971, pp. 42–43.

4. *The New Journalism*, ed. Tom Wolfe and E. W. Johnson, p. 5.

5. Ibid., p. 6.

6. Linda Kuehl, "Dazzle-Dust," p. 213.

7. Tom Wolfe, *The Kandy-Kolored Tangerine-Flake Streamline Baby*, pp. xii.

8. Ibid., pp. xiii–xiv.

9. Tom Wolfe, *Radical Chic and Mau-Mauing the Flak Catchers*, p. 5.

10. Ibid., p. 118.

11. Robert Scholes, "Double Perspective on Hysteria," p. 37.

12. Michael L. Johnson, *The New Journalism*, pp. 50–51.

13. Ibid., p. 58.

14. Tom Wolfe, *The Electric Kool-Aid Acid Test* (New York: Farrar, Straus & Giroux, 1968). All references are to the paperback edition (New York: Bantam Books, 1969), p. 148, hereafter cited in the text as *AT*.

15. Scholes, "Double Perspective on Hysteria," p. 37.

16. Alvin Toffler, *Future Shock*, pp. 251–84 passim.

17. Lionel Trilling, "Morals, Manners, and the Novel," in *Approaches to the Novel*, ed. Robert Scholes, p. 122.

18. McMurtry is one of the young novelists whom Kesey met during the Perry Lane days at Stanford University. McMurtry's first novel, *Horseman, Pass By*, was made into the Hollywood film *Hud* starring Paul Newman. He has also collaborated with director Peter Bogdanovich on *The Last Picture Show*; his latest novel is *All My Friends Are Going to Be Strangers*. During his exile in Mexico, Kesey sent long letters in a paranoid style to McMurtry, who later, with Kesey's permission, allowed Wolfe to use them in reconstructing the "fugitive-on-the-run" sequences (chapters 21 and 23) in *Acid Test*.

19. Gorham Munson, *Style and Form in American Prose*, pp. 136–37.

20. Paul Hernadi defines "substitutionary narration" as a complex narrative technique in which the voice of the speaker shifts between that of a character in the action and the narrator. At times, the narrator imitates a character's speech patterns and mental processes, which is frequently what occurs in *Acid Test* in the chapters on Kesey's exile in Mexico. See Hernadi's discussion in "Free Indirect Discourse and Related Techniques," in *Beyond Genre*, pp. 187–205.

21. Michael Wood, review of *The New Journalism*, ed. Wolfe and Johnson, pp. 20–21.

22. Robert Scholes and Robert Kellogg, *The Nature of Narrative*, pp. 265–66.

23. Scholes, "Double Perspective on Hysteria," p. 37.

24. Anthony J. Lukas, "The Life and Death of a Hippie," pp. 106–8, 158, 165–78; Robert Christgau, "Beth Ann and Macrobioticism," in *The New Journalism*, ed. Wolfe and Johnson, pp. 331–39.

25. Joan Didion, *Slouching towards Bethlehem*, pp. 84–85.

26. Tom Wolfe, *The Pump House Gang*, p. 9.

27. Tom Wolfe, "The Author's Story," p. 41.

28. Ken Kesey, *One Flew Over the Cuckoo's Nest* (New York: Viking Press, 1973), p. 209.

CHAPTER 7

1. The historical uniqueness of our era has been asserted by social scientists concerned with the study of the future. Buckminster Fuller, Kenneth Boulding, Willis Harman, and Alvin Toffler view the sweeping changes of the sixties as indicative of a major shift in man's consciousness. Harman writes that we are in the midst of "a thoroughgoing systemic change to a degree comparable at least with such historical transitions as the Fall of Rome, the Reformation, and the Industrial Revolution, invoking changes in basic cultural premises, the root-image of man-in-society, fundamental value postulates, and all aspects of social roles and institutions" ("Planning Amid Forces for Institutional Change," paper given at the symposium, "Planning in the Seventies," cosponsored by the American Society for Public Administration and the National Bureau of Standards, Washington, D.C., 3–4 May 1971, p. 1). See also Kenneth Boulding and Willis Harman, *Alternative Futures and Educational Policy* (Menlo Park, Calif.: Stanford Research Institute, 1970); R. Buckminster Fuller, *Utopia or Oblivion: The Prospects for Humanity* (New York: Overlook Press, 1969); George Leonard, *The Transformation: A Guide to the Inevitable Changes in Humankind* (New York: Delacorte Press, 1972);

Robert Theobald and J. M. Scott, *Teg's 1994: An Anticipation of the Near Future* (Chicago: Swallow Press, 1972); Alvin Toffler, *Future Shock*.

2. Since this postscript was written, Woodward and Bernstein have published a controversial account of the last eight months of the Nixon presidency, *The Final Days* (New York: Simon and Schuster, 1976). Excerpts published in *Newsweek* (5 April and 12 April 1976) indicate that the book raises anew all of the methodological questions inherent in the new journalism. First responses to the book have been critical of the fact that the *Washington Post* reporters do not supply footnotes or other documentation; instead, they present a fiction-like narrative that includes the intimate thoughts and emotions of former president Nixon and his close associates. The two reporters defend their practices by noting that they interviewed 394 persons and worked from memos, logbooks, files, contemporaneous notes, and other documents. No matter how one views the validity of their new book, it graphically proves that the issues of method and ethics surrounding the new journalism are very much alive in the seventies.

3. Alfred Kazin, personal correspondence with the author, 9 March 1974.

4. Norman Mailer's recent books include *A Prisoner of Sex*; *St. George and the Godfather*; *Marilyn: A Biography*; and, with Mervyn Kurlansky, comp., *The Faith of Graffiti*.

5. Mailer's latest book is *The Fight*, a new journalistic report on the Muhammad Ali-George Foreman fight held in Zaire, Africa, in which Ali regained the heavyweight championship. And according to the publicity on his long-awaited multivolume novel, Mailer has been at work on the "big book" some five years and plans a length of from 500,000 to 700,000 words. His one-million dollar contract with Little, Brown & Company represents one of the largest advances ever granted in the history of American publishing. Mailer refuses to discuss the projected novel publicly except to give the barest plot outline. "It's bad luck to talk about a book while you're writing it," he told a talk show audience in 1974, "but it's about an idea I've had all my life."

6. Gay Talese, "A Matter of Fantasy," pp. 49–57, 144–52.

7. Tom Wolfe, *The Painted Word*. Wolfe's most recent work on contemporary manners and mores, *Mauve Gloves and Madmen, Clutter and Vine* (New York: Farrar, Straus & Giroux, 1976), was published just as this book went to press. He is also at work on a "psychohistory" of the astronauts entitled *The Right Stuff*.

8. Capote's personality sketches include "Blind Items," *Ladies' Home Journal*, January 1974, pp. 81, 122–24; and "Elizabeth Taylor," *Ladies' Home Journal*, December 1974, pp. 72, 76, 78, 151. *The Dogs Bark* collects travel sketches on Spain and Brooklyn Heights as well as such long nonfiction as Capote's "personality piece" on Marlon Brando, "The Duke in His Domain," and "The Muses Are Heard," on the Soviet tour of "Porgy and Bess" in the late fifties. Capote views his forthcoming novel, *Answered Prayers*, as a major work: "I always planned this book as being my principal work, the thing I always have been working toward" (Gerald Clarke, "Checking in with Truman Capote," p. 137).

9. See, especially, John W. Tebbel, "The 'Old' New Journalism," pp. 96–97. Tebbel argues that the tradition of objective reporting developed over many years is in danger if the new journalism and its impressionistic style become too acceptable to editors.

10. Ihab Hassan, *Contemporary American Literature, 1945–1972*, p. 170.

BIBLIOGRAPHY

BACKGROUND ON THE NEW JOURNALISM

Agee, James, and Evans, Walker. *Let Us Now Praise Famous Men*. Boston: Houghton Mifflin Co., 1939.

Aldridge, John W. *After the Lost Generation: A Critical Study of the Writers of Two Wars*. New York: McGraw-Hill Book Co., 1951.

———. *The Devil in the Fire: Essays on American Literature and Culture, 1951–1971*. New York: Harper & Row, 1972.

———. *In Search of Heresy: American Literature in an Age of Conformity*. New York: McGraw-Hill Book Co., 1956.

———. *Time to Murder and Create: The Contemporary Novel in Crisis*. New York: David McKay Co., 1966.

Arlen, Michael J. "Notes on the New Journalism." *Atlantic*, May 1972, pp. 43–47.

Bagdikian, Ben H. *The Information Machines: Their Impact on Men and Media*. New York: Harper & Row, 1971.

Barth, John. "The Literature of Exhaustion." *Atlantic*, August 1967, pp. 29–34.

Baumbach, Jonathan. *The Landscape of Nightmare: Studies in the Contemporary Novel*. New York: New York University Press, 1966.

Berman, Ronald. *America in the Sixties: An Intellectual History*. New York: Free Press, 1968.

Berthoff, Warner. *Fictions and Events: Essays in Criticism and Literary History*. New York: E. P. Dutton & Co., 1971.

Boorstin, Daniel J. *The Image, or What Ever Happened to the American Dream?* New York: Atheneum Publishers, 1962.

Booth, Wayne C. *The Rhetoric of Fiction*. 1961. Reprint. Chicago: University of Chicago Press, Phoenix Books, 1967.

Brown, Charles H. "New Art Journalism Revisited." *Quill*, March 1972, pp. 18–23.

———. "The Rise of the New Journalism." *Current*, June 1972, pp. 31–38.

Brustein, Robert. "Who's Killing the Novel?" *New Republic*, 23 October 1965, pp. 22–24.

Chase, Dennis. "From Lippmann to Irving to New Journalism." *Quill*, August 1972, pp. 19–21.

Chesnick, Eugene. "The Plot Against Fiction: *Let Us Now Praise Famous Men.*" *Southern Literary Journal* 4 (Fall 1971): 48–67.

Christianson, F. Scott. "The New Muckraking." *Quill*, July 1972, pp. 10–15.

Cook, Fred J. *The Muckrakers: Crusading Journalists Who Changed America*. New York: Doubleday & Co., 1972.

Crane, Stephen. *The Collected Short Stories and Sketches of Stephen Crane*. Edited by Thomas A. Gullason. Garden City, N.Y.: Doubleday & Co., 1963.

"Damage Award for Invasion of Privacy by Cleveland Paper Is Upheld by Justices." *Wall Street Journal*, 19 December 1974, p. 1.

Dennis, Everette E., ed. *The Magic Writing Machine: Student Probes of the New Journalism*. Eugene: University of Oregon School of Journalism, 1971.

Dennis, Everette E., and Rivers, William L. *Other Voices: The New Journalism in America*. San Francisco: Canfield Press, 1974.

Dickson, Frank A., ed. *The Writer's Digest Handbook of Article Writing*. New York: Holt, Rinehart & Winston, 1968.

Dickstein, Morris. Review of *My Life as a Man* by Philip Roth. *New York Times Book Review*, 2 June 1974, p. 1.

Eliot, T. S. "*Ulysses*, Order, and Myth." *Dial*, November 1923, pp. 480–83.

Fiedler, Leslie A. *Waiting for the End*. New York: Stein & Day, 1964.

Flippen, Charles C., ed. *Liberating the Media: The New Journalism*. Washington, D.C.: Acropolis Books, 1974.

Fontaine, André. *The Art of Writing Nonfiction*. New York: Thomas Y. Crowell, 1974.

Frye, Northrop. *Anatomy of Criticism: Four Essays*. Princeton, N.J.: Princeton University Press, 1957.

Glessing, Robert J. *The Underground Press in America*. Bloomington: Indiana University Press, 1970.

Gold, Herbert. "Epidemic First Personism." *Atlantic*, August 1971, pp. 85–87.

Grant, Gerald. "The 'New Journalism' We Need." *Columbia Journalism Review* 9 (Spring 1970): 12–16.

Harper, Howard M., Jr. *Desperate Faith–A Study of Bellow, Salinger, Mailer, Baldwin, and Updike*. Chapel Hill: University of North Carolina Press, 1967.

Hassan, Ihab. *Contemporary American Literature, 1945–1972: An Introduction*. New York: Frederick Ungar Publishing Co., 1973.

———. *The Dismemberment of Orpheus: Towards a Post-Modern Literature.* New York: Oxford University Press, 1971.

———. *Radical Innocence: Studies in the Contemporary American Novel.* Princeton, N.J.: Princeton University Press, 1961.

Hayes, Harold. "Editor's Notes." *Esquire,* January 1972, p. 12.

———, ed. *Smiling Through the Apocalypse: Esquire's History of the Sixties.* New York: Delta Books, 1969.

Hazlitt, William. "The Fight." In *The Complete Works of William Hazlitt.* Edited by P. P. Howe. London: J. M. Dent & Son, 1933.

Hemingway, Ernest. *Green Hills of Africa.* New York: Charles Scribner's Sons, 1935.

Hernadi, Paul. *Beyond Genre: New Directions in Literary Classification.* Ithaca, N.Y.: Cornell University Press, 1972.

Hills, Rust. "Fiction." *Esquire,* November 1973, pp. 20, 26, 31.

Howe, Irving. "Mass Society and Post-Modern Fiction." *Partisan Review* 26 (Summer 1959): 420–36.

Howe, Quentin. "The Age of the Journalist-Historian." *Saturday Review,* 20 May 1967, pp. 25–27.

Jacobs, Lewis. *The Documentary Tradition: From Nanook to Woodstock.* New York: Hopkins and Blake, 1971.

Johnson, Michael L. *The New Journalism: The Underground Press, the Artists of Nonfiction, and Changes in the Established Media.* Lawrence: University Press of Kansas, 1971.

Kazin, Alfred. *Bright Book of Life: American Novelists and Storytellers from Hemingway to Mailer.* Boston: Little, Brown & Co., 1973.

———. "Imagination and the Age." *Reporter,* 5 May 1966, pp. 32–35.

———. "The Literary Sixties: When the World Was Too Much with Us." *New York Times Book Review,* 21 December 1969, pp. 1–3, 18.

Kermode, Frank. *The Sense of an Ending: Studies in the Theory of Fiction.* New York: Oxford University Press, 1967.

Klein, Marcus. *After Alienation: American Writing in Mid-Century.* Cleveland: World Publishing Co., 1964.

———, ed. *The American Novel since World War II.* New York: Fawcett Publications, 1969.

Kramer, Dale. *Ross and the New Yorker.* Garden City, N.Y.: Doubleday & Co., 1951.

Langbaum, Robert. *The Modern Spirit: Essays on the Continuity of Nineteenth- and Twentieth-Century Literature.* New York: Oxford University Press, 1970.

Lawrence, D. H. *Studies in Classic American Literature.* New York: Viking Press, 1965.

Levin, Paul. "Reality and Fiction." *Hudson Review* 19 (Spring 1966): 135–38.

Liebling, A. J. *The Earl of Louisiana*. New York: Simon and Schuster, 1961.

————. *The Wayward Pressman*. Garden City, N.Y.: Doubleday & Co., 1947.

Lodge, David. *The Language of Fiction: Essays in Criticism and Verbal Analysis of the English Novel*. New York: Columbia University Press, 1967.

————. "The Novelist at the Crossroads." *Critical Quarterly* 11 (1969): 105–32.

Lubbock, Percy. *The Craft of Fiction*. London: Jonathan Cape, 1954.

Ludwig, Jack. *Recent American Novelists*. Minneapolis: University of Minnesota Press, 1962.

McCarthy, Mary. "Fact in Fiction." *Partisan Review* 27 (Summer 1960): 438–58.

MacDougall, C. D. *Interpretive Reporting*. 4th ed. New York: Macmillan Co., 1963.

McHam, David. "Old Ain't Necessarily Good, Either." *Bulletin of the American Society of Newspaper Editors*, January 1972, pp. 3–6.

Markel, Lester. "Lester Markel: So What's New?" *Bulletin of the American Society of Newspaper Editors*, January 1972, pp. 1, 7–9.

Masterson, Mark. "The New Journalism." *Quill*, February 1971, pp. 15–17.

Meyer, Philip. *Precision Journalism*. Bloomington: Indiana University Press, 1973.

Miller, J. Hillis, ed. *Aspects of Narrative: Selected Papers for the English Institute*. New York: Columbia University Press, 1971.

Mills, Nicolaus, ed. *The New Journalism: An Historical Anthology*. New York: McGraw-Hill Book Co., 1974.

Moon, Barbara. "Wolfe's New Journalism: Capote's Old Tricks." *Saturday Night*, March 1966, pp. 42, 44–45.

Mott, F. L. *American Journalism: A History, 1690–1960*. 3d ed. New York: Macmillan Co., 1962.

————. *A History of American Magazines*. Cambridge, Mass.: Harvard University Press, 1938–68.

————, ed. *Interpretations of Journalism: A Book of Readings*. New York: F. S. Crofts and Co., 1937.

Munson, Gorham. *Style and Form in American Prose*. Garden City, N.Y.: Doubleday and Doran, 1929.

Newfield, Jack. "Is There a New Journalism?" *Columbia Journalism Review* 11 (July–August 1972): 45–47.

Olderman, Raymond M. *Beyond the Waste Land: A Study of the American Novel in the Nineteen-Sixties*. New Haven, Conn.: Yale University Press, 1972.

Ortega y Gasset, José. *The Dehumanization of Art and Notes on the Novel*. Translated by Helene Weyl. Princeton, N.J.: Princeton University Press, 1948.

Orwell, George. *Down and Out in London and Paris*. London: V. Gollancz, 1933.

————. *The Road to Wigan Pier*. London: V. Gollancz, 1937.

Peterson, Theodore B. *Magazines in the Twentieth Century*. Urbana: University of Illinois Press, 1964.

Podhoretz, Norman. "The Article as Art." *Harper's*, July 1958, pp. 74–79.

Poirier, Richard. *The Performing Self*. New York: Oxford University Press, 1971.

Raeburn, John. "Ernest Hemingway: The Public Writer as Popular Culture." *Journal of Popular Culture* 8 (Summer 1974): 91–98.

Regier, C. C. *The Era of the Muckrakers*. Gloucester, Mass.: Peter Smith and Co., 1957.

Ridgeway, James. "The New Journalism." *American Libraries*, June 1971, pp. 585–92.

Robbe-Grillet, Alain. *For a New Novel: Essays on Fiction*. Translated by Richard Howard. New York: Grove Press, 1965.

Robinson, L. W.; Hayes, Harold; Talese, Gay; and Wolfe, Tom. "The New Journalism." *Writer's Digest*, January 1970, pp. 32–35, 19.

Ross, Lillian. *Reporting*. New York: Simon and Schuster, 1964.

Roszak, Theodore. *The Making of a Counter-Culture*. Garden City, N.Y.: Doubleday & Co., 1969.

Roth, Philip. "Writing American Fiction." *Commentary* 31 (March 1961): 223–33.

Rubin, Louis D., Jr. *The Curious Death of the Novel: Essays in American Literature*. Baton Rouge: Louisiana State University Press, 1967.

Sale, Roger, ed. *Discussions of the Novel*. Boston: D. C. Heath & Co., 1965.

Saturday Evening Post. *Post Biographies of Famous Journalists*. Edited by John E. Drewey. Athens: University of Georgia Press, 1942.

Scholes, Robert. *Elements of Fiction*. New York: Oxford University Press, 1968.

————. *The Fabulators*. New York: Oxford University Press, 1967.

————. "The Fictional Criticism of the Future." Paper delivered at the H.V.S. Ogden Festegabe, University of Michigan, Ann Arbor, Michigan, 28 March 1974.

————, ed. *Approaches to the Novel*. Rev. ed. San Francisco: Chandler Publishing Co., 1966.

Scholes, Robert, and Kellogg, Robert. *The Nature of Narrative*. New York: Oxford University Press, 1966.

Selbst, Steven. "Journalist Thompson Greets Enthusiastic Campus Following." *Michigan Daily*, 13 February 1974, pp. 1, 8.

Snyder, L. L. *A Treasury of Great Reporting: "Literature Under Pressure" from the Sixteenth Century to Our Time*. 2d ed. New York: Simon and Schuster, 1962.

Sontag, Susan. *Against Interpretation, and Other Essays*. New York: Farrar, Straus & Giroux, 1966.

Stevick, Philip. *The Theory of the Novel*. New York: Free Press, 1967.

Swados, Harvey. "Must Writers Be Characters?" *Saturday Review*, 1 October 1960, pp. 12–14, 50.

————, ed. *Years of Conscience: The Muckrakers*. Cleveland and New York: World Publishing Co., 1962.

Tanner, Tony. *City of Words: American Fiction, 1950–1970*. New York: Farrar, Straus & Giroux, 1971.

Tebbel, John W. *The American Magazine: A Compact History*. New York: Hawthorne Books, 1969.

————. "The 'Old' New Journalism." *Saturday Review*, 13 March 1971, pp. 96–97.

Toffler, Alvin. *Future Shock*. New York: Bantam Books, 1971.

Trilling, Lionel. *A Gathering of Fugitives*. Boston: Beacon Press, 1956.

Wakefield, Dan. "The Personal Voice and the Impersonal Eye." *Atlantic*, June 1966, pp. 86–90.

Waldmeir, Joseph J., ed. *Recent American Fiction: Some Critical Views*. Boston: Houghton Mifflin Co., 1962.

Watt, Ian. *The Rise of the Novel*. Berkeley: University of California Press, 1957.

Weber, Ronald. "Tom Wolfe's Happiness Explosion." *Journal of Popular Culture* 8 (Summer 1974): 71–79.

————, ed. *The Reporter as Artist: A Look at the New Journalism Controversy*. New York: Hastings House, 1974.

Wolfe, Tom. "The New Journalism." *Bulletin of the American Society of Newspaper Editors*, September 1970, pp. 1, 18–23.

Wolfe, Tom, and Johnson, E. W., eds. *The New Journalism, with an Anthology Edited by Tom Wolfe and E. W. Johnson*. New York: Harper & Row, 1973.

Wolseley, Roland E. *The Changing Magazine: Trends in Readership and Management*. New York: Hastings House, 1973.

————. *The Magazine World: An Introduction to Magazine Journalism*. New York: Prentice-Hall, 1951.

Truman Capote

Alexander, Shana. "A Nonfictional Visit with Truman Capote." *Life*, 18
February 1966, pp. 22–23.

Breit, Harvey. "A Talk with Truman Capote." *New York Times Book
Review*, 24 February 1963, p. 39.

Capote, Truman. *Breakfast at Tiffany's: A Short Novel and Three Stories*.
New York: Random House, 1958.

————. *The Dogs Bark: Public People and Private Places*. New York:
Random House, 1973.

————. *The Grass Harp, and A Tree of Night, and Other Stories*. New
York: New American Library, 1956.

————. *In Cold Blood: A True Account of a Multiple Murder and Its
Consequences*. New York: Random House, 1965.

————. *Local Color*. New York: Random House, 1950.

————. *Other Voices, Other Rooms*. New York: Random House, 1948.

————. *Selected Writings*. New York: Random House, 1963.

Clarke, Gerald. "Checking in with Truman Capote." *Esquire*, November
1972.

"The Country below the Surface." *Time*, 21 January 1966.

Dunne, John Gregory. "Fictitious Novel." *National Review*, 8 March
1966, pp. 226–29.

Dupee, F. W. "Truman Capote's Score." *New York Review of Books*, 3
February 1966, pp. 3–5.

Friedman, Melvin J. "Towards an Aesthetic: Truman Capote's Other
Voices." In *Truman Capote's "In Cold Blood": A Critical Handbook*,
edited by Irving Malin. Belmont, Calif.: Wadsworth Publishers, 1968.

Garrett, George. "Crime and Punishment in Kansas: Truman Capote's *In
Cold Blood*." 3, no. 1 *Hollins Critic* (February 1966): 1–12.

Hamish, Hamilton. "Stranger Than Fiction." *Times Literary Supplement*,
17 March 1966, p. 215.

Hicks, Granville. "The Story of an American Tragedy." *Saturday Review*,
22 January 1966, pp. 35–36.

Hill, Pati. "Truman Capote Interview." In *Writers at Work: The Paris
Review Interviews*, edited by Malcolm Cowley. New York: Viking Press,
1958.

"Horror Spawns a Masterpiece." Review of *In Cold Blood* by Truman
Capote. *Life*, 7 January 1966, pp. 58–69.

Howard, Jane. "How the 'Smart Rascal' Brought It Off." *Life*, 7 January
1966, pp. 70–76.

"In Cold Blood . . . An American Tragedy." Review of *In Cold Blood* by
  Truman Capote. *Newsweek*, 24 January 1966, pp. 59–63.
"In a Novel Way." Review of *In Cold Blood* by Truman Capote. *Time*, 8
  October 1965, pp. 74–76.
Kauffmann, Stanley. "Capote in Kansas." *New Republic*, 22 January 1966,
  pp. 19–22.
Langbaum, R. "Capote's Nonfiction Novel." *American Scholar* 35
  (Summer 1966): 772–80.
Long, Barbara. "In Cold Comfort." *Esquire*, June 1966, pp. 124, 126, 128,
  171–73, 175, 176, 178–81.
McCormick, J. "The Non-Fiction Novel." *Yale Literary Magazine*, May
  1966, pp. 22–24.
Macdonald, Dwight. "Cosa Nostra." *Esquire*, April 1966, pp. 44–48,
  58–62.
Malin, Irving, ed. *Truman Capote's "In Cold Blood": A Critical
  Handbook*. Belmont, Calif.: Wadsworth Publishers, 1968.
Mouton, Jean. *Littérature et sang-froid*. Bruges, Belgium: Desclée de
  Brouwer, 1967.
Nance, William L. *The Worlds of Truman Capote*. New York: Stein &
  Day, 1970.
Plimpton, George. "The Story behind a Nonfiction Novel." *New York
  Times Book Review*, 16 January 1966, pp. 2–3, 38–43.
Tanner, Tony. "Death in Kansas." *Spectator*, 18 March 1966, pp. 331–32.
Tompkins, Phillip K. "In Cold Fact." *Esquire*, June 1966, pp. 125, 127,
  166–68, 170–71.
Weigand, William. "The Non-Fiction Novel." *New Mexico Quarterly* 37
  (Autumn 1967): 243–57.
West, Rebecca. "A Grave and Reverend Book." *Harper's*, February 1966.
Yurick, Sol. "Sob-Sister Gothic." *Nation*, 7 February 1966, pp. 158–60.

Norman Mailer
Bell, Pearl K. "The Power and the Vainglory." *New Leader*, 8 February
  1971, pp. 16–17.
Braudy, Leo, ed. *Norman Mailer: A Collection of Critical Essays*.
  Englewood Cliffs, N.J.: Prentice-Hall, 1972.
Carroll, Paul. "*Playboy* Interview: Norman Mailer." *Playboy*, January
  1968, pp. 69–72, 74, 76, 78, 80, 82–84.
Decter, Midge. "Mailer's Campaign." *Commentary* 37 (February 1964):
  83–85.
Dickstein, Morris. "A Trip to Inner and Outer Space." *New York Times
  Book Review*, 10 January 1971, pp. 1, 42–43, 45.
Didion, Joan. "A Social Eye." *National Review*, 20 April 1965, pp.
  329–30.

Fallaci, Oriana. "An Interview with Norman Mailer." *Writer's Digest*, December 1969, pp. 40–47.

Flaherty, Joe. *Managing Mailer*. New York: Coward-McCann, 1969.

Foster, Richard. *Norman Mailer*. University of Minnesota Pamphlets on American Writers, no. 73. Minneapolis: University of Minnesota Press, 1968.

Gilman, Richard. "Norman Mailer: Art as Life, Life as Art." In *The Confusion of Realms*. New York: Vintage Books, 1970.

————. "What Mailer Has Done." In *Norman Mailer: A Collection of Critical Essays*, edited by Leo Braudy. Englewood Cliffs, N.J.: Prentice-Hall, 1972.

Greenfield, Josh. "Line between Journalism and Literature Thin, Perhaps, but Distinct." *Commonweal*, 7 June 1968, pp. 362–63.

Hoffa, William. "Norman Mailer: Advertisements for Myself or Portrait of the Artist as Disgruntled Counterpuncher." In *The Fifties: Fiction, Poetry, Drama*, edited by Warren French. New York: Everett-Edwards, 1970.

Kael, Pauline, "Celebrities Make Spectacles of Themselves." *New Yorker*, 20 January 1968, pp. 90–95.

————. Review of *Marilyn* by Norman Mailer. *New York Times Book Review*, 22 July 1973, pp. 1–3.

Kaufmann, Donald L. "Mailer's Lunar Bits and Pieces." *Modern Fiction Studies* 17 (1971): 451–54.

————. *Norman Mailer: The Countdown*. Carbondale: Southern Illinois University Press, 1969.

Kermode, Frank. "Rammel." *New Statesman*, 14 May 1965.

Langbaum, Robert. "Mailer's New Style." In *The Modern Spirit: Essays on the Continuity of Nineteenth- and Twentieth-Century Literature*. New York: Oxford University Press, 1970.

Leeds, Barry H. *The Structured Vision of Norman Mailer*. New York: New York University Press, 1969.

Lucid, Robert F. *Norman Mailer: The Man and His Work*. Boston: Little, Brown & Co., 1971.

Macdonald, Dwight. "Politics." *Esquire*, May 1968, pp. 41–44, 194–96.

————. "Politics." *Esquire*, June 1968, pp. 46–50, 183.

Mailer, Norman. *Advertisements for Myself*. New York: G. P. Putnam's Sons, 1959. Reprint. Berkley Publishing Co., 1966.

————. *An American Dream*. New York: Dial Press, 1965. Reprint. Dell Publishing Co., 1965.

————. *The Armies of the Night: History as a Novel, the Novel as History*. New York: New American Library, 1968.

————. *Cannibals and Christians*. New York: Dial Press, 1965. Reprint. Dell Publishing Co., 1966.

————. *Existential Errands*. New York: New American Library, 1973.

_____. *The Fight*. Boston: Little, Brown & Co., 1975.

_____. *Marilyn: A Biography*. New York: Grosset & Dunlap, 1973.

_____. *Miami and the Siege of Chicago: An Informal History of the Republican and Democratic Conventions of 1968*. New York: New American Library, 1968.

_____. *The Naked and the Dead*. New York: Rinehart and Co., 1948.

_____. *Of a Fire on the Moon*. Boston: Little, Brown & Co., 1970. Reprint. New York: New American Library, 1971.

_____. *The Presidential Papers*. New York: G. P. Putnam's Sons, 1963.

_____. *The Prisoner of Sex*. New York: New American Library, 1971.

_____. *St. George and the Godfather*. New York: New American Library, 1972.

_____. *Why Are We in Vietnam?* New York: G. P. Putnam's Sons, 1967.

Mailer, Norman, with Kurlansky, Mervyn, comps. *The Faith of Graffiti*. New York: Praeger Press, 1974.

"Mailer's America." Review of *The Armies of the Night* by Norman Mailer. *Time*, 11 October 1968, pp. 81–82.

Marcus, Steven. "Norman Mailer Interview." In *Writers at Work: The Paris Review Interviews*. 3d ser. Edited by Alfred Kazin. New York: Viking Press, 1967.

"Mr. Mailer Interviews Himself." *New York Times Book Review*, 17 September 1967, pp. 4–5, 40.

O'Brien, Conor Cruise. "Confessions of the Last American." *New York Review of Books*, 20 June 1968, pp. 16–18.

Podhoretz, Norman. "Norman Mailer: the Embattled Vision." *Partisan Review* 26 (Summer 1959): 371–91.

Poirier, Richard. *Norman Mailer*. New York: Viking Press, 1972.

Resnick, Harry S. "Hand on the Pulse of America." *Saturday Review*, 4 May 1968, pp. 25–26.

Richardson, Jack. "The Aesthetics of Norman Mailer." *New York Review of Books*, 8 May 1969, pp. 3–4.

Sale, Roger. "Watchman, What of the Night?" *New York Review of Books*, 6 May 1971, pp. 13–17.

Schrader, George A. "Norman Mailer and the Despair of Defiance." *Yale Review* 51 (December 1961): 267–80.

Schroth, Raymond A. "Mailer and His Gods." *Commonweal*, 9 May 1969, pp. 226–29.

_____. "Mailer on the Moon." *Commonweal*, 7 May 1971, pp. 216–18.

Schulz, Max F. "Mailer's Divine Comedy." *Contemporary Literature* 9 (Winter 1968): 36–57.

Shaw, Peter. "The Conventions, 1968." *Commentary*, December 1968, pp. 93–96.

————. "The Tough-Guy Intellectual." *Critical Quarterly* 8 (Spring 1966): 13–29.

Sheed, Wilfrid. "Miami and the Siege of Chicago: A Review." *New York Times Book Review*, 8 December 1968, pp. 3, 5–6.

Sisk, John. "Aquarius Rising." *Commentary*, May 1971, pp. 83–84.

Sokolov, Raymond A. "Flying High with Mailer." *Newsweek*, 9 December 1968, pp. 84, 86–88.

Stark, John Olsen. "Norman Mailer's Work from 1963 to 1968." Ph.D. dissertation, University of Wisconsin, 1970.

"Surveying Supernation." Review of *The Armies of the Night* by Norman Mailer. *Newsweek*, 26 February 1968, p. 62.

Trachtenberg, Alan. "Mailer on the Steps of the Pentagon." *Nation*, 27 May 1968, pp. 701–2.

————. "Repeat Performance." *Nation*, 9 December 1968, pp. 631–32.

Trilling, Diana. "Norman Mailer." *Encounter*, November 1962, pp. 45–56.

Wain, John. "Mailer's America." *New Republic*, 1 October 1966, pp. 19–20.

Tom Wolfe

Bennett, M. "Akond of Swock." *Reporter*, 12 August 1965, p. 50.

"Breaking Out of Beige: New Journalism." *Christianity Today*, 31 August 1973, p. 26.

Buckley, William F. "Mau-Mauing Wolfe." *National Review*, 15 January 1970, p. 51.

Coyne, J. R. "Sketchbook of Snobs." *National Review*, 26 January 1971, pp. 90–91.

Current Biography, January 1971, pp. 42–43.

"Department of Amplification." Review of *he Kandy-Kolored Tangerine-Flake Streamline Baby* by Tom Wolfe. *Newsweek*, 3 May 1965, p. 82.

Dundy, Elaine. "Tom Wolfe . . . But Exactly Yes!" *Vogue*, 15 April 1966, pp. 124–25.

Frankel, Haskel. "Author." Review of *The Kandy-Kolored Tangerine-Flake Streamline Baby* by Tom Wolfe. *Saturday Review*, 31 July 1965, pp. 23–24.

Gordon, J. "Tom Wolfe: Reactionary Chic." *Ramparts*, January 1972, pp. 58–62.

Grossman, Edward. "Kandy-Kolored Journalism." *Saturday Review-World*, 5 June 1973, pp. 57–60.

"Hijinks Journalism." *Commentary*, February 1969, pp. 76–78.

"Journalism's Woodstock." *Time*, 8 May 1972, p. 70.

Kuehl, Linda. "Dazzle-Dust: A Wolfe in Chic Clothing." *Commonweal*, 7 May 1971, pp. 212–16.

Macdonald, Dwight. "Parajournalism, or Tom Wolfe and His Magic Writing Machine." *New York Review of Books*, 26 August 1965, pp. 3–4.

————. "Parajournalism II: Wolfe and The New Yorker." *New York Review of Books*, 3 February 1966, pp. 18–24.

Maddocks, Melvin. "A Carnival Barker in Search of Style." *Ann Arbor News*, 16 August 1973, p. 22.

Mok, Michael, ed. *Publisher's Weekly Interviews*, 18 June 1973, pp. 34–36.

Scholes, Robert. "Double Perspective on Hysteria." *Saturday Review*, 24 August 1968, p. 37.

Seelye, John. "The Shotgun behind the Lens." Review of *The New Journalism*, edited by Tom Wolfe and E. W. Johnson. *New Republic*, 11 August 1973, pp. 22–24.

Sheed, Wilfrid. "The Good Word: A Fun-House Mirror." *New York Times Book Review*, 3 December 1972, pp. 2, 10–12.

Stein, Ted. "New Journalism: A Bold, Flashy Genre Searches for Identity." *Michigan Daily*, 10 February 1974, p. 4.

"Talk of the Town." Review of *The Kandy-Kolored Tangerine-Flake Streamline Baby* by Tom Wolfe. *National Review*, 4 May 1965, pp. 359–60.

"Whisper." Review of *The Kandy-Kolored Tangerine-Flake Streamline Baby* by Tom Wolfe. *Time*, 16 April 1965, p. 60.

Wolfe, Tom. "The Author's Story." *New York Times Book Review*, 18 August 1968, pp. 2, 40–41.

————. "The Birth of New Journalism." *New York Magazine*, 14 February 1972, pp. 1, 30–45. Appears in different form in *The New Journalism*, edited by Tom Wolfe and E. W. Johnson. New York: Harper & Row, 1973.

————. *The Electric Kool-Aid Acid Test*. New York: Farrar, Straus & Giroux, 1968. Reprint. Bantam Books, 1969.

————. *The Kandy-Kolored Tangerine-Flake Streamline Baby*. New York: Farrar, Straus & Giroux, 1965. Reprint. Pocket Books, 1966.

————. *The Painted Word*. New York: Farrar, Straus & Giroux, 1975.

————. *The Pump House Gang*. New York: Farrar, Straus & Giroux, 1968. Reprint. Bantam Books, 1969.

————. *Radical Chic and Mau-Mauing the Flak Catchers*. New York: Farrar, Straus & Giroux, 1970. Reprint. Bantam Books, 1971.

————. "Why They Aren't Writing the Great American Novel Anymore." *Esquire*, December 1972, pp. 151–59, 272–80. Appears in a different form in *The New Journalism*, edited by Tom Wolfe and E. W. Johnson. New York: Harper & Row, 1973.

Wood, Michael. Review of *The New Journalism*, edited by Tom Wolfe and

E. W. Johnson. *New York Times Book Review*, 22 July 1973, pp. 20–21.
"Wowie!" *Newsweek*, 1 February 1965.

Other New Journalists
Breslin, Jimmy. *Can't Anybody Here Play This Game?* New York:
  Ballantine Books, 1963.
————. *The Gang That Couldn't Shoot Straight*. New York: Bantam
  Books, 1970.
————. *The World of Jimmy Breslin*. New York: Viking Press, 1967.
Bugliosi, Vincent. *Helter Skelter*. New York: W. W. Norton & Co., 1974.
Conot, Robert. *Rivers of Blood, Years of Darkness*. New York: Bantam
  Books, 1967.
Conroy, Frank. *Stop-Time*. New York: Viking Press, 1967.
Cowan, Paul, and Cowan, Geoffrey. "Three Letters from Mississippi."
  Esquire, September 1964, pp. 105, 106, 190.
Demaris, Ovid. *The Green Felt Jungle*. New York: Pocket Books, 1963.
Didion, Joan. *Slouching towards Bethlehem*. New York: Delta Books,
  1969.
Dunne, John Gregory. *Delano: The Story of the California Grape Strike*.
  New York: Farrar, Straus & Giroux, 1971.
————. *The Studio*. New York: Farrar, Straus & Giroux, 1969.
Eszterhas, Joe, and Roberts, Michael D. *Thirteen Seconds: Confrontation
  at Kent State*. New York: Dodd, Mead & Co., 1970.
Hersey, John. *The Algiers Motel Incident*. New York: Bantam Books,
  1968.
Hersh, Seymour M. *Cover-Up*. New York: Random House, 1972.
————. *My Lai Four: A Report on the Massacre and Its Aftermath*. New
  York: Random House, 1970.
Kunen, James. *Standard Operating Procedure*. New York: Avon Books,
  1971.
————. *The Strawberry Statement*. New York: Random House, 1969.
Levin, Meyer. *Compulsion*. New York: Simon and Schuster, 1956.
Lukas, J. Anthony. *Don't Shoot—We Are Your Children!* New York: Dell
  Books, 1972.
————. "The Life and Death of a Hippie." *Esquire*, May 1968, pp.
  106–8, 158, 165–78.
McCarthy, Mary. *Vietnam*. New York: Harcourt Brace Jovanovich, 1967.
McGinniss, Joe. *The Selling of the President, 1968*. New York: Pocket
  Books, 1972.
Marine, Gene. *The Black Panthers*. New York: New American Library,
  1969.
Mills, James. "The Detective." *Life*, 3 December 1965, pp. 108–10.

_____. *The Panic in Needle Park*. New York: New American Library, 1971.

_____. *The Prosecutor*. New York: Simon and Schuster, 1970.

Moser, Don, and Cohen, Jerry. *The Pied Piper of Tucson*. New York: New American Library, 1967.

Mungo, Raymond. *Famous Long Ago: My Life and Hard Times with the Liberation News Service*. Boston: Beacon Press, 1970.

Newfield, Jack. *Bread and Roses Too: Reporting about America*. New York: E. P. Dutton & Co., 1971.

Plimpton, George. *Paper Lion*. New York: Harper & Row, 1966.

Pynchon, Thomas. "A Journey into the Minds of Watts." *New York Times Magazine*, August 1966.

Rader, Dotson. *I Ain't Marchin' Anymore*. New York: David McKay Co., 1969.

Reed, Rex. *Big Screen, Little Screen*. New York: Macmillan Co., 1971.

_____. *Conversations in the Raw*. New York: New American Library, 1970.

_____. *Do You Sleep in the Nude?* New York: New American Library, 1968.

Rosenthal, A. M. *Thirty-Eight Witnesses*. New York: McGraw-Hill Book Co., 1964.

Sack, John. *Lieutenant Calley: His Own Story*. New York: Viking Press, 1971.

_____. *M*. New York: New American Library, 1967.

Sheehy, Gail. *Hustling: Prostitution in Our Wide-Open Society*. New York: Dell Books, 1973.

_____. *Panthermania: The Clash of Black against Black in One American City*. New York: Harper & Row, 1971.

_____. *Speed Is of the Essence*. New York: Simon and Schuster, 1971.

Sontag, Susan. *Trip to Hanoi*. New York: Farrar, Straus & Giroux, 1969.

Southern, Terry. *Red Dirt Marijuana and Other Tastes*. New York: New American Library, 1967.

Talese, Gay. *The Bridge*. New York: Harper & Row, 1964.

_____. *Fame and Obscurity: Portraits by Gay Talese*. New York: World Publishing Co., 1970.

_____. *Honor Thy Father*. New York: Fawcett-World, 1972.

_____. "Joe Louis: The King as a Middle-Aged Man." *Esquire*, June 1962.

_____. *The Kingdom and the Power*. New York: Bantam Books, 1970.

_____. "A Matter of Fantasy." *Esquire*, August 1975, pp. 49–57, 144–52.

_____. *The Overreachers*. New York: Harper & Row, 1963.

Terkel, Studs. *Division Street: America*. New York: Avon Books, 1968.
———. *Hard Times: An Oral History of the Great Depression*. New York: Avon Books, 1971.
———. *Working*. New York: Avon Books, 1975.
Thompson, Hunter S. *Fear and Loathing on the Campaign Trail*. San Francisco: Straight Arrow Books, 1973.
———. *Fear and Loathing in Las Vegas*. New York: Popular Library, 1973.
———. *Hell's Angels: A Strange and Terrible Saga*. New York: Ballantine Books, 1967.
von Hoffman, Nicholas. *We Are the People Our Parents Warned Us Against*. New York: Fawcett-World, 1971.
Wakefield, Dan. *Supernation at Peace and War*. New York: Atlantic Monthly Press, 1968.
Wambaugh, Joseph. *The Onion Field*. New York: Delacorte Press, 1973.
Wills, Garry. "Martin Luther King Is Still on the Case." *Esquire*, August 1968, pp. 89–104, 124–29.

Index

A

Abnormal person: in Capote's works, 75
Addison, Joseph, 33
Advertisements for Myself, 56, 88, 93, 119
Advocacy journalism, 35, 154
Agee, James, 35
Aldridge, John, 12–13, 49, 55, 57, 88
Aldrin, Buzz, 118. *See also* Astronauts
Algiers Motel Incident, The, 12, 42
All the President's Men, 148
Alternative broadcasting, 154
Alternative journalism, 154
American Dream, An, 60, 118, 120
American Tragedy, An, 84, 85
Anatomy of Criticism, 83
Answered Prayers, 150, 164
Antinovels, 78, 79. See also *Nouveau roman*
Apocalypse: sense of, 3, 15; in Mailer's works, 100, 110, 123, 124, 143, 144; "game" of, 145
Apollo mission, 113, 116, 117, 119, 123, 124. *See also* Astronauts; *Of a Fire on the Moon*; Space program
Arlen, Michael J., 22, 23, 44, 51
Armies of the Night, The, 90–101 passim; subtitle of, 10; as example of documentary fiction, 11; Berthoff review of, 13, 16; as Mailer's say on contemporary matters, 14; combining fictional and empirical modes, 19, 90; in historical mode, 20; inspiration for, 39; as Mailer's major work, 88; prizes won by, 113; design of, 116; and "End of Days," 124; successful balance of, 149. *See also*

Pentagon, march on the
Armstrong, Neil, 118, 119. *See also* Astronauts
Art, dehumanization of, 6
Art, modern: Wolfe on, 149–50
Art and life, relationship of, 58
Art of the Novel, The, 26
Arts: popular vs. elite, xi, 47
"As if" sensation of the novel, 139
Astronauts, 119, 120, 122; impersonal language of, 118
Atlantic (magazine), 38
Atmospheric details. *See* "Status details"
Auteur principle, 51
Autobiography, 12, 15, 58; Mailer's style of, 91
Autobiography of Malcolm X, The, 12, 13, 16

B

Baldwin, James, 8, 12
Barbary Shore, 112
Barth, John, 7, 17, 18, 19
Barthelme, Donald, 17
Beat Generation, 132
Bellow, Saul, 16–17, 18, 89
Berkeley Barb, 39, 154
Bernstein, Carl, 46, 148, 164
Bernstein, Leonard, 26, 27, 31, 129
Berthoff, Warner, 13, 16
Best-sellers: changes in nature of, 9
Beyond the Waste Land, x, 18
Biography: as mode of empirical narrative, 18; as one root of the novel, 19; as literary form, 58, 59
Black humor, 17, 18
Black Panther party, 12, 26, 129, 130
Boorstin, Daniel, 49

148. *See also* New journalism, the; New nonfiction, the; Novel, the; Novelist, the

Notes of a Native Son, 12

"Notes on the Novel," 6

Nouveau roman, 78, 79

Novel, the: of the sixties, x; decline and "death" of, 5, 6, 7, 8, 9, 10, 18, 19, 20, 116; traditional function of, 8; since World War II, 9; criterion of success for, 14; central tradition of, 20; distinguishing characteristic of, 26; vs. the new journalism, 45–46; contemporary trends in, 61; definition of, 83; techniques fused with the new journalism, 101. *See also* Fantasy; Fiction; Fictional mode; Fictional techniques

"Novel as History, The," 91

Novelist, the: in the sixties, 5; dilemmas and pressures, 5, 8, 9, 13, 14; contemporary, 9; moral vision of, 10, 11; as celebrity, 50, 51, 55; as selector of materials, 70, 71; prestige of, 89

Novelistic techniques. *See* Fictional techniques

Novels: of the sixties, 16; postwar, 17

Novels-as-history, 83

Novelty, demand for, 49–50, 59

O

Oates, Joyce Carol, 17

"Objective history": impossibility of, 74

Objective journalism: rebellion against, 11; tradition of, 22; development of, 33; as dominant trend, 36; contrasted with Mailer's subjectivity, 92, 109, 125; Wolfe and, 130–31

Objectivity: "higher," 22; Capote's striving for, 66, 73; promoted by "omniscient narration," 72; Mailer's use of, 94–95

Observations, 65

O'Connor, Flannery, 58

"Of a Fire on the Moon" (article), 113

Of a Fire on the Moon (book), 88, 106, 108, 113–25 passim; design of, 116; apocalyptic aspects of, 124, 146. *See also* Mailer, Norman

Olderman, Raymond M., x, 18

"Old" journalism. *See* Journalism, conventional

Omniscient narration, 9, 15, 72

On Being Busted, 12

One Flew Over the Cuckoo's Nest, 133, 146

Ortega y Gasset, 6, 7

Orwell, George, 35

Other Voices, Other Rooms, 55, 75

P

Paine, Tom, 21

Painted Word, The, 149

Paper Lion, 42

"Parajournalism," ix, 44, 127

Participant-observer, 52, 53, 131

Pentagon, march on the, 39, 75, 90, 94, 97, 98, 100, 147, 161. *See also Armies of the Night, The*

Periodical journalism, 33, 34

Personal involvement of the new journalist, 22, 47, 52, 133, 151. *See also* Objectivity; Subjectivity

Personality pieces, 36. See also *New Yorker*, profiles; Star interview

Playboy (magazine), 38

Play It As It Lays, 17, 144

Plimpton, George, 42, 84

Podhoretz, Norman, 8, 89

Point of view: as narrative device, 25, 28–29, 64, 70, 72

Poirier, Richard, 99, 117, 119

Political conventions. *See* Democratic convention in Chicago; *Miami and the Siege of Chicago*; Republican convention in Miami

Politics, American: Mailer's metaphor for, 105

"Pop sociology," ix

Portis, Charles, 36

Pranksters, Merry. *See* Merry Pranksters

Precision journalism, 154

Presidential Papers, The, 56, 98, 104

"Pseudo-events," 49

Psychological depth in the new journalism, 24, 28, 32, 47, 64

"Psychology of Astronauts, The," 113, 115, 118

"Public writers," 55

Pulitzer Prize, 39, 113

Pump House Gang, The, 127, 145

Pynchon, Thomas, 17, 18

Q

Quotation, direct, 29–30

Social reality: defining of, 5; in the novel, 14, 18
Social sciences: competition with fiction, 8, 9, 12
Social turmoil, 4, 46, 85, 135, 145
Sontag, Susan, 13
Sot-Weed Factor, The, 17
Soul on Ice, 12
Southern, Terry, 43
Southern Christian Leadership Council, 43
Space program, 41, 106, 113, 121. *See also* Astronauts; Cape Kennedy; Manned Space Center; NASA; *Of a Fire on the Moon*
"Star," the new journalist as, 49, 56
Star interview, 40, 41, 67, 68. See also *New Yorker*, profiles; Personality pieces
"Status details": as technique of the new journalism, 25, 28, 129
Steele, Richard, 33
Steffens, Lincoln, 35
Steinem, Gloria, 39
Stendhal, 84, 85
Storytelling techniques, 24; giving rise to the novel, 33
Stream-of-consciousness technique, 47, 138, 139
Studio, The, 41
Styles of Radical Will, 13
Styron, William, 12, 16–17, 18, 89
Subjectivity, 22, 90, 103, 109, 125, 134, 136. *See also* Objectivity; Personal involvement
Substitutionary narration, 140, 163
"Superman Comes to the Supermarket," 60, 101, 109
"Supernation at Peace and War," 44
Surrealistic writing, 17
Symbolism: in Mailer, 96, 114

T
Talese, Gay: as new journalist, 11, 25, 37, 39; as user of fictional techniques, 28, 29, 30, 35, 46, 47; discusses the new journalism, 31–32, 36; as interviewer, 40; latest work, 149. See also *Honor Thy Father; Kingdom and the Power*
Tanner, Tony, 73, 79, 85
Tarbell, Ida, 35
Tate, Sharon, murder case, 115

Technology vs. humanism: in Mailer, 119
Temps forts, des, 71
Thompson, Hunter, 11, 42, 151
Thoreau, Henry David, 54, 79
"Three Letters from the South," 43
Time (magazine), 92
Toffler, Alvin, 41, 134, 135, 163
Tom Jones, 93
"Totem newspapers," 24
"Totem story," 133, 134
Trachtenberg, Alan, 91
Traditional journalism. *See* Journalism, conventional
Traditional novel. *See* Novel, the
"Transcultural translators," 134, 138
Travel literature: relation to the new journalism, 134
Trilling, Lionel, 8, 12, 134, 135
Trip to Hanoi, A, 13
Turn of the Screw, The, 69
Twain, Mark, 33, 34, 47, 96, 134

U
"Ultimate Trick, The," 30
Underground press, 35, 39, 53, 134
Underground Press Syndicate, 40, 134
Understanding Media, 7
Updike, John, 16–17, 89
U.S.A. (book), 12, 44, 94

V
V (book), 17, 18, 20
Value judgments: lack of in traditional reporting, 22
Values. *See* Moral dilemmas
Vidal, Gore, 55
Vietnam War, 13, 14, 39, 41, 42, 52, 89, 90, 93, 96, 98, 99, 108, 145, 148
Village Voice, 39, 102, 154
Violent events: as subject of the new journalism, 42, 100
Vonnegut, Kurt, Jr., 17

W
Waiting for the End, 7
Wakefield, Dan, 44, 45, 59, 127
Wall Street Journal, 46
Warhol, Andy, 53
Warren, Robert Penn, 13
Washington Newspaper Guild Awards, 128
Washington Post, 46, 128, 148

Printed in Great Britain
by Amazon.co.uk, Ltd.,
Marston Gate.